GHETTO
Schooling

A Political Economy of
Urban Educational Reform

GHETTO Schooling

A Political Economy of Urban Educational Reform

Jean Anyon

Foreword by William Julius Wilson

TEACHERS COLLEGE PRESS

Teachers College
Columbia University
New York and London

Published by Teachers College Press, 1234 Amsterdam Avenue, New York, NY 10027

Library of Congress Cataloging-in-Publication Data

Anyon, Jean.
    Ghetto schooling : a political economy of urban educational reform
/ Jean Anyon : Foreword by William Julius Wilson.
        p.   cm.
    Includes bibliographical references and index.
    ISBN 0-8077-3663-5 (cloth). — ISBN 0-8077-3662-7 (pbk.)
    1. Education, Urban—Social aspects—New Jersey—Newark—Case
studies.   2. Education and politics—New Jersey—Newark—Case
studies.   3. Education, Urban—Economic aspects—New Jersey—Newark—
Case studies.   4. Education, Urban—New Jersey—Newark—History.
5. Newark (N.J.)—Social conditions.   6. Educational change—New
Jersey—Newark—Case studies.   I. Title.
LC5133.N39A59   1997
370′.9173′2—dc21   97-26507

ISBN 0-8077-3662-7 (paper)
ISBN 0-8077-3663-5 (cloth)

Printed on acid-free paper

Manufactured in the United States of America

04 03 02 01 00 99 98   8 7 6 5 4 3 2

This book is dedicated to my daughter
Jessica Tanya,
who is a most wise and wonderful city kid.

Contents

Foreword

The economist Harry Holzer of Michigan State University recently surveyed 3,000 employers in Atlanta, Boston, and Los Angeles and found that only 5 to 10 percent of the jobs in central-city areas for *non-college graduates* require very few work credentials or cognitive skills. This means that the job prospects for workers who lack skills in reading, writing, performing arithmetic calculations, and operating a computer are very slim indeed. The computer revolution—that is, changes in skill-based technology—has made a basic education indispensable. It has also enhanced the importance of and increased the urgency for effective urban public school reform.

This book provides a different and important perspective on public school reform in our nation today. Jean Anyon, a participant in a four-year attempt to restructure eight schools in inner city Newark, NJ, maintains that to be successful, educational reforms in the urban schools have to be part of a larger effort to address the problems of poverty and racial isolation in our inner cities.

Anyon acknowledges the need to confront the problems cited by most school reformers to overcome educational retardation in our public schools, such as rigid district bureaucracies, resignation among teachers and school principals, low expectations for students, and ideologies to justify poor student performances. Moreover, she is fully aware that the level of science and math resources in central-city schools, including teachers with adequate skills and training in science and mathematics, is far below that of advantaged suburban schools.

However, the intent of this timely book is not to "blame" school personnel, parents, or even the students themselves for the poor educational performances of youth; the intent, rather, is to illuminate how the cumulative effects of economic and political decisions in the larger urban context have, over time, severely constrained the ability and actions of current actors in central-city schools, including their efforts to achieve meaningful school reform. These effects are embodied in the poverty and social isolation of neighborhoods.

Anyon therefore calls for a more comprehensive vision of school reform. This vision recognizes the need to move beyond attempts to change only the system of education in order to address more fundamental problems in "the city environment itself"—an environment that creates failing schools and destroys the hopes of not only the students and their families, but of the teachers and administrators as well.

This book makes it crystal clear the economic and political devastation of cities has severely reduced the odds that current approaches to school reform will be successful. The majority of the students in the public schools of large cities are African-American and Hispanic. Forty percent of students in urban areas attend high-poverty schools (in which over 40% of students receive free or reduced price lunch). Anyon argues that in the absence of a long-range strategy to eradicate the underlying causes of racial isolation and poverty, heroic attempts to restructure schools or to introduce new pedagogical techniques in the classroom will be difficult to sustain. "If we can provide the conditions for a diminution of anger and a resurgence of hope in the inner cities, by an aggressive assault on urban poverty and racial isolation," she states, "we will begin to see healthy returns on our investments in education there" (pp. 181–182).

The implications of Anyon's analysis are clear. The "upgrading of city schools is itself dependent on improvements in the lives and opportunities of inner city residents" (p. 168). Therefore, educational reformers will have to join forces with others who are dedicated to improving the social and economic conditions in our cities.

Anyon emphasizes that vigorous efforts are needed to engage concerned citizens in a struggle to change attitudes and to alter existing economic and political priorities. She points to the hopeful sign of a resurgence of grass-roots movements in the United States concerned about the economy, jobs, housing, safety, and the environment. These movements are rooted in religious organizations, inner-city communities, labor groups, and consumer activity. She calls upon educational reformers to join forces with these groups, in addition to working with relevant established institutions, agencies, and non-government organizations to bring about the needed changes. Anyon argues that "together we can summon from ourselves and others the outrage, the combativeness, and the courage that will transform our inner cities, and our inner city schools" (p. 186). I hope she is right. And I believe that this passionate book will help to move us in that direction.

William Julius Wilson
Harvard University

Acknowledgments

I would like to thank the friends and colleagues who gave me advice and counsel, and who read or discussed with me various parts of this work during six years of researching and writing. The project began long ago in notes on a folded envelope during a conversation with Janet Miller, when she said to me, "Why don't you write up what you're doing in the Newark schools?" For that question, Janet, thank you. To Steve Block, Michelle Fine, Bill Firestone, Annette Lareau, David Lavin, Roslyn Mickelson, Gary Natriello, Clement Price, Stephen Smith, Lois Weis, and Julia Wrigley I give special thanks for help along the way. Susan Liddicoat of Teachers College Press is an extremely talented editor, and I thank her for her many smart suggestions. I am also grateful to Seymour Sarason, who doesn't agree with me at all, and who nevertheless gave me some good advice. And many thanks to Charles Cummings and the staff of the Newark Library's New Jersey Room, for keeping such good records of the past. To my daughter Jessie, love and thanks for always being there for me.

Introduction

As I enter the room there is a strong smell of urine. The windows are closed, and there is a board over the glass pane in the door. The teacher yells at a child from her desk, "I'm going to get rid of you!" Some children are copying spelling words from the board. Several of them jump up and down out of their seats. Most are not doing the work; many are leaning back in their chairs, chatting or fussing.

The children notice my arrival and look at me expectantly; I greet them and turn to the teacher, commenting on the broken pane of glass in the door. She comes over from her desk and says, "Jonathan put his hand through the window yesterday – his father passed him on the street and wouldn't say hello. Jonathan used to live with him, but since he started living with his mother, the father ignores him."

"These kids have hard lives, don't they," I say. At that, she begins a litany of the troubles of the children in her class: Derrick's father died of AIDS last week; one uncle has already died of AIDS and another is sick. One girl's father stole her money for drugs. On Monday a boy had been brought to school by his mother, who said that the boy had been raped by a male cousin on Thursday, but that "he was over it now." The teacher was trying to get the boy some counseling. Two boys were caught shaving chalk and "snorting" the dust, and "they aren't getting any counseling either." One boy had a puffy eye because his mother got drunk after she got laid off and beat up the kids while they were sleeping; last night he had hit her back, while she was sleeping.

At this point I interrupt the teacher to say, "It's really stuffy in here. Why don't you open a window?" "I can't," she replies, "because I have some children [points to a tiny girl] who like to jump *out* of school windows!" The children are totally out of control now, running around the room. One boy is weeping quietly at his desk. She shouts, "Fold your hands!" They ignore her. I realize I must leave so she can get them back in some order, so I say I will see her

next week, and go out the door. It locks behind me. (Field notes,
April 6, 1992)

The children in this second grade class and their teacher at Marcy
Elementary School (a pseudonym) are experiencing some of the results
of the economic and political devastation of America's inner cities. Such
devastation is the social context in which this book examines the current
educational reform movement.

From over a year of work with teachers in the midst of an intensive
but ultimately unsuccessful effort to improve a cluster of schools in
Newark, New Jersey, came my personal account demonstrating the an-
guish and anger of students and teachers—and the systematic abuse of
children by some school staff—all of whom are caught in the tangle of a
failing school system and unrealized school reform. Through that account I seek to reveal ways in which poverty and racial isolation have
often trivialized efforts in this city to teach, to learn, and to bring about
change.

In part I of this book I thus inaugurate the painful but necessary
discussion of the effects of social class and race on educational reform.
With few exceptions, discussions of school reform have ignored the
consequences of poverty and racial isolation on attempts to improve
America's inner city schools. One consequence of this silence, I believe,
is that the restructuring and other educational reforms have not significantly improved most central city schools or classrooms. Jonathan Kozol
(1991), after visiting schools in Boston, Chicago, Detroit, East St. Louis,
New York City, San Antonio, Washington, DC, and four cities in New
Jersey—Camden, Irvington, Jersey City, and Paterson—summarized his
perceptions of the effects of the restructuring movement on these
schools:

> Few of these reforms have reached the schools that I have seen. In
> each of the larger cities there is usually one school or one subdistrict
> which is highly publicized as an example of restructured education;
> but the changes rarely reach beyond this one example. Even in those
> schools where some restructuring has taken place . . . it struck me as
> very little more than moving around the same old furniture within the
> house of poverty. The perceived objective was a more "efficient"
> ghetto school or one with greater "input" from the ghetto parents or
> more "choices" for the ghetto children. The fact of ghetto education
> as a permanent American reality appeared to be accepted. (4)

Others who have argued that educational reforms have failed to improve city schools include Lewis (1996), Muncey and McQuillan (1993),

Sarason (1996), Rothman (1993), Wehlage, Smith, and Lipman (1992), and Zook (1993); see also Cuban (1990) and Tyack and Cuban (1995).

To discover why inner city schools have not improved, it is not enough to only examine present reform or educational practice. We need, in addition, to understand how inner city schools have come to be what they are. For schools—like people—are products of their past, as well as of their present. We must uncover not only the histories of the schools and districts, but also those of the cities in which they are embedded.

In part II I tie the account of the educational reform scene in Newark, New Jersey, to past economic and political trends. Rather than being a conventional history, however, the chapters in part II provide an overview of ways in which economic and political decisions and trends have shaped America's cities and their schools during the last 100 years. This historical political economy—wherein Newark is used as a case study—reveals how policies of the federal, state, and local governments, combined with business and other practices, formed and shaped the schools as cities such as Newark were devastated economically and isolated politically.

I show that, contrary to common belief, public education in Newark was of poor quality long before African Americans took over the reins of city government in the 1970s; education in the majority of schools in this old American city was in significant decline by the mid-1930s, when most students were white lower middle class, working class, or poor. The chapters in part II make reference to the many similarities between the history of Newark and that of other old American cities, and to what is known about the twentieth century economic and political history of other urban American school systems.

Using this historical analysis, in the final chapter I return to Marcy School, the site of the account of recent reform efforts in Newark, to provide further insight into phenomena that occurred in the school and in the district. Thus, some of the problems that were encountered in the early 1990s reform attempts are understood as concentration effects of the gradual ghettoization and stigmatization over time of the city's minority poor; some are direct results of the twentieth century economic devastation of the city; and some are linked to nearly a century of isolation of urban leaders from federal and state power.

I close by developing a new vision of reform, wherein I urge that we direct a portion of our country's vast resources to reconstruction of the central city environment. While America's corporate coffers, for example, overflow into the building of infrastructure—the basis for future investment—in the Third World, much of the infrastructure in our own cities is crumbling (see, among others, Faust 1994; Javetski 1994; Nathaus 1996; Smart 1993; *New York Times*, July 14, 1996). In the concluding chapter I argue that what is needed to make educational reform possible in America's cities is economic reprioritization, and a resuscitation of the cities themselves.

The analysis in this study thus yields a vision of educational reform profoundly different from what Americans have heretofore been offered. Creators of current visions, as will be demonstrated in chapter 1, restrict themselves to attempts to change various levels of the educational system. I will argue, however, that visions of educational reform in America's cities must also include efforts to restore economic and political opportunities to inner city residents. I believe that long-lasting, substantial educational improvement will not occur in the schools in our impoverished cities without the restoration of *hope* in the hearts of all involved—students, families, teachers, and administrators. Thus, the plan for educational change that is most likely to yield long-term success is one that includes a strategy to improve the lives, and life chances, of inner city residents, in addition to educational reform. The book concludes with a presention of economic, political, and educational policy suggestions for acting on this vision.

NEWARK AS AN ARCHETYPE

Newark, the third oldest major city in the United States, home to a population of minority poor, has lost the economic vitality it once had, and is without a job base for the employment of the majority of its residents. Among the first major cities to experience an industrial slide and attainment of a majority black population, Newark is often considered an "archetypal" aging urban center. In 1970, Newark's first African American mayor, Kenneth Gibson, remarked that "wherever American cities are going, Newark will get there first" (Groh 1972, 248; see also Barbaro 1972; Berkeley 1971; Chamber of Commerce of Greater Newark 1989; Curvin 1975; Laccetti 1990; Louis 1975; Winters 1990).

New Jersey's largest city is also, however, in some ways atypical. For example, compared to many other cities, a somewhat greater percentage of its population is poor; and its historical encirclement by suburbs makes it physically smaller (23.8 square miles) and more dense than most other major cities. Furthermore, the New Jersey state legislature has historically been more influenced by organized crime than those in other states, and though wealthier, the state has been less generous toward its poorer citizens than most (Cook 1974; Salmore and Salmore 1993).

However, the commonalities among America's aging industrial centers (e.g., Baltimore, Boston, Buffalo, Camden, Chicago, Cleveland, Detroit, East St. Louis, Gary, Milwaukee, Newark, New York, Philadelphia, Pittsburgh, St. Louis, and Trenton) in their development and decline over the last 100 years outweigh, for the purposes of this analysis, the individual differences among them. Their history is of utmost importance to our understanding of the failure of educational reform to remake the schools within these cities.

It is intended that the research in this book be generalizable in another way, as well. Assessing urban schools in the sociohistorical context that produced them provides a new method of studying school reform. Rather than excise educational events from their economic and political contexts, I give these latter forces an explanatory role. While not nearly sufficient for explaining everything that transpires in school buildings, economic and political understandings contribute important insights into underlying causes and, therefore, meaningful solutions.

GENERATING MY ACCOUNTS

The personal account in part I of this book is based on my participation in a 4-year reform effort begun by the Newark district in 1989. I participated in the reforms during 1992 and part of 1993 primarily as staff developer at Marcy School, and then continued for another year in other district schools after the reforms had been officially abandoned. I carried out workshops at Marcy School between February 1992 and February 1993, and worked at least one full day a week during the 10 school months in teachers' classrooms, providing coaching in the methods of cooperative teaching and learning.

In addition to spending more than 200 hours with Marcy School teachers and their classes, I also attended district-mandated reform team meetings and spent numerous hours talking with teachers at these meetings. In my months at Marcy School I spent 21 lunch periods "hanging out" with the students in the cafeteria and on the asphalt yard; I also chatted with them frequently in classrooms and halls. I became well acquainted with the assistant superintendent responsible for the reform, commuted periodically on the train with him between Newark and New York City, where we both lived, and often discussed the reform efforts with him, and with members of his staff. I formally interviewed the assistant superintendent, his staff, 24 of 25 classroom teachers at Marcy School, the members of Marcy's school-based support team, both Marcy School administrators, the school's drug counselor, 15 parents, and 25 students. I read numerous school, district, and state reports and other documents pertaining to the schools and to the reform initiative. I examined all curriculum materials—those in use, and those prepared by the district but not often used.

My historical account of the city and schools of Newark over the last 100 years, and my discussion of the ways in which this city's municipal and educational history resembles that of other older cities, is primarily a portrayal of policies and their effects (following Tabb 1970; and Wilson 1987). I describe the policies of governments at all levels, and of economic groups such as national and local corporations. In most instances, I do not recount how residents have felt about what these groups were doing, and in most cases I do not describe the ways in which individuals resisted or acquiesced to the developments. Thus, my account is not a social history in which you will hear the voices of Newark residents over the years. Almost all of my primary sources are archival materials such as newspapers and printed documents, although the results of a number of interviews with participants or knowledgeable observers also dot the record.

My account, moreover, is not a delicately nuanced elaboration that teases out the complexities and contradictions of a city's past. Rather, it is a straightforward story of economic and political decisions and actions and a demonstration of how these actions affected the development of an American city and its schools. The historical political economy in this book attempts to reveal the extent to which current urban educational failure is embedded in the past actions of powerful economic and political groups.

RACE, SOCIAL CLASS, AND THE
CONSTRUCTION OF NARRATIVES

This introduction must not be silent on the issues of race and class, nor on the experiences that flood these terms with meanings. I am a white professional. Most of the people who are discussed in the accounts of Marcy School are not white. Most of the people who have lived in Newark since 1970 are not white, nor are they middle class. What gives me the right to judge their behavior and their history?

When I presented to teachers and administrators a draft of the narrative of my experience at Marcy School—which included my perceptions of abusive statements made by both black and white adults to children in the school—there were some painful moments. The teachers who met with me to discuss the draft (all of whom happened to be African American), admitted that I had not made any mistakes other than the grade placement of a few children, but expressed anger that I would see their school in such a negative way. I was told later that a leader of the black parents, after reading the manuscript, tore it into pieces and said that it was "just another white person trashing our school."

My rebuttal to the implicit charge of racism is that "race," like "gender" and "social class," is a socially constructed term; and therefore meanings attributed to it will vary with the vantage point of the social actor or speaker. What I may see as abuse, for example, may be interpreted by black teachers as part of a longstanding African American tradition of strict discipline (Hale-Benson 1986).

Moreover, my interpretations may be influenced by my position as an outside observer. One's location as stranger to an institution, looking in, may allow one to notice and view as extraordinary various attitudes and behaviors that long-time participants have gotten used to, and may no longer see as remarkable (Anyon 1994a).

Importantly, the intent of the book is not to "blame" students, parents, or school personnel for their actions, but rather to illuminate how economic and political decisions by others—over many decades— have made the positions of current actors in central city schools almost unbearable. Having contributed this societally based analysis of failed school reform, I am then able to demonstrate that it cannot be up to educators alone—it is up to all of us, through concerted social action—to work together to provide cities, city families, children, and their schools with a modicum of hope and a chance to excel.

PART I

THE PRESENT

CHAPTER 1

Cities, Urban Schools, and Current Visions of Educational Reform

It is "World Day" on the Rutgers University campus. The colleges and universities in downtown Newark have joined together to celebrate the diversity of people who make up the city and the world. Jesse Jackson's son is to speak. Computer screens and science laboratories are temporarily empty as college students and faculty mingle among the banners and booths on the decorated street. I drive from my office and this bustling scene to the school where I am working with Newark public school teachers.

The street on which Marcy School stands is empty. Stretching for many blocks is a desolate area of closed factories, housing projects, and small, tired-looking homes. I see no people or cars, no trees or other signs of life. I feel as if I have left one country and entered another. I have left the world of progress and technology on the Rutgers campus, and even though less than two miles away, feel as if I am on a continent in which a holocaust has wiped out a civilization, leaving only a few disoriented survivors. The dilapidated buildings and empty lots breathe a postholocaust weariness and devastation. The celebration of diversity, the computers and science labs, the arrival of Jesse Jackson's son, are not known to the inhabitants of this place. (Field notes, April 8, 1992)

The contrast between the university and the neighborhood around Marcy School illustrates the extreme isolation and poverty of many residents not only in Newark, New Jersey, but in the majority of our large American cities. In this chapter I set the stage for the analyses to follow by describing this current social milieu of isolation and poverty, then illustrate how these conditions affect urban schools. I use Newark as a specific example in each section. I then analyze the visions driving current educational reform, and end by questioning whether these visions

3

are capable of overpowering the effects of the urban environment on education.

THE RACIAL ISOLATION AND POVERTY
OF CENTRAL CITIES

Central cities now hold only 29% of the nation's population and comprise less than 12% of the national electorate (Judd and Swanstrom 1994, 255). About 48% of the U.S. population lived in suburbs when the 1990 census was taken. Because they turn out for elections at a higher rate than do rural and central city voters, suburban voters cast a majority of the votes in most state elections, as they did in the 1992 presidential election. Large cities cast less than half the votes in most states: For example, New York City casts 31% of the state's vote, Chicago's share of the popular vote in Illinois is 22%, St. Louis's share of Missouri's vote is 6%, and the six largest cities in New Jersey together produce under 10% of the state's vote (Goertz 1992, 6; Judd and Swanstrom 1994, 304; Salmore and Salmore 1993, 47). Inner city residents thus elect proportionately very few representatives in state and national contests; most state and national politicians represent suburban constituencies (Judd and Swanstrom 1994).

Most residents of large cities are African American or Latino. Of the nation's eight largest cities with a population of one million or more in 1990, only two, Philadelphia and San Diego, were less than half minority. Of these eight largest cities, racial ethnic minorities (mostly black and Latino, with percentages of Asian and other minorities averaging 5.7%) are 57% in New York City, 62% in Chicago, 63% in Los Angeles, 70% in Atlanta, 79% in Detroit, and 88% in Miami. Among the 14 cities with between 500,000 and a million inhabitants, 8—Baltimore, Cleveland, El Paso, Memphis, San Antonio, San Francisco, San Jose, and Washington, DC—are also more than half African American, Latino, and Asian (Ginzberg 1993, 38–39).

However, the percentage of blacks in suburbia is miniscule. In 1990, African Americans made up only 8.7% of suburban residents in 12 large standard metropolitan statistical areas studied—New York, Los Angeles-Long Beach, Chicago, Philadelphia, Detroit, San Francisco-Oakland, Boston, Pittsburgh, St. Louis, Washington, DC, Cleveland, and Baltimore (Judd and Swanstrom 1994, 160–161; see also Dolce 1976, 71; Lake 1981, 3).

This political isolation of American cities—and their minority populations—is accompanied by the isolation of poorer urban residents from the economic mainstream of middle-class jobs. Most central city indus-tries have closed or dispersed. As jobs moved to the suburbs, residential segregation prevented most black families from following. Almost all new jobs created in cities are now either low-wage or top-tier (technical, professional) positions (Sassen 1991). Since 53% of adults living in ex-treme poverty tracts in American cities have not completed high school (Kasarda 1993, 101) they are automatically precluded from participation in the high-wage sectors of the economy (see below).

Adjusting for inflation, federal aid to cities was cut by 60% between 1980 and 1992. This has put most U.S. cities in a position where their dwindling tax base must serve to pick up costs once covered by the federal government. Many city governments are impoverished, increas-ingly unable to provide services to their residents (Brophy 1993, 215).

As a result of these and other social conditions and trends, by 1991 central cities housed 43% of the U.S. poverty population and the vast majority (80%) of America's African American poor (Kasarda 1993, 82). While in 1970, four out of five city residents lived in *non*poverty census tracts, by 1990 more than one third of the population in America's 100 largest cities resided in neighborhoods with at least 20% of the residents falling below the poverty level (106).

Moreover, between 1970 and 1990, the number of census tracts in these cities classified as extreme poverty tracts, or ghettos, grew from 6% of total city tracts to 13.7% (89). Here, over 40% of residents are living below the poverty line, and there are disproportionately high levels of joblessness, female-headed families, welfare recipiency, and high teenage school drop-out rates. Over 80% of concentrated poverty areas in the United States are found in the nation's 100 largest cities (Kasarda 1993, 87). While nationally 14.7 million children or 20.8%, are officially poor, the official poverty rate for children under 6 in central cities is 30%, and 16% for suburban areas (Brophy 1993, 215; *New York Times* November 30, 1996).

The city of Newark (whose 1990 census population count was 275,221) exemplifies the poverty and political isolation characterizing large Ameri-can cities. Although not the poorest city in the nation or in New Jersey, its combined community wealth is in the bottom 10% of communities in the state. In 1990, per capita income there was $9,424, in a state with the second highest per capita income in the country, at $24,936 (Salmore and Salmore 1993, 56; U.S. Census 1990). Eighty-five percent of city residents are African American or Hispanic (U.S. Census 1990). Most (78%) of the children and youth in the city schools are from families with income low enough to qualify them for federal free or reduced-price lunch programs (Council of Great City Schools [CGCS] 1994b, 196).

Twenty-two percent of Newark residents have less than a ninth grade education. Only 51.2% of city residents have completed high school, and 8.5%, college (as opposed to 76.7% and 24.9% for the state as a whole) (U.S. Census 1990).

Third in the nation in the growth of ghetto census tracts between 1970 and 1980, by 1990 the 14th most segregated of the 100 largest U.S. cities, and with a majority of its census tracts exhibiting poverty status (Kasarda 1993, 111, 117, 122) Newark has been called "the city that became a ghetto" (Groh 1972, 157).

THE PLIGHT OF URBAN SCHOOLS

Total public school enrollment in the United States is about 38 million. Of these, 10.4 million students are in urban, 16.8 million in suburban, and 10.5 million in rural schools (U.S. Department of Education 1996, 4). City demographics are reflected in the enrollments in urban schools. Most (approximately 76%) of the students in America's central city schools are African American or Latino. In school year 1992–93, 50 of the Great City School districts enrolled 5.7 million students, including 36.1% of our nation's African American students, 29.8% of our Hispanic students, and only 4.8% of our white students. These districts enrolled 13.5% of the nation's students, but 22.1% of the nation's school poor and 35.9% of the nation's students with limited English proficiency.

Nationally, 42% of urban students are eligible to receive subsidized school lunches, and 40% attend schools defined by the U.S. Department of Education as high-poverty schools, in which more than 40% of students receive free or reduced-price lunch. Against these figures, only 10% of suburban students and 25% of rural students attend high-poverty schools (U.S. Department of Education 1996, vi, 6). If present trends continue, the United States will, in 25 years, have a majority of "minority" students in its public schools, enrolling most of the black and Hispanic students in the large cities, with more than half of them living in poverty (Orfield 1993; see also CGCS 1994b, xii, 3–4).

Less than half of the ninth graders entering high schools in our large city systems typically graduate in 4 years (Fossey 1996, 5; Glazer 1993, 253; but see Education Trust 1996 for a slightly higher percentage); urban drop-out rates for low-income African American and Hispanic students, already high, increased between 1990 and 1993 (CGCS 1994b, xiii). Less than half of urban students are above national achievement norms (CGCS 1994b, xiii–xiv, 44). The large percentages of students needing special services or programs strain city school budgets, in some

City Schools don't get as much

cases accounting for up to one quarter of expenses (Firestone, Goertz, and Natriello 1994, 51).

Despite greater need, 79% of large city districts studied by the Council of the Great City Schools are funded at a lower rate than are suburban schools; nationally, advantaged suburban schools spend as much as ten times that spent by urban poor schools (Educational Testing Service 1991; National Commission on Teaching and America's Future 1996; also U.S. General Accounting Office 1997). A full 82.4% of the Great City School districts experienced a decline in local revenues during the survey year of 1992–93. The share of total state K–12 educational expenditures devoted to Great City Schools also declined—from 14.7% in 1988–89 to 13.7% in 1992–93, although the share of federal funding devoted to city schools increased slightly during these years, from 19.8 to 22.1% (CGCS 1994b, xvii, xv).

Old school buildings, many dating from the nineteenth and early twentieth centuries, have not been well maintained. Classrooms typically have few instructional supplies and little equipment (Education Trust 1996; Kozol 1991). Oakes found in 1990 that students in schools in central cities tend to have less access to science and math resources, programs, and teachers with science or math backgrounds than do those in more advantaged schools. Moreover, math and science teachers in central city schools rate themselves as less confident about their science and math teaching than do teachers in advantaged schools (1990; vii–viii). According to Darling-Hammond and Sclan, students in urban schools have only a 50% chance of being taught by a certified mathematics or science teacher (1996).

Research has shown that instruction in inner city schools is often based on cognitively low-level, unchallenging, rote material (Anyon 1994b, 1995a; 1995b; Darling-Hammond 1996a; Hopfenberg and Levin 1993; Oakes 1990). Members of the Washington, DC-based Education Trust relate their dismay at witnessing "English classrooms [in urban schools] where 14-year-olds were assigned to *color* the definitions to a list of vocabulary words and required to recite—over and over again—the parts of speech" (1996, 11; emphasis in original). Although high percentages of city students need supplementary academic instruction, there is a 50% higher shortage of teachers in cities than the national average (CGCS 1994b, xiv; Education Trust 1996, 7).

Newark, the 70th largest district in the United States, can serve as a case study of urban districts, although some of the Newark percentages are above the average. Newark is one of the 30 poorest urban districts in New Jersey. There are over 380,000 students in these 30 "special needs districts," and approximately 48,000 in Newark. Seventy-eight percent of Newark students qualify for free or reduced-price lunch as opposed to an average of 58.4% of students in the 50 large city school systems studied by the Council of the Great City Schools (1994b, xii, 196). In Newark, 63% of students are African American, 26.3% are Hispanic, and 9.5% are white (Association for Children of New Jersey 1992, 17, 65).

The Newark district enrolls 4.2% of the state's school enrollment, but 14% of the state's poor. The district reports a 36% 4-year drop-out rate, although an independent assessment found that only 45% of ninth graders graduate from high school. In Newark, 40.8% of students score in the bottom quarter in standardized reading tests and 30% in the bottom quarter in math tests; only 30.6 and 43.4% of students score at or above the national norms in reading and math. A full 66.8% of Newark students are considered by the state to be in need of remedial assistance (the statewide average is 21.7%) (CGCS 1994b, 196; Association for Children 1992, 17, 65).

Newark, as do most city districts, has educational resource needs that are much greater than those of suburban districts, whose students are more advantaged and less "needy," and whose property base is a richer source of school funds. However, with 4.2% of the state's enrollment, the city received in 1992–93 only 4.9% of the states's elementary and secondary expenditures (CGCS 1994b, 197).

During an outside evaluation of the Newark district mandated by the New Jersey state legislature in 1994, independent evaluators visited 51 of 82 schools, and directly observed over 400 classrooms. They reported that Newark schools "lack . . . sufficient, appropriate instructional materials, equipment and supplies" (New Jersey State Department of Education 1994b, 50). Evaluators also found in on-site observations that

> classrooms, for the most part, are dirty and ill-equipped, and instruction is unchallenging and often misdirected or inappropriate. Few instances were found in any classroom, regardless of the subject or grade level, of students being encouraged to generate their own ideas, to collaborate in problem-solving activities, to write in class, to read widely and independently or to use skills and facts in context.
>
> [High school] science laboratories lack basic equipment and show no evidence of recent use. . . . A number of teachers and other professional staff members are uncertified or inappropriately certified for their current assignments; some were observed to lack an understanding of the subjects they were teaching and to give misinformation for students to copy into their notebooks. (New Jersey State Department of Education 1994b, 11)

In a study conducted by the Association for Children in New Jersey in 1992, a majority of Newark elementary school teachers agreed with the statement that "[in Newark] instruction focuses almost entirely on basic skills taught in rote fashion with little opportunity for application" (65).

In an attempt to improve the achievement of their students many large city districts, including Newark, have been recently involved in the national effort to restructure schools. According to a poll of urban districts published in 1994 by the Council of the Great City Schools, 96% of large city districts report that they are engaged in districtwide reform activities and that 86.4% of these are attempts to restructure decision making. More than one third, or 39.5%, of large city districts polled by the council reported site-based management in at least 76% of their schools during school years 1991–93 (CGCS 1994a, 5; 1994b, xv; Newark Board of Education 1992).

Why, with such a large percentage of urban districts reporting restructuring activity, has the picture of education in inner cities not brightened considerably? In the last 15 years Boston, Chicago, Cincinnati, Cleveland, Dade County (Miami), Detroit, Hammond (Indiana), Louisville, New York, Philadelphia, Pittsburgh, and Rochester, New York—among other cities—have been in the news for their attempts to make city schools more successful for low-income students by using a variety of restructuring activities. This most recent wave of reform, of course, follows close on the heels of several decades of other educational reforms in urban districts: federal programs in the late 1960s and early 1970s, and the decades of accountability and standards reforms in the 1970s, 1980s, and 1990s (Massell and Fuhrman 1994). The latest wave of reform, of which restructuring is a component, is referred to by advocates as "systemic reform." Activity to produce systemic change is an attempt to pull together disparate types of reform from the past several decades, and to overcome contradictory initiatives generated by different levels of the educational system.

Given the dismal state of schooling in most of our central cities, however, it seems clear that this recent wave of educational reform has not succeeded there. I believe it is imperative, therefore, to examine the adequacy of assumptions underlying these efforts. How do educational reformers define school, for example, and what is their vision of change?

THE INADEQUACY OF CURRENT VISIONS OF EDUCATIONAL REFORM

A basic tenet of reform efforts has been that schools are complex, "loosely coupled" organizations in which all parts affect each other, in which control is vested at the top, but in which change cannot be dictated from above (Purkey and Smith 1983; Weick 1976). These loosely coupled organizations are enmeshed in systems of district and state regulations (Cohen 1982; Cohen, M. 1990; David 1990; Elmore 1990; Lieberman 1995; Massell and Fuhrman 1994). Participants in the school are the key to reform. As longtime authority on school reform Seymour Sarason, says, "salvation for our schools will not come from without but from within" (in Lieberman 1995, viii; see also Sarason 1971, 1996).

Reform thus depends upon alteration of the work patterns of school actors. The regularities of their daily practice need to be changed (Elmore 1990; Lieberman 1995; Wasley 1994). This bottom-up change needs to be supported by district and state rules, professional and—if possible—community support. The alteration of the regularities of schools will be accomplished by creating new mechanisms, or new structures, for the way school actors participate in the daily educational enterprise (Lieberman 1995; Sarason 1971; Sizer 1992). As Lieberman says,

> Changing schools demands changing practices, and . . . structures must be built to support these changed practices. . . . Cultures of colleagueship, continuous inquiry, and collaborative work . . . may well mark the organizational path to the schools of the future. (15)

The goal of the new practices and structures is to transform the whole school rather than individual projects or classrooms (Lieberman 1995; see also Sizer 1992).

Examples of the new organizational forms for changing the regularities of daily life in school are joint decision making among teachers and administrators, the teaming of teachers, flexible scheduling, multiage groups, and core planning in individual schools (Darling-Hammond 1996b; Lieberman 1995, 12; see also Coalition of Essential Schools classroom projects described in Wasley 1994).

In the case of Chicago, an altered structure produced by the 1988 reform legislation resulted in the creation of local councils in all schools—assigning unprecedented power to parents and teachers (Hess 1991). (In 1995, however, a new law brought about the reorganization of authority, returning the preponderance of power back to a chief executive officer and board of trustees.) In New York City, system-wide decentralization, several districts with school choice, and a number of alternative schools within the public system have involved many of the restructuring movement's most cherished reforms: small, personalized schools; cooperative learning; integration of curriculum; longer class periods; deeper curriculum study and fewer topics; parental involvement; joint management by teachers and administrators; and new forms of assessment, wherein students show both their knowledge and their capabilities in a comfortable setting through demonstrations and portfolios of work rather than through pencil-and-paper tests (Meier 1995, 65; see also Darling-Hammond, Ancess, and Falk 1995).

In Philadelphia, small, self-contained learning communities (charters), within large comprehensive high schools and closely linked to local universities and national networks of other restructured schools, represent a district goal of decentralization of administration to support democratic governance of schools, school-based decision making, and management of resources. The task in Philadelphia has been to "reinvigorate intellectually and professionally the educators," "to reengage the students," and "to organize the parents" in order to achieve what Michelle Fine has called "radical, systemic reform of the school system" (1994, 1–2).

The current emphasis on restructuring decision making in schools has been informed by models for reforming complex business organizations in pursuit of higher productivity. One source of the corporate vision is the idea, publicized by Xerox vice president John Seely Brown and business consultant W. Edwards Deming, that participants in an organization are more productive when they are involved in decisions affecting their efforts and when authority is decentralized (Brown 1991; Deming 1982). Deming goes further. His approach to quality control in organizations entails, rather than blaming the workers when problems arise, instituting new organizational structures—such as "quality control circles"—so that groups of employees can work together to solve the problems. Producing a quality product is everyone's job, and collaborative planning by constituents from various strata of an organization results in solutions (Deming 1982).

When the corporate model is applied to schools, principals, teachers, parents, citizens, and sometimes students are supposed to come together to discuss and decide on the educationally best practice for their school. Rather than blaming the students for educational failure, adults in the school should examine and change their own behavior. Superintendents are key, as, in this model, they will need to give up absolute power in deference to others in the system. Principals are also to give up total control, while at the same time retaining their instructional leadership and motivational roles, long associated with school success (see Edmonds 1979; Mortimore and Sammons 1987; Purkey and Smith 1983).

In the view of reformers, teachers are perhaps the most important element, because it is they on whom change ultimately depends: The reforms are, in the final analysis, classroom reforms. Democratization of school governance and organization serves the purpose of improving classroom teaching. An important goal of systemic reform, for example, moving away from teaching by rote drill and toward "active student learning" and use of higher order thinking skills, cannot be met if teachers do not enact it.

However, classroom change is also in great measure dependent on changes in the culture of the school (see Fullan 1991; Sarason 1971). This involves changing the attitudes of people in all parts of the system— from teachers and students in classrooms, to district administrators, to legislators in state capitals (Elmore 1990; Lieberman 1995; Massell and Fuhrman 1994). The involvement of all levels of educational decision making gives the movement its name—"systemic reform" (Lieberman 1995, 3). Educational change also needs to be assisted by professional networks and university researchers, and by consultants, business executives, and foundations (Fine 1994; Hess 1991; Lieberman 1995).

According to the reformers, among the most important impediments to changing urban schools are district bureaucracy and rigidity, educator resignation, low expectations for students, ideologies that are used to explain school failure (e.g., "It's the kids' fault"), teacher isolation and suspicion of joint planning, administrator reluctance to being branded a "reformer," and some federal and state regulations (Fine 1994; Hess 1991; Lieberman 1995; Massell and Fuhrman 1994). I believe, however, and I will argue in this book, that there are other, equally significant, impediments to school reform, and that they can be found in the urban context of the school, in the political isolation and poverty of cities.

The current educational restructuring movement is suffused with democratic ideals: a search for democratic governance in suburban schools, and for "radically democratic education for all" in urban schools (Fine 1994, 3; see also Darling-Hammond 1996a). The vision of democratic schools is powerful and important. It is also of long standing, with early expression in the work of John Dewey and the Progressive educational reformers of the early twentieth century. The vision persisted: In the "open classroom" and "alternative school" movements in which I participated in New York City in the late 1960s, democratic schooling was again a goal. Given that so many decades have seen so little improvement in city education, should we not question the adequacy of this vision to provide fundamental change in urban schools?

Is fundamental educational change in America's ghetto schools really going to result from reordered relations among teachers and administrators? Are these and other educational rearrangements going to be powerful enough to overcome the decades of accumulated want and despair that impede students every day? I believe not; I believe that it is absolutely imperative to also think about ways to restructure the city environment itself, which produces these students and the failing schools.

It will be my argument in this book that until the economic and political systems in which the cities are enmeshed are themselves transformed so they may be more democratic and productive for urban residents, educational reformers have little chance of effecting long-lasting educational changes in city schools. It will be my task in the chapters treating history to demonstrate how the recalcitrance of urban schools to "reform" is in large part a result of economic and political devastation in cities. To date, current visions of educational reform have not been strong enough to redress this destructive power of the social environment, although a few reformers have developed programs that begin to reach beyond the traditional purview of the schools (see Comer 1980; also Jehl and Kirst 1993).

"But," one could retort, "we were talking about educational reform here, not social reform." Indeed, a final task will be the attempt to persuade readers that educational change in the inner city, to be successful, has to be part and parcel of more fundamental social change. An all-out attack on poverty and racial isolation that by necessity will affect not only the poor, but the more affluent as well, will be necessary in order to remove the barriers that currently stand in the way of urban educational change. To add muscle to the charge that our systems of social class and racial organization are significant impediments to the success of restructuring and other recent educational reform attempts, the next chapter contains an account based on my observation of the ways in which poverty and race collide to overwhelm attempts to bring about change in a ghetto school in Newark, New Jersey.

CHAPTER 2

Social Class, Race, and Educational Reform at Marcy School

I walk through several blocks of old, two-story wooden and brick buildings, empty lots, an abandoned factory. I notice windows that are broken, front doors that do not close completely; but the buildings are inhabited – I hear a baby crying and see a woman sitting on a stoop smoking a cigarette.

I reach the school in which I will work with teachers, sign the guest book, and look around for the principal, whom I know. Two children run down the hall. Seven or eight sit on a bench against a wall. The school guard watches them. A group of children run by, nearly knocking me over. Several yards away a woman is telling two girls that they have to go home because they were late. I ask the guard for the principal, and he points toward the main office.

The door is open; inside is a small room with a long, waist-high wooden counter that creates a barrier between the door and two secretaries. This small space is filled with people coming and going. Leaning heavily on the counter, and yelling angrily at an Hispanic woman is a very overweight white man (the principal). His face is flushed and he is sweating profusely. More people press into and out of the tiny space, moving between us. A woman leans over the barrier from the other side, holds out a folder for the principal to see, and says, "He's a 10-year-old terror from the hotel [homeless shelter]; they're sending him over here." The principal responds, "Start the process now. Get him into King [another school]."

Phones are ringing, and in the corner a woman is speaking loudly into the intercom. The principal sees me, says hello, and continues yelling at the woman (who turns out to be the assistant principal). A loud bell begins to ring and rings for what seems a

14

long minute; I glance at the clock, to see what time it is. The clock, however, says 6:30.

I go with the principal into his private office, a large room with a couch and framed pictures on the walls. He says to me, "It's a zoo here." After a pause, he adds, somewhat apologetically, "I'm not the greatest administrator in the world." I say something intended to be nonthreatening, perhaps even comforting, and we begin to talk about my upcoming work with the teachers. I have been asked by the district to participate in current reform initiatives by carrying out a series of workshops for teachers in cooperative learning, a classroom technique in which students are taught to work in small groups to meet team as well as individual goals. The principal tells me, "Do whatever you want." He also feels it necessary to warn me: "Remember, you can't plan here – things happen!" (Field notes, February 24, 1992)

MARCY SCHOOL

This K–8 school, which I call Marcy Elementary School, is in the central section of Newark. The building was constructed in 1861 for the children of German and Irish immigrants who worked in nearby beer and leather factories; Abraham Lincoln is said to have given a speech from the steps of the building when it was new. The school population is now 71% black and 27% Hispanic.

Forty-five percent of the census tract population live below the poverty line (U.S. Census 1990). All but 3 of the 500 students in the school receive some form of public assistance, and are eligible for free lunch. Most live in nearby housing projects. The school has a population of homeless children whose numbers fluctuate. The official rate varies from between 5 and 20%. According to the school social worker, a much larger percentage are ''hidden homeless,'' children living with relatives or friends. A psychological assessment of a random sample of 45 Marcy students found that they were plagued by the problems that result from extreme poverty: chaotic lives, neglect, abuse, histories of poor health and chronic health problems, emotional stress, anxiety, and anger (Mun Wong et al. 1992).

Poverty, the use of drugs—especially maternal use of crack—and deaths from AIDS have combined to create in this city a generation of children in which many are growing up without parental support. The *New York Times* has reported that ''bands of youngsters can be seen

roaming Newark at night, stealing cars, and sleeping in hallways and
doorways during the day, without any apparent adult supervision.''
The majority of the youths—girls as well as boys—were reported to be
between 8 and 11 years old (August 11, 1992).

During the period of this study, the principal of Marcy School was a
white Italian male, and the assistant principal was an Hispanic woman.
Sixteen (64%) of the 25 classroom teachers were black, and a sizeable
minority of these stated in interviews that they had grown up in poor or
working-class neighborhoods of this or other cities. Six classroom teachers (24%) were Hispanic, and 3 (12%) were white. Almost all of both
groups were from working-class backgrounds; all but two now live in
the suburbs.

According to New Jersey Department of Education data, in school
year 1992–93, 51% of the certificated full-time teachers in the city were
African American, and 8.5% were Hispanic (1994, 1374). According to
an informant in the Bureau of Research at the city's board of education,
the percentage of African American teachers cited in the state statistics
is low. According to this informant, the percentage of African American
teachers in the city is much higher, due to the relatively high number of
teachers in the district who are not certified, and who are part-time
(long- or short-term substitutes). Almost all part-time teachers in the
district are African American. Although statistics could not be obtained
from the district, observation reveals that in schools where black children are the majority (such as the research site), there are more black
teachers than at district schools where the majority of the children are
Italian or Portuguese. As noted above, 64% of the classroom teachers at
Marcy School were African American.

According to state figures, in 1992–93 43.3% of Newark district administrators were black, and 7.7%, Hispanic. Fifty percent of special
services personnel in city schools were black, and 5.8% Hispanic. At
Marcy School, most (61%) of the specialists and non-classroom teachers
in the school—basic skills teachers, special education teachers, art and
gym teachers, psychologist, social worker, learning disabilities specialist, and so forth—were white. The rest were African American. All the
teacher aides in the building were black women, with the exception of
several who were Hispanic, and were parents of students or former
students; all lived in the neighborhood, most in nearby housing projects. Approximately half of the aides had themselves attended Marcy
School, and all had children—and some, grandchildren—who were
Marcy students. Almost all of the building's janitors and kitchen workers were black residents of the city.

The analysis of adults in the school reported in this chapter is based on my observations and interactions with African American and white employees, and statements about teachers are confined to members of these groups. As far as I could tell, the relatively few Hispanic employees—six classroom teachers, several aides, and the assistant principal—did not differ in substantive ways from their white and black colleagues. However, with the exception of one teacher and the assistant principal, the Hispanic staff were (unofficially) isolated from the rest of the school in a bilingual program, and the time I spent with them was limited.

Marcy was considered by some personnel to be a good school. "It's a happening school," said an assistant superintendent. The drug counselor claimed, "It's a very good school—there aren't drugs all over it like in some of the other schools." Others, such as the school psychologist, considered it to be "in the middle—not great, not terrible; right at the mean." No teacher or administrator considered it to be among the worst schools. The principal said, "We may have problems, but we're no way the worst."

This chapter presents first-hand data from my experience as a participant in the reform efforts at Marcy Elementary School. Drawing on that experience, I assess the impact of class and race on school reform by describing how three factors—sociocultural differences among participants in reform, an abusive school environment, and educator expectations of failed reform—occurring in a minority ghetto where the school population is racially and economically isolated, constitute some of the powerful and devastating ways in which the concomitants of race and social class can intervene to determine what happens in inner city schools, and in attempts to improve them.

EDUCATIONAL REFORM IN NEWARK

A state-sponsored evaluation of Newark district was undertaken in the early 1980s, and in 1984 the state ordered that the district leadership take action to raise student achievement and to improve administration, or the district would lose accreditation (New Jersey State Department of Education 1984). In 1989, in response to a state threat of takeover, the district's leaders initiated a 4-year program of reform in eight schools in the central section of the city, including Marcy School, which was the focus of the research reported here. Over a million dollars had been donated by major corporations and foundations for projects in the eight schools (seven feeder schools and one high school). Twenty-five corporate, higher education, and local citizen groups provided plans and personnel.

The reforms were organized and directed by representatives of the city's majority black population. In 1989 the superintendent was African American, and the members of the board of education were African American and Hispanic. The assistant superintendent with responsibility for the reform initiative was black, and his staff consisted of two blacks and an Hispanic. African Americans were the majority of significant players at most levels of the school system and in the city government.

It was possible that local control by blacks would be a catalyst for change, making the schools more responsive to black students: The administration could, for example, choose reforms that empowered members of their own constituency—significant parent involvement if not community control could be a focus. A celebration of minority cultures could infuse the curriculum. Or the district could, given the studies that show black students' difficulty with standardized tests, present a serious challenge to government reliance on these tests as measures of achievement and funding. Perhaps the black teachers could reverse commonly held low expectations for minority students from low-income households; perhaps they could understand and nurture their charges, laying down an educational ground for academic success (King 1993).

However, and conversely, it was also possible that, as shown by Fannon (1967), Freire (1970), Memmi (1965, 1968), Said (1978), and others studying oppressed minorities, victims of race and class exploitation sometimes grow to mimic the behavior and attitudes of their oppressors, and themselves victimize others of their own group over whom they have power. It becomes important, then, to note here that some African American educators, as products of past racial, and, perhaps, class, discrimination and exploitation, may have internalized negative beliefs about their students whereby they mimic attitudes held by the dominant white society.

An extensive battery of school improvement projects was attempted in the eight schools. The most comprehensive projects planned by the board were

- School Based Management (in which teams of teachers, parents, and administrators were to jointly decide on school policy and practice)
- A professional development project (in which reform teams and all administrators in the eight schools were involved in retreats, workshops, and other preparations for shared decision making)
- All-day kindergartens
- Ungraded primary classes

- Departmentalization of the middle grades (so that students in grades 6 through 8 changed classes for each subject)
- Introduction of new textbooks for whole language, math, and science instruction in elementary grades
- Teacher retraining in methods articulated by Madeline Hunter
- School-wide Chapter One conversion to provide basic skills remediation for all students using compensatory federal funds for low-achieving, low-income students

There were smaller projects at Marcy and several of the other schools, as well:

- A "robotics" science program
- Integrated math and science in the middle grades
- An African American arts program
- An early intervention drug prevention program for the primary grades
- Extended day programs for homeless children in two schools
- Mentoring of students by successful adults from the community
- Local university, citizen, business, state, and volunteer programs run by Educate America, Cities in Schools, United Way Charities, the Protestant Community Center, Prudential Corporation, and Rutgers University and New Jersey Institute of Technology, among others
- The staff development project in cooperative learning that I carried out (see Anyon, 1994b)

Reform in Marcy School took what Charles, a white learning disabilities specialist assigned to the school and a central actor there, called "a shotgun approach." He explained to me:

Nothing has worked before, so we're trying everything. Did you see the movie *Animal House*? That's what this place is like. [The present reform initiative] is our last chance to get even with the town! Mike [the school psychologist] and I wrote the School Improvement Plan [mandated by the state]. We also wrote the school-based management proposal [also mandated by the state]. The teachers voted for it, but they probably didn't understand it. It didn't matter, they didn't have any choice anyway. Read it, it lists our initiatives. The board [of education] didn't approve the school-based management plans,

they never moved on any of them [from any of the schools].
But we're doing it anyway.

This learning disabilities specialist revealed his concern for the children
at Marcy School in many ways, and worked very hard to improve education there. Unlike most other adults working at the school, he arrived
early and stayed late, he spent many hours assisting teachers and students who asked for his help, and he was constantly dreaming up ideas
for new projects. Yet in his statement are intimated some of the attitudes
that, I will argue below, contributed to the failure of reform activity:
sociocultural differences and hostilities between groups involved, lack
of assistance from the board of education, and frustration.

SOCIOCULTURAL DIFFERENCES BETWEEN REFORMERS, PARENTS, AND SCHOOL PERSONNEL

In the following portions of the chapter I discuss ways in which I see
the racial-class histories and characteristics of participants in the reform
process affecting attempts to improve Marcy School. This section, for
example, contains descriptions of ways in which the sociocultural dis-
tances between reformers, parents, and school personnel interfered
with the implementation of several projects.

The assistant superintendent in charge of the reform called occasional meetings of his "collaborators"—25 representatives from groups
or agencies with projects in the eight schools. All who attended these
meetings, and who took part in projects in the schools, were professionals; five, in addition to the assistant superintendent, were African
American and the other 20 were white. The following account of a
meeting between two of these reformers and low-income minority parents at Marcy School suggests how sociocultural differences were mani-
fested.

Two retired white executives from the National Executive Service
Corps have been brought in by the assistant superintendent to ad-
vise parents at Marcy School on how to collaborate. The men are
meeting with the Parent Corps in the library. Mrs. Betty Williams, a
black woman of about 60, former student and parent at Marcy,
head of the Parent Corps, and a community leader in the housing
projects where she and the four other parents, four black women
and one Hispanic male, live, are sitting around a rectangular table.
On the other, far side, of the room, around a smaller table, sit the

two executives, wearing expensive-looking suits, smiling across the room at the parents, and holding pencils above long yellow pads. The five parents are seated so that only Mrs. Williams faces the two men across the room. At no time during the discussion does she or any of the other parents look at the executives.

One executive smiles broadly and addresses the group: "We each had our own company. We've had a good deal of experience. What problems do you have that we – with our background – could help you with?" Mrs. Williams responds, "Maintenance are our only problems. We've gotten everything done except the bathrooms. And we're fighting for equipment. I fought for 2 years to get a gym floor. I went to this school. We had all kind of equipment here. Now the kids don't have nothing to do in the gym [several parents nod]. We're going to send letters to parents so kids'll wear uniforms for gym. We go to the board meetings. The eighth graders don't know how to play kickball! We got taught that in gym. We were so amazed. They didn't know how to play kickball, so we teach them."

Retired white executive: "But [pause] if there's anything we can do for you, we'd like your suggestions." Mrs. Williams ignores his question and says to the parents, "I'm going to the dentist – to get me some teeth. And then I'm *really* going to eat!" She then talks to the parents about an upcoming assembly in which she will give certificates to parent volunteers.

Retired white executive intercedes, referring to the fact that the Parent Corps has only eight members: "What are your plans for getting more parents?" Mrs. Williams says, "We *have* a lot of parents. We found that this is the way we get parents: In the morning I stand by the door and tell them they can talk to me about anything." She again speaks to the group at her table about the upcoming assembly.

The retired executives look at each other, smile again at the parents, and stop asking questions. They sit quietly at the back of the room during the rest of the meeting, and Mrs. Williams does not acknowledge them again. (Field notes, November 8, 1992)

The social gulf between the parents and reformers that to me seemed to impair communication and joint planning at this meeting was never breached. During the subsequent months neither the white executives from the corporate world nor the black and Hispanic parents from the projects were able to utilize each others' skills. Commentators have long pointed to the fact that differences in social backgrounds and language

can impair interaction and trust (Hardin 1982; Laitin 1986). Other factors, such as inexperience, certainly contributed to the executives' lack
of expertise in working with the parents, but even this inexperience can
be attributed in part to the enormous social and cultural gulf separating
the two groups. Nothing came of the executives' attempted involvement in the parent group, and they terminated their visits after several
months.

A similar social distance separated many of the black teachers from
the two consultants directing the "Professional Development Project"
(training for shared decision making for school-based management).
This project was run by two expensively dressed consultants based in
an exclusive suburb 25 miles away. In part because of their blond, suburban "look," teachers called the consultants "the all-American kids."

On several occasions one of the consultants complained to me that
the teachers and administrators in this district "are just like the kids.
They don't even know how to *talk* about collaboration. And they want
immediate gratification. If they don't get it, they want to quit." The
teachers, on the other hand, related to me their opinion that the two
consultants were "too suburban": "They have no idea what city
schools are like. They don't know what we're up against." "They don't
know the kids!" A number of teachers, moreover, informed the assistant superintendent that the consultants were racist, and had made
racist comments. The assistant superintendent told me that he had
agreed with the teachers, but had counseled them: "We have to work
with them despite the racism. They have a lot to teach us [about cooper-
ation]."

The workshops and retreats that were part of the professional development training were resisted by both teachers and administrators,
who saw them as "too abstract," and "not geared to city schools"
(Anyon, 1994a, 1995b). In part because of teacher complaints of racism
and the perceived inappropriateness of the consultants for the city's
schools, the board of education rescinded permission for the consultants
to continue the training for shared decision making after the 2nd year.

As part of another reform project, middle-level management employees, both black and white, from the nearby headquarters of two
national corporations participated in a tutoring program in Marcy and at
two other elementary schools. In the two other schools the administration refused to cooperate with them, saying that the managers were not
equipped "to deal with the kids." In Marcy School the tutors quit because, they said, "nobody was interested in the students getting any
tutoring" from them. Referring to middle- and upper-middle-class help-
ers in the reform effort, such as the groups of executives, as well as

graduate students from a university in New York City, a Marcy teacher stated, "They come in the schools, and they can't handle the kids. We have to train them and monitor them. It takes too much time." Another said, "They have no idea of the *situation* we have here! They just get in the way."

As these examples indicate, social distance arising in part from lack of common experience and knowledge of each other in people of different class and racial backgrounds can impair communication, trust, and joint action between reformers and school personnel, can foster an incompetence that arises in part from this lack of knowledge, and can hamper the implementation of educational improvement projects. In the examples presented here, teachers and parents resisted the efforts of reformers, and several improvement projects were vitiated.

DIFFERENCES BETWEEN THE SOCIOCULTURAL CONTENT OF REFORMS AND THE STUDENT POPULATION

I questioned the assistant superintendent about who had decided which projects would be part of this reform effort. He said that he, members of the board of education, a union representative, and a parent representative had taken a weekend retreat together in June of 1989 and had chosen the projects that would be attempted. I asked whether their choices differed in any way from what the state had mandated in recent regulations. "No, we chose the exact same things," he said.

> We chose what is raising scores across the country: school-based management, ungraded primary, all-day kindergarten, departmentalization of the middle grades, programs like whole language and cooperative learning. We ordered all new textbooks in math, science, reading, phonics, and a whole language series.

I asked if any of the reforms were a response to the fact that most of the school children were African American. "No," he said, "although the superintendent and I are black nationalists—well, I was a pan-Africanist—but we chose what was fundable." I asked if any of the reforms were a response to the poverty of the children. "No," he stated again, "just the parent forums [informational meetings]. A lot of our parents are young and disenfranchised." I then inquired if any of the reforms had anything to do with the students' black dialect (or, more accurately, inner city dialect, as all the students seem to speak it—

blacks, Hispanics, and the few poor whites as well). "No—but that does get in the way. They can't express themselves."

I pressed, "Why not choose reforms that respond in some way to the children—at the least a multicultural focus to curriculum, for example?" He replied,

> It wouldn't be politically doable. Education reform is as much about politics as it is about kids. You have to be aware of the larger bureaucratic system you're working in. The old-boy network, they're white, and that's where the money is! You have to go to them for money to do things. What you do has to be acceptable to them.

What I would like to suggest is that these and the other reforms that were chosen have little if anything to do with this district's students and the cultural and economic realities of their lives, and in part because of this sociocultural inappropriateness, the reforms actually impede the students' academic progress and thereby preclude reform success.

One of the reforms initiated by the board of education in 1989 was an attempt to enforce teacher accountability by mandating that instruction be based on the new textbooks, and that these texts were to be used "on grade level" (e.g., fifth grade texts used with all fifth graders) despite the fact that the majority of students in most classrooms were reading and computing well below grade level. A 1993 state report directed Newark teachers to adhere closely to those texts. Both state and district mandates include directives that teachers are to reteach and retest students on any skills not passed on the quarterly tests devised by the publishers of the reading and math series (New Jersey State Department of Education, Education Programs 1993, 13, 15). Teachers complained bitterly about the "on-grade-level" policy, stating that it was impossible to teach students from textbooks that they could not understand. "They can't read the books and they're labeled failures before they even try!" was a typical complaint.

There are additional ways in which this reliance on mainstream texts and workbooks to teach students marginalized by poverty and race interferes with their achievement. An examination revealed that despite an occasional story featuring a minority character, the texts are a microcosm of white, middle-class interests and situations. Teachers state that the stories in the reading and language series, for example, "have nothing to do with the kids, they hate them, they think they're boring and stupid." Exclusive use of these texts, and the continual testing and retesting of the skills in them, means that there is no time for curriculum about black and Latino history—although the district has produced excellent curriculum guides in this area. None of the 24 teachers in the school whom I queried supplemented the written curriculum with black studies in a systematic way, except to varying degrees during Black History Month. In 1990, high school students at two city high schools demonstrated (unsuccessfully) in pursuit of a black studies curriculum for their schools.

The children I interviewed at Marcy School knew very little about African American history. I interviewed 25 children at the school aged 9 to 13, and only 8 knew who Martin Luther King Jr. was. Of these, 5 stated that they had heard about him or about other figures in black history from family members. More knew about Malcolm X because of the Hollywood movie ("They have T-shirts and hats about that," said one 12-year-old).

However alienating it may be for students to have a curriculum that does not concern them, and however frustrating to try to study a book that is too difficult, in the curriculum, there is yet another impediment to the progress of the students. This is the fact that the texts are written in standard English, a dialect that, because of their extreme marginalization and isolation from the mainstream, almost none of the students speak.

The following are representative examples of black dialect spoken by students in classrooms at Marcy School (see also Smitherman 1975):

"They lookin at us paper." [at our paper]
"He ain't ax you." [didn't ask you]
"I'm is the girl you want." [I am]
"When my sister take my baby sister toys she be in school."

As Joan Baratz argued in 1970, the fact that the authors of the texts that children are given to read continually reject nonstandard dialect as inferior provides a repeated insult to nondialect speakers. Not only is the standard English in written materials a source of insult to nonstandard dialect speakers, according to a large body of research, it also interferes in important ways with reading achievement (Baratz 1969; Labov 1969; Wiener and Cromer 1967). This interference is caused in part by the subtlety in the differences between standard and nonstandard English. Baratz and others demonstrated long ago that it is extremely difficult to learn to read a language that you do not speak, and that reading achievement can be significantly retarded by a reliance on texts whose syntax and phonetic structure differ from the structures of one's own language. Conversely, reading comprehension increases significantly when one learns to read from texts printed in one's native tongue (Baratz 1970; Cullinan 1974).

Black dialect can also interfere with mathematical thinking in educational contexts, where mathematical thinking, in textbooks and in most pedagogy, is governed by standard English language and forms of thought (Orr 1987). Eleanor Orr argues that not only does the subtlety of differences and the lack of familiarity with terms impede mathematical understanding, but the outright conflicts between black dialect terms and those of standard English do as well. Orr demonstrates that the grammars are distinct, the lexicons overlap, and, significantly, the unconscious rules that govern syntax in black dialect often conflict and cause interference with standard English, which uses different rules.

One of the many kinds of mathematical problems encountered by the black dialect speaker involves the conflicts among standard and nonstandard English expressions used to compare parts of objects or amounts (partitive comparative expressions):

Standard English	Black Dialect
half of	two times less than
half as large as	two times smaller than twice as small as half as small as
half as much as	half less than
half as fast as	twice as slow as half as slow as (Orr 1987, 166–167)

In some cases, the terms in which black dialect speakers think are the inverse of what they read in the math textbooks. For example, in an expression like "half as much as," the expression is in the vocabulary of both languages—the students' language and the language of the texts— but with opposite meanings. The confusion that can occur is substantial. Orr demonstrates how such confusion over the meanings of standard English mathematical expressions can also affect scientific reasoning:

> In a [high school] chemistry class a student [who speaks nonstandard dialect] stated that if the pressure was doubled with the temperature remaining constant, the volume of a gas would be "half more than it was." When I asked her if she meant that the volume would get larger, she said, "No, smaller." When I then explained that "half more than" would mean larger, one and a half times larger, indicating

the increase with my hands, she said she meant "twice" and with her hands indicated a decrease. When I then said, "But 'twice' means larger, two times larger," again indicating the increase with my hands, she said, "I guess I mean 'half less than.' It always confuses me." (171)

When the teachers who are attempting to teach speakers of nonstandard dialect from books written in standard English are also speakers of nonstandard dialect, as are many teachers in Newark, the confusion can be compounded. I estimate that most of the African American teachers at Marcy use black dialect with their students at least some of the time, mixing it with standard English. I estimate that approximately one third use dialect all the time with their students. Examples of teachers' comments follow:

"What does a sentence begins with?"
"When I be out they has a good time!"
"You didn't do nothin' yet."
"You wrong!"
"Take care your crayons—we can't get no more."
"Have anyone seen Shawana?"

I estimate that approximately the same fraction, one third, of the principals I talked with at reform team meetings also consistently spoke black dialect. According to the assistant superintendent, they speak dialect "most of the time." For example, I heard principals say:

"He have a parent who. . . . "
"Many people have came here."
"He don't never come to school."

Despite the curricular reforms—new textbooks, departmentalization, mandated instructional changes, and state and district regulations that attempt to align instruction with basals and other textbooks—the children's achievement scores have not increased. The standardized scores of the students at Marcy School are among the lowest in the district, as they have been for the last several decades, and actually declined between 1988 and 1992. This was also true at the other seven schools in the reform group. District achievement scores are among the lowest in the state, and are considerably below national medians (Newark Board of Education 1992; New Jersey State Department of Education 1994b).

The teachers, black and white, are in the unenviable position of being asked to impart a white, middle-class curriculum, written in a language that differs from and interferes with the students'—and many teachers'—own language, and which in most cases is presented to students in textbooks that are too difficult for them to fully comprehend.

The situation certainly fosters student failure, and, consequently, the failure of reform to raise achievement. Moreover, the frustration engendered by the students' low achievement has the potential to worsen classroom relations between teachers and students.

RELATIONS BETWEEN TEACHERS AND STUDENTS

Teachers face an extremely difficult pedagogical situation at Marcy School. In addition to the curricular and instructional mandates and conditions discussed above, teachers confront roomfuls of students whose home circumstances are often extremely stressful. Their desperate lives make many of them restless and confrontational; they can be difficult to teach, and to love. In this section of the chapter I first discuss interactions that I observed between black and white personnel and students, and then the reactions of the students.

Teachers' Attitudes Toward Students

It was apparent to me that many black teachers care deeply about their students: One, a young teacher at Marcy School who prays over her class every morning and evening, and every day for each one of her students, is an example. Another teacher in the building takes homeless students back to her residence to live with her whenever she can. Another coordinates a clothing drive in the spring, and food baskets at Thanksgiving. Moreover, in my work in Marcy and other Newark schools I encountered talented, dedicated, consistently hard-working teachers who were an inspiration to behold.

Most black teachers with whom I interacted during my work in the school also, however, expressed deep frustration in dealing with their students. Perhaps fueled by this frustration, many of these black teachers were—to varying degrees—abusive of their students. (I will argue below that many white teachers also exhibited—again to varying degrees—systematically abusive behavior toward their students.) During the 10 months in which I spent a full day each week working with teachers and their classes, I heard a tirade from black teachers of what seemed to me to be verbal humiliation and degradation, directed at students; for example:

"Shut up!"
"Get your fat head in there!"
"Did I tell you to move [talk; smile]?"
"I'm sick of you."
"He's not worth us wasting our time waiting for."
"Act like a human being."
"I'm going to get rid of you!"
"Excuse me!", said with what sounds like withering contempt.

I heard one particularly abusive black male teacher tell a girl that her breath "smelled like dog shit," and that her clothes "smelled like stale dust." A sampling of other, not atypical, comments I overheard includes:

"You're disgusting; you remind me of children I would see in a jail or something." (Black teacher to her class of black and Hispanic first graders)
"Shut up and push those pencils. Push those pencils—you borderline people!" (Black teacher to his class of black and Hispanic sixth graders)
"Your mother's pussy smells like fish. *That's* what stinks around here." (Black teacher to black fourth-grade girl whose mother is a prostitute)

Janice Hale-Benson (1986) argues that a cultural norm of harsh discipline exists among African Americans, and thus verbal expressions that a white observer might perceive as abusive are not perceived thus by African American teachers or students. As one black teacher explained to me, "It's what they're used to. They wouldn't listen to us if we didn't yell and put on a mean face. They know it's only our school voice." An older black teacher explained, "You can't treat these kids nice. They don't deserve it." Then, referring to a beginning teacher who had taken her class to the museum and had been asked to leave because the students were "touching everything," the older teacher said, "Why did she take them on a trip? They don't deserve to go to the museum! They don't know how to act!"

On eight occasions when I was working with teachers in their classrooms, I saw black teachers, none of whom was considered to be an unusually harsh disciplinarian, smack a student with some force on the head, chest, or arm as if it were a routine occurrence. On numerous occasions I saw teachers grab students by the arm and shake them. No one reacted to these actions. I also witnessed a severe beating by a parent while a teacher was present and did nothing to stop the beating (nor did I).

My experience at Marcy School leads me to believe that the treatment of students by many black adults at this school goes beyond any tradition of harsh discipline that would be culturally sanctioned among other African Americans, and represents, instead, aspects of a lived professional culture that characterizes the behavior of both black and white teachers, and that systematically degrades the children.

Thus, I found many white personnel to be just as verbally abusive as the black teachers discussed above. Remarks included:

> "If I had a gun I'd kill you. You're all hoodlums." (white fifth-grade teacher)
>
> "Stop picking in your ear. Go home and get a bath." (White basic skills teacher to a black boy)
>
> "Why are you so stupid! I'm going to throw you in the garbage." (Other white basic skills teacher to a black boy)
>
> "Don't you have *any* attention span? You have the attention span of cheerios!" (White principal trying to quiet a class of black and Hispanic fourth graders)
>
> "This ain't no restaurant, you know—where you go in and get what you *want*! [pause] You have no sense! You have no sense!" (White teacher reprimanding three African American girls in the hall outside his door)

Two white teachers expressed fear of confronting their students. One stated, "I don't talk to them like I used to. They'll challenge you now, and you might not win." A white male gym teacher said he refused to give a fourth grade their scheduled gym class because "They're too rough. They throw the ball, it could kill you!" I did not see any white teacher strike a student, perhaps because of cultural norms that do not sanction this or perhaps for fear of retaliation. As one white male teacher said, "They all have social workers, and the social workers tell the girls, don't let any man touch you. One girl accused me of touching her on the knee. Her mother told her to do it, to get [her] out of my class. And it worked."

The school psychologist alleged that abuse by teachers is "common" in the Newark schools. The school social worker told me that she thought that there was less teacher abuse in the last 4 to 5 years because the Department of Social Services is "more diligent." However, the district—which as noted in Chapter 1 serves only 4.2% of the state's students—reports over 40% of the institutional child abuse reported by school systems to the state (New Jersey State Department of Education, Education Programs 1993, 68). (The phrase "institutional abuse" as used by the New Jersey Department of Education refers to emotional, physical, or sexual abuse of students by public school employees.)

The attitudes of staff are also transmitted to students by "inspirational sayings" that the board of education requires principals to post around the building. The purpose is to motivate the students. The following are sayings that the principal and a teacher posted on walls and on hallway bulletin boards:

> "If you have an open mind, chances are something will fall into it."
> "The lazier we are today, the more we have to do tomorrow."
> "The way to avoid lying is not to do anything that involves deception."
> "It is easier to think you are right than to be right."
> "Don't pretend to be what you don't intend to be."
> "If you can't think of anything to be thankful for, you have a poor memory."

These "motivational" sayings are also instantiations of the lived professional culture that degrades the students at Marcy School. The staff's abusive, implicitly sanctioned attitudes and behaviors have evolved over time in a situation where working conditions make teaching and administrating extremely difficult and in a milieu in which the student population is extremely poor, racially marginalized, often of low academic standing and difficult to motivate educationally, and from families with little or no social clout. The lived culture of the teachers combines with the alien curriculum described above to create a hostile, rejecting environment for the students.

Student Opposition to Teachers

The students in turn describe their reactions to their school experience, especially to their teachers. The following are representative quotes from 8 of the 25 students whom I interviewed. The students are African American, unless otherwise noted.

"Tell me about your class," I say to a fifth-grade girl during her interview. "My class stupid. They mentally depressed. They don't want to learn." "Why not?" "They don't like the teachers." "Why not?" "Well, Miss Washington, she assigns all this homework, and she never collect it. Lots of parents puts in complaints about Mr. D., but they don't do nothin." "Do you have many friends in your class?" I ask. "No," she responds, "I'm lonely. I'm a nerd." When asked to explain why her teachers and the principal act the way they do, this girl says, "When they need a low place to come to they come here. That the only place they get a job." (This 11-year-old attempted suicide twice during the year in which I knew her.)

During another interview an 11-year-old boy tells me, "Teachers throw kids out, say 'I don't want you in my class.' They throw us on the floor and be grabbin us. Teachers too mean. They lie on people." "So what do you do?" I ask. "We make him mad." "How?" "Talk, laugh, and have fun."

I ask a 10-year-old boy to "tell me about the teachers in this school." He responds, "Most teachers here don't teach us." "Why not?" "Because of the kids. They runs the halls and makes the teachers upset." "Why do they do that?" "Um, they think [teachers] just doin the job for money, they don't care."

An 11-year-old boy tells me, "Most of the kids here don't do well." "Why?" I ask. "They fight too much and they don't feel like going to school." "Why not?" "They don't like school. They want to hang out." "And then?" "Then they'll drop out."

When I ask a 13-year-old white girl (one of three white students in the school) why some kids don't do well at school, she says, "Kids don't want to learn. They be playin in the halls. They don't study." "Why not?" "It's boring and they get mad at the teachers." "How do you think the teachers feel about that?" "They don't care. [pause] If we don't learn, the teachers still gets their paycheck."

I ask a 10-year-old Hispanic girl, "Why don't some kids here do well at school?" "It's they fault. Because Mr. Thompson—you saw him teach—he's crazy, but he's a good teacher. The kids that don't learn don't want to learn." "Why not?" "They don't like school. They don't like Mr. Thompson. They playin so much in school they don't have time to learn." At this point the principal comes over, and pinches her hard on her cheek, leaving a red mark. He says, "Mr. Thompson knows what to do with *you*, doesn't he?"

"Tell me about your teacher," I request of a 9-year-old boy. "He says we're animals. Hooligans. He said we should be in a zoo. I feel bad when he say that. I get kinda sad." "So what do you do?" "I put my head down." A boy walking past us as we sat talking in the hall added, "He treat us like we're toys. So we make him mad." I ask him, "What do you do?" "We run around. [pause] Watch!" This 10-year-old boy proceeded to do forwards and backwards cartwheels, flipping high in the air off a desk that was in the hall. Several other boys who were wandering the halls gathered around and cheered him on.

Almost all of the students I interviewed at Marcy School seemed to be in an oppositional stance to their teachers; most were aware that they are in an environment which is hostile and aggressively rejecting of them. Ray McDermott (1987) argued that black children who have white teachers may ''achieve'' failure, by rejecting the oppressive definition that they perceive their teachers hold of them, and by concomitantly rejecting the teachers' and the school's definition of success. The black and Hispanic children I interviewed apparently feel oppressive rejection on the part of both black and white teachers. In this regard, almost all of the interviewees said it did not matter whether you had white or black teachers (''They all the same''), although one student stated that his aunt told him, when he complained about his teacher, ''Just be glad you got a black teacher.'' Another black child said it was better to have a white teacher, ''as long as it's a lady.''

It may be that the hostile social situation in which teaching, learning, and testing occurs in this school has important consequences for achievement on the standardized tests which are given to the students every quarter and every spring, and which are the benchmark of success in educational reform. Ernest Haggard demonstrated as long ago as 1954 that the social situation made a significant difference in how the 671 black inner city children whom he studied performed on standardized IQ tests. The attitude of the student to the tester was the most important aspect in determining how students did on those standardized tests. Significantly, the attitude of the student to the tester was more important than the content (e.g., the identifiable cultural bias) of the test items (see also Cazden 1970; Smitherman 1977).

Some teachers at Marcy School wonder aloud why the students ''can do all the things in the street they won't do for us. Did you ever see a drug dealer who couldn't make change? They're walking spreadsheets!'' In the face of intense district pressure on teachers to ''get the scores up,'' they convey to their students angry, desperate hopes that they will perform well on the tests. I suspect that, although some children may not be intellectually capable of learning what the school asks, one effect of the hostile atmosphere in the school is that many students may simply refuse to comply. One teacher told me that her students ''can do the work in class, but when it comes time to take the standardized tests, they know people think they can't do it. So they just go through the test marking down any answer. They don't even try.'' The assistant superintendent said that one of his biggest problems in the high schools was "to get the students to take the [standardized] tests seriously" (see also Kohl 1994).

The result of student opposition to the academic demands of the school could be devastating for reform. Standardized tests are almost always the criterion that defines success in inner city schools. As long as testing takes place in a hostile, oppressive environment and measures a curriculum that is culturally and linguistically unsuited to the students, the scores, I suspect, will not rise.

EXPECTATIONS FOR REFORM

Most school personnel appeared to be resigned to the failure of reform efforts in the eight schools. The principal of Marcy School stated that "nothing will happen. This school was built over a hundred years ago. They just replaced the [original] windows 5 years ago! With the decades of neglect in this ward, it'll take years to fix it up."

Teachers agree: "Nothing will be left when the money goes home." "The 1st year was nice—we were treated like professionals; the 2nd year? Nothing." One teacher stated, when asked what she thought would come from the reform projects. "Maybe I'll get them [her students] from 'very low' to 'low' on the [achievement] tests." Then she added, "But even if they do learn to read and write, there are no jobs."

During one of my first few days in the building, the child study team, the psychologist, social worker, and learning disabilities specialist, invited me to lunch with them. They seemed eager to tell me about the school. The following is an excerpt of our conversation during that meeting. We are discussing the enormous problem the team sees in "getting anything done" at Marcy School.

> "We're part of the problem, you know," the psychologist says, "I mean, jailers and prisoners are the same." The social worker adds, "This district has enormous problems – the mayhem of the system itself is a big problem. But the children's lives are the biggest problem." "Yes," agrees the psychologist, "we should be teaching them [the students] who they are in the system, and what the system does to them. We need a diagnosis like they have in Europe – of economic and social victimization. That's what these kids are – victims."
>
> "What about the teachers?" I ask. "What are they like?" The psychologist replies, "There is a lot of teacher abuse of the students – it's common here. The children have desperate lives, and

the teachers distance themselves from that by abusing them, by separating themselves from the children, even though they're [the
teachers are] black, too. But you know, most of these teachers are
one paycheck away from welfare themselves."

"And you," I ask, "how do you deal with the children and the
system?" They say that they blame the system. "Contradictory initiatives on the part of the board, disarray at the board," says the learning disabilities specialist. And he blames the state: "The state is
weak; it has no money to monitor the system, and couldn't afford
to take over [the city's schools]." "Even your project," says the psychologist, referring to my work with the teachers on cooperative
learning. "We've seen it all before. We did cooperative learning in
the early seventies – the open classroom, curriculum integration,
there's nothing new being done now, it's all been tried before."
"Yes," I say. "But maybe this is how *we* distance ourselves from the
problems. We say, 'there's nothing we can do, it's all been tried before.'" "Maybe," said the psychologist. (Field notes, February 27,
1992)

A consequence of this resignation among teachers and other personnel
is that it is impossible to garner the enthusiasm and energy necessary to
carry out improvement projects. Indeed, most personnel imply that
they accept the present situation as the best that can be expected. I
heard over and over again, "We're doing the best we can" and "This is
the best that can be done with what we have."

Many of the district's central office administrators, many of the
teachers and principals, as well as the majority of the participating parents (e.g., classroom aides) grew up in the city. They and their children
attended the city's schools. For the people who work in the schools, this
is "their" system; the system provides their jobs, and despite its faults,
most with whom I spoke defended and supported it.

Even I, an outsider, after almost 4 months of intense work with the
students and teachers, recorded the following:

I was very negative about the school when I arrived. Now I find myself thinking, "This is a good urban school," and hoping that the
State people will feel that way too. I feel that many of the teachers
work very hard, and actually teach. I go through the halls – with
the doors slamming, adults going in and out of classes, kids roaming the halls, the intercom blaring and crackling, and the teachers
shouting and angry – and I have to remind myself that it is an in-
credibly noisy and distracting place for studying. It is beginning to

sound normal to me. So is what goes on in the classrooms. "Good"
is, of course, relative. If I were in [an affluent district in which I
have done several district evaluations] what happens here would
signal a crisis or breakdown of the system. It would never be considered "good." I must be part of the system now; those who are in an
institution have a hard time seeing it from the outside. (Field notes,
June 17, 1992)

The next day I recorded my reactions after a visit to my daughter's
third-grade classroom in a "model" public school in New York City.
The parents are, for the most part, professionals; 40% of the students
are minority, but only 10% of them are low-income students. It is widely
known as a very good school.

After being in Marcy yesterday where chaos filled the halls, and
teachers tried angrily and in vain to get the children to go back in
their rooms, I went into my daughter's class today.
    The contrast was overwhelming. The kids were sitting, doing
various activities, all over the room, on the floor, at tables – one
boy was curled up on top of a low book shelf, reading a book. The
children were reading; making Father's Day presents from brightly
colored materials; and were working with manipulables of various
kinds. Materials, books, and supplies were everywhere, and in
abundance; the children's work was on display on the walls, hanging from the ceiling, and in the hall. Murals and papier-mâché projects decorated the back of the room. The T-shirts which they had
tie-died and silk-screened for their "Olympics Day" the next day
were hanging from rope strung across the room, drying. The children were working easily, absorbed, in little clusters. Chatter filled
the air, and smiles; and – most importantly – they seemed involved
and interested in what they were doing. They seemed happy to be
there!
    It seemed unbelievable to me how wonderful it was. It made
me realize how far I had gone toward accepting the starkness of
Marcy's bare and vacant rooms, the angry, wounded-looking children, and the resentful, hostile teachers – as acceptable. (Field
notes, June 18, 1992)

CONCLUSION

The foregoing discussion delineates some of the ways in which black-
ness and whiteness, extreme poverty and relative affluence, cultural

marginalization and social legitimacy come together—and conflict—
within a school to affect educational reform. The events and behaviors
that I have described take place when people of low social status (e.g.,
impoverished people of color) are the student and parent population
and do not have the power to prevent such things, and when the rage
and resignation of those in a community and in a school are so great
that no good deeds can overcome them.

Tragedies like these are experienced in a school and district when
administrators from an oppressed group mimic, through educational
policy choices, their oppressors, and when teachers from an oppressed
group devalue students of their own group, as do the dominant culture
and teachers of that culture. Most importantly, dire effects are produced
when people in a community and school confront the workings of a
class-biased, racist system without sufficient resources and without
hope.

In this chapter I have discussed some of the ways in which the
context of social class and race in Newark has intervened in school
reform attempts at Marcy School. In July of 1995, after 30 years of federal, state, and local school reform efforts had failed to raise student
achievement, the state department of education ousted the elected
board of education and took control of the Newark school district.

It is important at this juncture to ask why more than a quarter
century of educational reforms have not been able to transform Newark
schools into smoothly functioning, highly regarded educational institutions. Why is the city not able to financially support quality schooling for its children? How did it come to pass that the children at Marcy
School are so isolated from the mainstream of American culture that
they cannot profit from its curriculum? For what reason was a principal
who is not capable of curricular and pedagogical leadership appointed
at such a needy school? What circumstances have fostered the evolution of a professional educator culture that systematically degrades
students?

To answer these questions, we certainly need to take account of the
impact of the current social context, as in this chapter I have attempted
to do. A more thorough answer, however, requires that we understand
how this social context came to be. What economic and political policies
led to the fiscal distress of the city? What economic and political forces
contributed to the development of a ghetto which holds the children
tightly within it? For what reasons have urban leaders been kept from
legislative councils that would have yielded them state and national
power—and perhaps access to adequate fiscal resources? And how did
these developments, in turn, shape the city's schools—their curricula,

their policies, the attitudes of their personnel? Finally, and crucially, we must ask, How can we use the answers to these and other questions as a guide to corrective future action? History is ignored by most who study educational reform; one which will yield insights into these matters is presented in part II.

PART II

THE PAST

CHAPTER 3

Industrial Strength, Educational Reform, and the Immigrant Poor: 1860-1929

During the early period, to be discussed in this chapter, American cities were prospering industrially and leading the nation in the development and reform of educational systems. In these same cities, however, we can identify developments and policies that were creating problems that have intensified and that plague America's urban centers—and their schools—to the present day.

THE CITY AND THE STATE

In 1860, Newark was one of the leading industrial cities in the nation. Although small in area, it ranked sixth in the nation in the value of its manufactured products and was the 11th largest city in population. Seventy-four percent of the city's labor force was employed in manufacturing (Hirsch 1978, xix). By the 1870s, Newark was the fourth largest insurance center in the United States and the largest retail center in New Jersey (Popper 1952, 92). Mansions graced the broad, tree-lined downtown streets, and industrialists, the middle class, and many workers lived within walking distance of the factories and shops (Cunningham 1988). In the decades preceding and following the Civil War in this prosperous American city, there were children from all social classes attending the public schools (Burr 1942, 288; see also Tyack 1974, 54).

By 1900, New Jersey was one of the wealthiest states in the Union. As a result of the state's refusal to comply with the U.S. government's "trust-busting" regulations, one half of the nation's 300 largest corporations were located in New Jersey by the early part of the twentieth century (Laccetti 1990, 16). As the fugitive trusts (e.g., Rockefeller's Standard Oil) were crossing the river from Wall Street, refugees escaping poverty in Europe were crossing the Atlantic. Between 1880 and 1920, more than 200,000 immigrants arrived in Newark. Those who remained joined the Irish and Germans who had settled earlier, between 1830 and 1880. Most of the new immigrants were Italians and Russian Jews; but there were Hungarians, Poles, Lithuanians, Slavs, Austrians, and Greeks as well (Cunningham 1988, 201–202). Between 1890 and 1920 more than 18 million immigrants, overwhelmingly Catholic and Jewish, arrived in America's cities (Judd and Swanstrom 1994, 107). In 1910, New Jersey was the state with the fifth highest proportion of foreign-born residents (Salmore and Salmore 1993, 11).

By the turn of the century, more than half of Newark's workforce was foreign born (Popper 1952, 63). Although most of the immigrants found entry-level jobs in the city's manufacturing industries, for many there was no decent place to live. Newark's first slums had been described in 1832 (Jackson and Jackson 1971, 51). From the 1860s the city had possessed ghettos: German and Irish poor and free blacks crowded into tenements, into shanties measuring 10 feet by 10 feet, and into decaying barns and wooden shacks (Galishoff 1988, 19). In 1890 most of the new immigrant poor were shunted into tenement houses in several wards of the central city and in an industrial section called the Ironbound (84). As in other industrial cities, the uncontrolled growth of the second half of the nineteenth century had not only produced great wealth for the mighty Barons and graceful downtown mansions, but a city with slums, dirty water, rutted unpaved streets, and cholera and smallpox epidemics. "By 1910, the results of unplanned growth were most apparent, slum conditions had developed to an alarming degree, traffic congestion was acute" (400 trolleys passed the downtown corner of Broad and Market Streets every hour). "Many sections of the city were extremely unattractive" (Newark Central Planning Board 1944, 13).

Newark thrived economically, in 1909 providing one fifth of all jobs in New Jersey, and supplying one quarter of all wages paid to industrial workers in the state (Bartholomew 1944, 12). As the 200,000 "strangers in the land" arrived in Newark, swelling the population to 350,000 by 1910 (Cunningham 1988, 201) and as the effects of uncontrolled industrial growth made the city a less pleasant place to live, those who could, moved to the country. Trolley car lines had linked the city with outlying areas in the 1890s, and the movement outward accelerated. Members of the business elite who so desired commuted to and from Newark's nineteenth century suburbs (Cunningham 1988, 199; see Jackson 1976, 89–110 for more on early suburbs near other cities).

With the influx of immigrants to New Jersey's cities, the three largest, Newark, Jersey City, and Paterson, contained 30% of the state's population by 1890 (Salmore and Salmore 1993, 203). As in virtually every other state, however, a rural elite dominated the state legislature, having established mechanisms to ensure that no matter how many inhabitants a city had, rural representatives would continue to hold a majority (Judd and Swanstrom 1994, 51). In New Jersey this was accomplished by means of the "one county, one senator" rule, and by using the county unit rather than population or acreage to elect assembly members (Salmore and Salmore 1993, 20). Neither rural legislators in the state capital nor members of an increasingly nonresident local business elite were sympathetic to the stringent controls on industry— or the financial expenditures that would have been necessary—to clear up befouled drinking water, muddy, impassable streets, and dilapidated housing for workers in the city's central sections. Moreover, even though the 1920 census showed that a majority of Americans were living in urban areas, city residents had no recourse in the federal government either, as rural elites dominated there, as well (Judd and Swanstrom 1994, 51–52). Thus, the national government could also ignore the damaging consequences of industrialization and urbanization so apparent in America's cities.

As in other cities at the time, Newark's immigrants had created numerous local administrative structures in their attempts to gain the power and control not available to them through state or national electoral representation. By 1860 there were 12 wards in Newark, many aldermen, many elected officials, and numerous independent boards (Douglas 1972, 3). By the turn of the century, "executive and administrative authority was so complicated and confused that the average voter did not know who was doing what or to whom" (*Newark Evening News* April 30, 1953, in Douglas 1972, 3). In 1900, Germans dominated the Newark government. In 1916, "a long history of corruption and mismanagement climaxed in a series of scandals" which would add ammunition to the call—being heard in many American cities at this time—for a change to the commission form of government (*New York Times* December 18, 1916, in Douglas 1972, 4; see also Tyack 1974, 89).

Although the Protestant business elites essentially controlled the city through their access to finances and state legislators, they were dissatisfied with ethnic power, decentralization, and the inefficiency of aldermanic government (*New York Times* November 10, 1917; Stellhorn 1982, 82). Anti-German hysteria at the time of World War I and Progressive middle- and upper-middle-class pressure led to a successful referendum to change the city government to a small (five-member), non-ward-based, non-partisan commission in 1917 (Douglas 1972, 4). As in many cities during the Progressive Era, machine-dominated city governments were changed to the commission form, which was based on a business model of management in that all judicial, legislative, and executive powers were vested in a small board of commissioners. Every 4 years the commissioners would choose one out of their group to be mayor. Each commissioner had complete control over one sector of the government—police, zoning, revenue and finance, parks and public property, fire, and so forth. With a large field of candidates in commission elections, the winners needed to receive only a few votes more than did the losers. The top five vote getters were elected. There were 80 candidates in Newark's 1917 election, and 26 in 1953—when Newark's commission form of government was finally overturned (Douglas 1972, 9; Banfield and Wilson 1963).

During the 1920s, most cities Newark's size abandoned commission government: Concentrating the collection, disbursement, and auditing of funds and jobs in each independent commmissioner, with no checks and balances, fostered corruption and patronage. Although political corruption and graft did continue in most of these other cities, Newark's use of this form for the next 36 years made it especially easy for commissioners to develop personal fiefdoms, job banks, and opportunities for illegal activities.

THE SCHOOLS

When an 1871 act of the New Jersey legislature compelled all of the state's municipalities to offer a 9-month school term and prohibited tuition charges, the state became the last in the nation to guarantee free public education (Burr 1942, 217, 281). Even though New Jersey was late in providing free public education, the spirit of the action seems to have been generous. As a result of this 1871 act, for almost 10 years education in New Jersey became primarily a state responsibility: The state government assumed 75% of school costs of all districts exclusive of construction and repairs (*Robinson v. Cahill* 1973, 266; see also Burr 1942, 283).

During this period, in 1875, an amendment was added to the state constitution guaranteeing every child between 5 and 18 years of age a "thorough and efficient" public school education. The amendment containing the "thorough and efficient" phrase did not require that the state merely provide "rudimentary instruction" (that proposal was defeated); rather, the amendment that passed

> imposed on the [state] legislature a duty of providing a free system of schools capable of affording to every child such instruction as is neces-

> sary to fit it for the ordinary duties of citizenship . . . with the view of
> securing the common rights of all, before tendering peculiar advan-
> tages to any (*Robinson v. Cahill* 1972, 268).

Twenty-six other states added similar phrases to their constitutions during the nineteenth century, as state education systems were consoli-
dated by legislatures (see Odden and Picus 1992, 38–46).

Although they shared the widespread nineteenth-century view that
education was a cure for the problems resulting from industrialization
and immigration, businessmen in the cities and the rural elites in Trenton, the New Jersey state capital, were not willing to pay for enactment
of the "thorough and efficient" amendment for very long. After 9 years,
it became apparent that state leaders did not have the commitment to
continue carrying out the mandate of the 1871 legislation whereby the
state assumed the education costs of the municipalities. An 1881 law
returned 90% of state school taxes to the county of origin. The state's
extensive railroad property was exempt from taxation, and the legislature's historic reliance (since 1670) on the property tax for school funds
had confined most money to the wealthier districts (Salmore and Salmore 1993, 244). Thus, the 1881 law reinstated a trend that would contribute to extreme fiscal disparities in school districts—a reliance, as in almost all states, on local support of education (266; Carnoy 1982, 527).

New Jersey localities spent handsomely on their schools (at a rate a
third above the national average by the 1920s) for above-average teacher
salaries and a state-financed pension system for teachers by World War
II. However, the state's contribution to local education budgets through
the 1940s was 3 to 6%, lower than that of most states. New York, for
example, already provided one third of the funds for New York schools
by the late forties (Salmore and Salmore 1993, 366).

Ellwood P. Cubberly demonstrated in 1919 that nationally, "practically all the educational progress . . . within the past half century has
been progress [in the cities]" (465). Newark was an early example of this
development. Its school system was—by mid-nineteenth century—one
of the most successful in that it had developed a complete, free, public
school system "which was regarded as a model by other communities
throughout the state" (Burr 1942, 287). By 1839 there was a free school
in each ward of Newark, and one city high school—the third in the
nation after those in Boston and Philadelphia (286). Between 1840 and
1870, children of the professional and wealthy classes enrolled in the
Newark High School, whose quality was said to rival the private acade-
mies (287–288). Nelson R. Burr says of Newark at midcentury:

> As in most other large cities, [as the public high schools became estab-
> lished], and the "practical" subjects began to yield to academic

courses, the public high school became respectable, and the wealthier classes began to patronize it as a good preparation for college (1942 288; see 287–288 for other cities in New Jersey; also Vinovskis 1985, 32, for Beverly, Massachusettes).

Students from the working classes predominated in Newark's grammar schools and in the five evening schools. At midcentury nearly two thirds of the children of school age were attending the city's public schools (Burr 1942, 286). However, even though the Newark schools were in the forefront of the development of public education in the nineteenth century, as in other urban systems, many of these early schools (typically those with large percentages of the working poor) were dirty and overcrowded, with ill-trained teachers responsible for 100 students per class (Cunningham 1988, 142; Tyack 1974).

Educational Reform

Between 1880 and 1915, in many large cities educational leaders were national figures, often former university presidents. Presidents of the University of Illinois, Brown University, and the University of Iowa held positions as superintendents in Cleveland, Chicago and New York City respectively. President Charles W. Eliot of Harvard, Nicholas Murray Butler of Columbia, and William R. Harper of Chicago, among others, achieved prominence in the Progressive educational reform movement in cities (Tyack 1974, 7, 43, 134). The four Newark superintendents during this time were also national figures. All had earned doctoral degrees, one edited a professional journal called the *Educational Review*, two wrote for other journals, and several played leading roles in state and national educational organizations—for example, the prestigious national committees, the Committee of Ten in 1893, which influenced the development of the American high school for many years; and the Committee of Fifteen, which issued an influential report in 1895 on the organization of American city school systems (Kusick 1974, 82, 88, 101). Journal articles praised these superintendents and the reforms that they wrought in the Newark schools (Bruce 1904a, 1904b; Corson 1924).

Newark became nationally known as a large system that early on had instituted organizational reforms designed to make the schools hierarchical, professionally ordered, and more efficient, as was the national passion. In the 1850s, for example, the first superintendent of the Newark schools, Steven Congar, had added the following (among the first in the nation): special schools for indigent, working, blind, and "crippled" children; teacher institutes and a normal school for teacher training; and experiments in evening and postsecondary education (Cunningham 1988, 142).

By 1908 the Newark public school population had grown to 44,605 students (U.S. Immigration Commission 1911, IV:189). As the number of foreign children swelled the schools, the school system received plaudits for a series of innovative programs designed to attract and hold the children of immigrants: kindergartens, to provide, in the words of one superintendent, "attitudes necessary for grade school" (Newark claimed to have more children in kindergarten in 1901 than any other city); the Gary plan for an extended day in several schools; all-year schools "to provide more time for 'slow' students to catch up to the others;" summer schools for the poorer children who "were forced to stay in the city during the hot summer months" (Corson 1924; Kusick 1974, 52); secondary schools that offered vocational and trade programs; and continuation schools as well as evening schools for those who worked during the day.

As did 56 other cities between 1912 and 1922, Newark organized a bureau of child guidance to assist children with problems adjusting to school. In 1917 Newark created a pathbreaking bureau of reference and research, which soon issued numerous scholarly reports on the new ethnic populations (Kusick 1974, 133, 149; Tyack 1974, 52).

In 1881 the state began to support industrial education in New Jersey with the first technical school, the Newark Technical School, "to advance the manufacturing interests of the city" with special reference to the "improvement of the working classes." A few years later the state and the board of trade successfully encouraged industrial education within the regular school curriculum with a "technical" course of study in Newark high schools, and by 1911 two commercial and manual training high schools had been built in the city (Kusick 1974, 232, 246).

Although insufficient to ease the overcrowding in schools caused by the influx of immigrant children, school building in this prosperous era of Newark's history was more extensive than it was to be in any period afterwards. Between 1880 and 1917, 44 new school buildings were built, and 76 additions. This construction was praised in the September 1914 issue of the *Architectural Record*:

> The building activities of the Newark board of education [under the guidance of the well-known architect Ernest F. Guilbert] during the last four years have been extraordinary when the size of the city is taken into consideration. Nineteen new buildings and additions have been undertaken, providing for nearly 15,000 pupils. Included in the 19 buildings are 13 auditoriums and as many gymnasiums. (quoted in *Newark Evening News*, January 29, 1950)

Rising costs, due in part to involvement in World War I, checked construction in 1917.

During this era of Progressive municipal and educational reforms, changes highly similar to those enacted in the Newark school system were carried out in other city districts across the country—for example, in Baltimore, Buffalo, Chicago, Cincinnati, Detroit, Gary, New York, Pittsburgh, Providence, San Francisco, and St. Louis. Administrative, organizational, and programmatic changes wrought substantial reorganization, coordination, and directional change in city schools, producing what reformers, educational experts, and business leaders considered "the one best system" for urban education (Tyack 1974; see also Cubberly 1919; Gersman 1969; Hogan 1985; Lazerson 1971; Mahan 1968; Mirel 1993; Perlmann 1988; Randall 1971; Taggart 1970).

In the decades surrounding 1900, then, Newark industry was thriving and the educational system was being modernized and centralized. Many of the educational reforms were intended to address the schooling of the new population of immigrants and their children. How did the reforms affect this group?

Immigrants and the Schools

R. Freeman Butts estimated that in 1909 almost 60% of public school students in 37 of America's biggest cities were immigrants or children of immigrants (1978, 234). Most of the arriving families were very poor (Newark Board of Education 1923; see also Hogan 1985).

While there had always been poor children in the Newark public schools, and since midcentury not only native children but English, Irish, and German immigrants as well, now suddenly the vast majority (71%) of Newark students were foreigners from unfamiliar places with unfamiliar languages, customs, and religions. Immigrant nationalities during the period were often referred to as "races"—the Italian "race", the Irish "race," the Hebrew "race." As late as 1941, an Italian ward leader in Newark told his Italian audience: "We are a racial minority, and it is in our interest to understand other minority groups (referring to Newark's Jews)" (Stellhorn 1982, 335).

Almost all (89%) of the city's teachers of these Italian, Russian, Jewish, Polish, Greek, Slavic, and Lithuanian children, on the other hand, were either native-born Americans of native fathers (69%); or were native born of earlier established Irish or German settlers (another 20%) (U.S. Immigration Commission 1911, 5:296). Across the United States, 43% of urban teachers were native born of immigrant parents, and almost 86% of those parents had come from Ireland, England, Germany, or non-French-speaking Canada (U.S. Immigration Commission 1911; Tyack 1974, 233).

At the turn of the century in U.S. cities, most elementary and a sizeable minority of secondary teachers had no more than a high school or normal school education (Tyack 1967, 417). However, some of these men and women were highly knowlegeable and highly educated, were dedicated to learning and to their students, and were revered by parents, students, and the community at large. Others, however, as Tyack notes, citing teachers in New York City and Chicago, were intolerant of the foreign children that flooded their classrooms. Tyack describes one teacher, for example, who remarked that her Italian students were "a bunch of little animals," and another who was overheard asking a student, "You dirty little Russian Jew, what are you doing?" (Tyack 1974, 231, 254).

One Irish teacher in Newark was so incensed by her foreign students that she wrote the *Newark Evening News* to complain about them.

> [A city] teacher cites her experience in contact with unruly pupils . . . tells of occasions when she and others of her profession were subjected to insult and the risk of physical injury by children of foreigners: "This change [in the schools]," she wrote, "is the result of . . . the tides in the last few decades of hordes of aliens . . . borne to our shores and they, in turn, have in still greater numbers sent their offspring flooding in our schools, changing their character and making a new problem for the school authorities to solve." (March 24, 1923)

Nor were the newly arrived students and their parents universally enthralled by the city schools. The students faced a culturally unfamiliar curriculum (one intended to "Americanize" them) and were taught in a language that they did not understand very well; in addition, some may have been taught by teachers who despised them. Economic opportunities, moreover, were plentiful: As in other industrial cities, entry-level jobs in Newark's flourishing factories did not require an education. Parents often sent their children to work after a few years in school in order to supplement family income (Tyack 1974, 59; Field 1976; Hogan 1985; Vinovskis 1985; and Graff 1979 for a slightly earlier period; see also Perlmann 1988, who shows that during this period the very few working-class youth who did complete the twelfth grade entered more attractive occupations than factory work).

Tyack relates another reason why children in Chicago did not attend school for very long.

> [In 1909] in the basement of a building in the stockyards, [factory] Inspector [Helen] Todd stumbled over a thirteen-year-old boy who

had huddled there, hoping she would not discover him. He wept bitterly when told he would have to go to school, blurting between his sobs that "they hits ye if yer don't learn, and they hits ye if ye whisper, and they hits ye if ye have string in yer pocket, and they hits ye if yer seat squeaks, and they hits ye if ye don't stan' up in time, and they hits ye if yer late, and they hits ye if ye ferget the page." Again and again Todd heard the same story: 269 [of the 500] children she interviewed said they preferred factory to school because no one hit them there. (1974, 178)

It is not surprising that, despite the many reforms designed to attract them, relatively large numbers of immigrant children attended school for only a few years; the majority never went past fifth grade, and only 3% of Newark's first graders finished high school (Ayres 1909, 57, 62). In Chicago, 57% of those who entered first grade went no further than eighth grade (Hogan 1985, 160).

The early school leaving of most immigrant children meant that the majority of the city's working-class students did not attend high school. Thus, few entered Newark's vocational schools, or enrolled in the district's vocational or technical programs. According to Kusick, in 1923 only 1% of the student population was in vocational schools (1974, 334). Norton and Lazerson report that in 1900–1916, less than 10% of urban public school students nationally were enrolled in industrial curriculum courses (in Tyack 1974, 328).

Moreover, large percentages of the immigrant poor who attended school failed in their studies. In 1909 Leonard Ayers published a study of "retardation" (grade repetition) and "elimination" (school leaving) in 61 U.S. city school systems. He argued that the failure of schools to reach immigrants and the poor was due to the fact that the work in the elementary grades had not been adapted to the ability or interests of these students. Those who could not succeed at the standard pace were required to repeat the work that they had failed, occasionally several times. As a result, classrooms overflowed with students of all ages and sizes (Kusick 1974, 266). Ayres found that Newark in 1906–07 spent almost one quarter of its school budget (23.5%) on "repeaters," against a national average of 15.4%, with Camden, New Jersey, spending a high of 30% (Ayres 1909, 97).

Two years later, a U.S. government survey of 37 cities demonstrated that Newark was typical in the high rates of grade repetition of the children of immigrants (U.S. Immigration Commission 1911). In all the grades in Newark almost half (47%) of the children were overage. By fifth grade, more than half (almost 60%) had been held back. According to the survey, there was less retardation among the "Hebrew" students than among any other group, and more among the Italian (IV: 191, 189-317; see also Perlmann 1988, for similar differences among the ethnic groups in Providence, Rhode Island).

In the parochial schools, which 9,403 Newark children attended, 70% of the students were found in grades 1 through 4; almost half (47.7%) had been retained, with 59.7% of the third graders retained. Most (60%) of the parochial students were working-class native children of limited means, rather than recent European immigrants. An additional 40% were of foreign parentage, with 27% of these being Irish and 13.7%, German (U.S. Immigration Commission 1911, IV:209–210).

Although touted by the city's newspapers in the decades surrounding 1900 as the "Jewel in the Crown" of public education in New Jersey (Cunningham 1988), the figures on grade repetition and early school leaving suggest that Newark schools—despite the innovative programs and administrative restructuring—did not successfully educate the vast majority of the new immigrant students.

Patronage and Corruption

In most cities with machine politics in the decades surrounding the turn of the century, political patronage and corruption in the city government was also apparent in affairs of the boards of education (see Tyack 1974 for discussions of educational patronage and corruption in Philadelphia, Pittsburgh, New York, and San Francisco; Mirel 1993 for Detroit; and Wrigley 1982 for Chicago). Newark was not immune; extensive political patronage and corruption occurred in its board of education during this period.

In the late nineteenth century, the administration of Newark's schools was determined by the annual election of two commissioners from each of the 15 wards. The commissioners prescribed texts, maps, suspension and dismissal, and teacher appointments and transfers, and could veto decisions by the superintendent on teacher placement. In 1891, the board included two physicians, two lawyers, a dentist, an architect, two publishers, many businesspeople—including a bank controller and a Prudential Insurance Company executive—saloon keepers, a locksmith, several carpenters, clerks and bookkeepers. In the matter of patronage, the board controlled nearly 500 positions. By 1898, factionalism, voting along party lines, corruption, and things not getting done (no copy books ordered, new boilers not ordered) were so extensive that Newark's Mayor James Seymour tried, unsuccessfully, to intervene (Kurp 1967, 143; Kusick 1974, 192–193).

In 1900 school superintendent Dr. Charles Gilbert resigned in protest at the political power of the board and at the bribery, patronage, and financial profits made from contracts. In the same year, the state attempted to convince Newark to change to a small board, as some other cities the size of Newark were doing. Representatives from the state visited the city to explain a new act allowing small boards. But members of the Newark Board of Education were not interested. In 1904 more graft was made public—extravagance and the paying of commissioners' friends for supplies that were never delivered (Kurp 1967, 145–148).

In 1907, a grand jury presentment was made, highly critical of the large board: Many members "were not fit for office," were "ignorant, inexperienced, a disgrace. . . . the public schools are tainted by the atmosphere emanating from the Board of Education" (Kurp 1967, 165–166). The city council forced a referendum, which passed, and Mayor Jacob Houssling appointed a new board of only nine members in December of 1907. The mayor selected all professionals and businesspeople, including lawyers, a Jewish banker, and the German publisher of the *Newark News*. Within 10 years, however, the factionalism and corruption in the small board was so great that it led to an attempt in the New Jersey legislature to remove the appointive power of mayors; but the measure failed. By 1917, Mayor Charles Gillin dominated the board, and was using school posts for "his friends and their friends." The New Jersey Supreme Court intervened in 1920, directing the board to obey the new civil service laws and to rehire its lawyer, who had been dismissed for proposing legislation to remove appointive powers from the mayor (Kurp 1967, 153–155). When board president Thomas Kenny and commissioner Harry Johnson came to a board meeting "under some influence of liquor" and "using a thick-tongued discourse uncommon to sober men" (*Newark Evening News* December 24, 1921), the public was aroused, but Mayor Gillan refused to intervene. In 1921, the chamber of commerce asked the state board of education to investigate the administration of the new board (Kurp 1967).

Following these events, the New Jersey State Department of Education agreed to audit the board's records but maintained that it had no punitive powers. During the investigation, the board admitted to the state department that it was "kind of scattering the contracts about" on the patronage plan, with no bids required. The state auditor found "persistent and willful law violations" as well as loose business practices. In the following year, the New Jersey legislature passed the Hobart Bill, designed to enable the mayor of any first-class city—i.e., Jersey City and Newark—to oust the existing board of education and to appoint another. After this intervention by the state, the installation of yet another new board, and the activities of a reform mayor beginning in 1924, "the Newark Public Schools [were] unusually free from politics for almost a decade" (*Newark Evening News* May 30, 1933; Kurp 1967, 171–173).

END OF AN ERA

As the long formative period in Newark came to a close in the late 1920s, business and educational achievements began to erode. Business "booster" budgets of the twenties, which used public tax monies to build skyscraper office buildings, department stores, and theaters in the downtown business district, would be curtailed by the Great Depression (Stellhorn 1982, Chap. 2). As in all American cities with population of over 100,000, Newark's manufacturing concerns had been leaving the central city during the 1920s (Jackson 1985, 184; Bartholomew 1944, 10). The economy was also changing. Newark's blue-collar industrial employment suffered during the twenties as traditional industries (leather, jewelry, hat, corset, fertilizer, breweries) declined, and white collar business (retail, banking, and insurance) increased (Stellhorn 1982, 11–12).

Business flight and economic changes were accompanied by a continued exodus of the elite and professional classes. Although in 1916 all of the officers and directors of the board of trade, the forerunner of the chamber of commerce, had been Newark residents, by 1929 only 36% of the officers and directors of the Newark Chamber of Commerce were residents of the city, and by the onset of World War II the residency rate would drop to 14.2%. In 1925, more than 40% of the attorneys who worked in Newark lived in the suburbs (Stellhorn 1982, 27). By 1947, the figure was 63% and by 1965, 78% (Jackson 1976, 92). By 1934, 76.7% of the officers of Newark's six largest banks lived outside the city and only three, or 12%, of executives at Newark's largest insurance companies, Prudential and Mutual Benefit Life, were Newark residents (Stellhorn 1982, 170).

As early as 1918, the *Newark Evening News* had worried about the loss of tax revenue from the affluent families who were moving to the countryside, and the loss of political control of the city by its "natural leaders" (Stellhorn 1982, 33–34). The chamber of commerce magazine, the *Newarker*, would lament in 1925 that "no one lives in Newark" anymore, but instead in the city's 26 suburbs (33). Suburbs of other American cities had started to grow as early as the 1850s, as elites began to leave the cities; and in the 1920s, cities like New York, Chicago, Boston, and Newark lost substantial numbers of their prosperous and successful citizens, as migration outward increased. In the 1920s, Newark's suburbs increased by 55% (Schwartz and Prosser 1977, 87).

By 1925, two out of three Newark residents were foreign born or children of immigrants; except for those who lived in the several middle-class sections in the city, most were working class and poor. With the onset of Prohibition, organized crime, in the form of "the Jewish Mafia," moved into the low-income, working-class wards in the city's central section, where 60% of Newark's 65,000 Jews and 38,000 blacks lived. Abner "Longie" Zwillman, the "Al Capone of New Jersey," was a strong presence in behind-the-scenes politics in Newark by the late twenties, making substantial contributions in money and votes, and through ballot fraud to both political parties (*Newark Evening News* November 29, 1932; Stellhorn 1982, 126; Curvin 1977). At the same time, the Italian Richie ("The Boot") Boiardo and his organization moved into the Italian North Ward. A lengthy battle between the two crime organizations ensued for control of bootlegging in and around Newark and on much of the East Coast (Conforti 1972, 24). During the 1920s, Newark was the bootleg capital of the eastern seaboard, with the Jewish organization importing 40% of the bootleg liquor brought into the United States between 1926 and 1931 (Cook 1974, 75). Organized crime would be a powerful influence in the city and in the state capital for the next 50 years.

In another sign of change, as if signaling a decline in the Newark schools that would begin in earnest in the 1930s, a number of highly accomplished principals, some active in the schools since the late nineteenth century, left the system during the 1920s through retirement or death. The *Newark Call* reported the retirement of the principal of Marcy School in 1927:

> The Dean of Newark Schoolmen will retire to enjoy ease at his summer home on the Maine Coast. [N. Hanson] Principal of [Marcy] School 15 years, founder of Newark Public School Athletic Association . . . attended Colby College. . . . [Marcy School] was in an aristocratic section at the time of his appointment in 1912. It was the "show school" of the city. [It had 14 rooms and fewer than 600 pupils when built; by 1927 Marcy had 31 rooms and 1,249 pupils.] (January 5, 1927)

CONCLUSION

From this fertile period of Newark's history, when the city and the schools were growing and renowned, developments and policies that will lead to decline can be identified and examined. For approximately half a century (1840–1890), a period of municipal economic growth and vitality when business was prosperous and the citizenry fairly homogenous culturally, the city completed sweeping educational reforms and became "a first-class school system," a model for others (Burr 1942, 286). This history corroborates what Jeffrey Mirel found for Detroit at a somewhat later date, when that city was at the height of its economic power, in the mid-1920s. According to Mirel, the Detroit school system was then thought of as "one of the finest systems in the world" (1993, 43).

However, as children who were of foreign "races" and who were poor began to predominate in the Newark schools, the educational reforms had less success. Although the system was extensively restructured in attempts to attract and hold the immigrant students, the restructuring failed in efforts to educate the vast majority of these students. Perhaps other reforms might have made the children more comfortable and successful—sympathetic teachers, or instructional materials in a language that they spoke. However, the failure of the schools to respond successfully to poverty and cultural difference even in a period of relative affluence and strength reveals a phenomenon that continued to grow in Newark and other American cities: the power of social class—poverty—and racial difference to overwhelm educational efforts to reform the schools.

Another factor that hurt Newark and its schools was the absence of a cultural notion of corporate responsibility to redress the consequences of economic development. One of Newark's largest firms, the Prudential Insurance Company, did build the city's first low-income housing in 1929 in an industrial, working-class section called the Ironbound, where it owned land. However, Prudential's precondition for building the homes was that the city buy from the company that part of the land not used for the scheme, at a cost nearly equal to what the homes would cost to build (Stellhorn 1982, 86).

The absence of corporate responsibility was reinforced in the twenties as firms became national in scope and loyalties shifted even further from the factory site or headquarters (Baltzell 1958; Whyte 1956, 303). The lack of capital investment to redress the problems of poverty, slums, and disease that resulted from industrialization, and the lack of jobs that resulted from the flight of business from the cities would be major contributors to urban decline in the decades to come.

A final development that can be examined in this early period is the isolation of the nation's urban ethnic residents and politicians from both state and national political power. To compensate for lack of representa-

tion and redress at the state and federal levels, local residents very soon developed administrative structures and mechanisms for their own enhancement and to run the town (see also Banfield and Wilson 1963; Hofstadter 1955). These ethnic machines very often became corrupt, as they did in Newark, and caused mismanagement and graft in both the city government and in the schools during the next decades. Moreover, the disregard for cities on the part of state and national political power groups meant that urban areas were not provided with state or federal financial resources to develop infrastructure, schools, or social services to stem the tide of decay.

A further consequence of this early political isolation of cities was that, as in New Jersey when the state renegged on its promise to provide a "thorough and efficient" education for all students, the municipalities were left with property taxes as the major source of revenue for the schools. This system would create vast disparities in educational funding that still plague Newark as well as most American cities.

In the following decade, these national economic and political trends continued and intensified—economic change, the impact of poverty and race on school success, the further withdrawal of corporate leaders from involvement in municipal affairs, the political isolation of city politicians from state and national power, and local corruption and patronage—and would combine to make the 1930s a turning point for American industrial cities, and for many city school systems as well, a fact that is less well known. Newark and most of the city's schools began a downward spiral in the decade of the Great Depression from which they have never recovered.

CHAPTER 4

Beginning of the Decline:
The 1930s

In Newark, as in many other industrial cities during the thirties, both an economic crisis and a transformation occurred. In this chapter, I will examine these, as well as the federal and corporate participation in the decay of Newark's infrastructure, and in the ghettoization of impoverished blacks who arrived from the South. I will subsequently inspect the impact of these and related developments on the city schools.

THE CITY

Until 1940, the six largest cities in New Jersey were home to almost 30% of the state's population. With 442,000 residents, Newark was the most populous (Pomper 1986, 39). Nationally, although more than half of U.S. residents lived in urban areas during the thirties, rural majorities in all state legislatures continued to control these bodies as well as national party caucuses, which nominated governors, congresspeople, senators, and presidents. City dwellers—immigrants, workers, increasing numbers of southern blacks, the middle class—had few formal political mechanisms through which to influence governmental policies at the state or national levels (Judd and Swanstrom 1994, 51). In New Jersey, for example, until reapportionment in the 1970s (when the supreme court ordered redistricting on the basis of "one man one vote"), 15% of the voters—those in the rural counties—determined the senate majority. Eleven rural senators could hold up a bill indefinitely (Dolce 1976, 69).

One of the consequences in New Jersey of the dominance of rural interests was that for municipal officials, the only substantial source of tax revenue continued to be the local property tax: both real, on wealth as seen in land values, and personal, on wealth found in individual or corporate chattel and capital accumulation. As the depression wore on, not only were taxes more difficult to collect—as early as 1931, tax delinquencies in Newark, Camden, and Paterson approached 30%—but cities found themselves with less, and less valuable, property to tax (Salmore and Salmore 1993, 209).

The decline in both taxable urban property and property values was partly a result of the move by the affluent to suburbia and partly a result of the depression, but an equally significant cause was ongoing economic transformation in America's industrial cities. A study of Newark completed in 1944 by preeminent urban planners Bartholomew and Associates found that during the thirties Newark's industrial base had eroded significantly:

> Prior to the [World War II-] stimulated manufacturing boom, Newark was steadily losing ground industrially. . . . Numerous plants have left Newark and this loss has only partially been offset by new establishments. The majority of Newark's manufacturing plants are old and many have become obsolete. Faced with the necessity of expanding or modernizing their plants, a tendency has developed to rebuild in new locations having a more favorable tax situation, where land is cheap and where there is less congestion. . . . A significant fact . . . is that in all the cities studied [Buffalo, Cincinnati, New Orleans, Oakland, Newark, New York City] the percentage of employment under the heading [manufacturing and mechanical classifications] has been declining since 1920, and there has been a corresponding increase in clerical employment, professional services and classifications of a miscellaneous nature. (1, 9–10)

According to Bartholomew and Associates, Newark had suffered an 18.4% loss of manufacturing jobs between 1909 and 1939 (10, 12). One out of five wage earners in the state were employed in Newark in 1909; by 1939 only about one in nine were employed within the city. Whereas in 1909 25% of all the wages paid to industrial workers in New Jersey were expended in the city of Newark, in 1939 this ratio had decreased to 10%. The only category of employment which showed a net increase after the depression was the white-collar category of clerical work (12). Nationally, almost all white-collar work was in cities and downtowns. Office space in cities, in fact, had tripled in the 1920s (Jackson 1985, 184).

There were a number of reasons for the decline of factory employment in the older American cities during the 1930s. These included a greater tax advantage in suburban areas; new pallet assembly-line production techniques for moving material and goods that required horizontal space and lots of land rather than requiring vertical buildings. The use of trucks and better highways, moreover, created a new efficiency for outlying operations that was not matched by locations in the inner cities. In addition, some firms moved to escape union organizing, which was strong in the thirties in industrial centers (Gordon 1978, 49; Jackson 1985, 183–184).

Of course, during the Great Depression extensive unemployment occurred in Newark as it did elsewhere in the country. In 1930 almost 10% of Newark's population was on relief; that number tripled in the next 5 years (Conforti 1972, 24). By the summer of 1933, 1 in 10 inhabitants of New Jersey's six largest cities was being sustained by Franklin D. Roosevelt's New Deal Federal Emergency Relief Administration. On March 1, 1934, Newark's city government faced default and bankruptcy (Schwartz and Prosser 1977, x; Stellhorn 1982, 164). Newark was not alone. Other large cities—Chicago, Detroit, and New York, among them—also faced financial collapse (Dewey 1933; Mirel 1993; Tyack, Lowe, and Hansot 1984; Wrigley 1982).

Financial Constraints

The financial problem in Newark was compounded by the concerted effort of the local, largely nonresident corporate elite to restrict municipal spending and borrowing. Pulling back from the building boom of the 1920s, when the corporations built large projects at public expense, businesspeople with firms headquartered in Newark successfully lobbied the state legislature during the 1930s for state restrictions on borrowing by cities, limits on municipal borrowing against unpaid taxes, a universal "cash basis" for municipal governments, and fiscal takeover by the state of municipalities which suffered severe financial difficulties. Codified in the Princeton Bills in 1938, this punitive legislation was accompanied by the bankers' refusal to buy city bonds to keep the city afloat unless the bond rates were substantially raised and the city budget was cut by 15%. The chamber of commerce opposed the building of four swimming pools for poor children, at a cost of $500,000, when several years previously they had pushed for the construction of the city railroad station at a cost *to the public* of $13.5 million (Stellhorn 1982, 301). As the depression wore on and the city—in the absence of federal and state aid—became more dependent on the bankers for "cash", the bankers in turn sold inflated bonds to the city, reaping large profits (107, 112, 262–314). In Chicago, New York, and Detroit city governments were also in receivership to the bankers, who controlled municipal budgets and slashed social spending (Dewey 1933; Mirel 1993, 91; Tyack, Lowe, and Hansot 1984, 68; Wrigley 1982, 212).

In 1935, despite the vociferous objections of Newark's popular Jewish mayor, Meyer C. Ellenstein, the tax assessments of nine of the largest corporations in the city (including NJ Bell and the *Newark Evening*

News) were reduced by a probusiness county tax board, thus limiting the city's income further. City taxes, moreover, were not equitably assigned: A survey in 1934 of 4,881 Newark firms found that 4,069 were assessed at only 5 to 15% of their true worth, and that 790 were not assessed at all, and paid the city no taxes. The city's nine investment trust companies, with assets of $150 million, paid taxes averaging $120 per year. A homeowner with property worth $10,000 paid about $365 (*Newark Evening News* October 1, 1934; Stellhorn 1982, 173, 227). As these figures indicate, the tax rates were exceedingly low for corporations and high for homeowners.

The business elite demanded budget cuts and curtailment of relief benefits to the unemployed, and, most important, prevented the city from fully using federal aid programs. The corporations successfully lobbied for the defeat of local bond issues (city funds required by the federal government to meet local share of the expenses if federal grants were provided). By preventing the use of federal aid programs in Newark, the business elite was crippling the urban environment. Fully utilized, aid from the Works Progress Administration (WPA), initiated by President Franklin D. Roosevelt in 1935, and other federal programs could have preserved the repairable urban necessities—school buildings, libraries, water and sewer systems, streets, gas lines, communications and power cables. But the water system, like the school system, received only emergency repairs to meet immediate crises. Largely because the nonresident business elite had blocked capital expenditures, Newarks's physical decay was well underway by 1940 (Stellhorn 1982, 306). Hundred-year-old sewers went unreplaced, public health service lagged, police and fire protection deteriorated, and urban redevelopment was fraught with corruption (see Mirel 1993 and Wrigley 1982 for similar developments in Chicago and Detroit). As we shall see, the Newark public schools declined as well.

The city's commission form of government also contributed to the decline of Newark's infrastructure. Each commissioner was independent, and represented a particular constituency—Jewish, Italian or the Irish who remained. There was no overriding municipal structure nor any incentive to ensure cooperative planning. This led to competition for spoils, which in turn led to strife and haggling, and a lack of planning for the city as a whole. During the 1930s, graft and corruption increased; mismanagement by the commissioners lost to the city control of Newark's airport, one of its major resources. In the latter half of the decade there was a major scandal or indictment involving one or another of the commissioners almost every year (Douglas 1972, 21, 24; Stellhorn 1982, 252, 326).

Influx of African Americans

At a 1936 meeting of the chamber of commerce to discuss plans for the 100th anniversary of the city's first charter, Vice President E.W. Wolmuth spoke against a celebration of the centennial, pointing out that businesspeople would most likely lack sufficient enthusiasm to either commit funds, or to travel into Newark, for the celebration. The vice president attributed this lack of enthusiasm to "the change in character of Newark's population" (in Stellhorn 1982, 254). The change in character in Newark's population to which the speaker was referring might have been the city's large population of Jews and Italians; however, he could also have been referring to the recent influx of black southerners.

Further significant changes that were taking place in the city involved the increasing numbers, and the increasing ghettoization, of Newark's black population. With World War I cutting off European immigration, industrialists began to encourage black movement from the rural South to the North (Price 1975, 26). Between 1910 and 1930, about 1 million blacks—one tenth of all blacks living in the South—moved to cities in the Northeast and Midwest (Judd and Swanstrom 1994, 155). Between 1920 and 1940, approximately 28,700 arrived in Newark, and by 1940 blacks were 10.7% of the population (Price 1975, 15). More southern blacks migrated to Newark than to any other New Jersey city (Price 1980, 211). They arrived in search of work and freedom from southern Jim Crow segregation laws. However, in the North they faced housing and job discrimination, and were hired primarily for menial labor.

Both labor unions and employers excluded blacks from skilled jobs. For example, only 6 of 22 unions in Newark were open to blacks. In 1920, black men were 5.3% of the Newark population, but 35% of its male servants, 31% of its porters, and 26.7% of its janitors. Denied WPA jobs during the thirties, refused relief by the local agencies, and confined to low-paying jobs, Newark's newly arriving blacks found that their economic status remained low; that of long-time black residents of Newark deteriorated (Price 1975, 22–23, 101–130).

In the decades just before and after the turn of the century, black citizens had been scattered throughout Newark, but by 1914, they were concentrated in wards 2, 3, 4, and 7. These contained 60% of Newark's 9,029 blacks, although blacks were only 3 to 6% of the total population in these wards, which were still overwhelmingly white. With the arrival of large numbers of southern blacks in the twenties and thirties, however, white residents moved west of the burgeoning central city ghetto, and to the suburbs, which discrimination kept closed to black families (Price 1975, 31, 42, 47).

In 1920 and again in 1930, Newark officials zoned the downtown area, where most blacks lived, for industrial building, and no new homes could be built there (Price 1975, 57–59). By 1940, 63.4% of Newark's blacks lived in this downtown section, in 16 of the city's 98 census tracts, with relatively few whites (47). By 1940, then, the ghettoization of Newark's black population in the city's core had become a visible fact.

Concentrated in the old Third Ward, the housing available to blacks had already deteriorated by the time the rural migrants arrived. A report to the city commissioners found that by 1940, more than 50% of all "Negroes" in the city lived in dilapidated dwellings that were in need of major repairs (Bartholomew 1945, 1). A 1934 housing survey showed that 40.2% of city and 53% of Central Ward homes needed major repairs (Stellhorn 1982, 96). By 1940 only 21 of 6,333 dwellings in the five census tracts having the highest concentration of blacks were owned by black occupants, which meant that residents of the ghetto were dependent on owners from outside for the conditions of their homes (Price 1975, 70).

Other cities were also experiencing an influx of southern black migrants during the period, and those who left their rural homes were experiencing increasing entrapment in deteriorated, impoverished dwellings, and in menial work in the places to which they traveled. New York (Harlem), Chicago, Gary, East St. Louis, St. Louis, and Philadelphia also developed ghettoes during this period. By their very arrival, the southern rural travelers—most without formal schooling, financial resources, or even winter clothes—played a crucial role in northern and midwestern cities (Judd and Swanstrom 1994, 155; Drake and Cayton 1945; Groh 1972).

Effects of Redlining

White flight, the increasing ghettoization of blacks, and the deterioration of the city itself was fostered by federal policies that discriminated against blacks, against whites who wanted to stay in the city, and ultimately against the cities themselves. As a result of the depression, 63% of workers in the housing industry were unemployed. In order to rejuvenate this industry, the National Housing Act of 1934 made cheap, long-term loans available to buyers as well as to homeowners (for renovation). The act allowed the federal government to provide insurance to lenders of 80% of the value of a property. It also allowed a long-term payment period (previously, a downpayment of 30 to 50% had been required when buying a house, and the loan had to be repaid in 6 to 11 years). Between the passage of the act and 1975, 79% of the loans made were for acquiring or building homes in the suburbs, rather than for repairing or rebuilding them in the city (Judd and Swanstrom 1994, 201).

The prime reason for the suburban destination of most loans was that the federal officials deciding who should get the loans did not often approve mortgage lending to city neighborhoods. In 1933 the federal Home Owners Loan Corporation (HOLC) had begun rating city neighborhoods to decide on the risk entailed in lending mortgages—as did realtors and banks, later. In 1934 the Federal Housing Administration (FHA) began using the risk-rating policies of HOLC. (The ratings were A = the best, to D = the worst.) The presence of black families in the proximity was of special concern to the raters, and caused a low rating (Jackson 1985, 197–218).

A 1933 report used by raters stated that declining property values would result from the presence of a number of groups: "Russian Jews of lower class, South Italians, Negroes, and Mexicans"; if these were present, no mortgages were to be financed (Berry 1979). When a decision was taken that a neighborhood was "unsuitable," a red line was drawn on an area map and no loans were made, on the assumption that the neighborhood was a bad investment risk. The lack of loans to repair or build homes in the city was a major cause of the deterioration of old, but basically sound, housing stock in many cities (Jackson 1985, 203; Judd and Swanstrom 1994, 206).

In the late thirties, federal appraisers rated every block of Newark. No area got an A rating, and many received the lowest ratings, which meant that mortgage loans and loans to renovate would not be offered in most sections of the city. In fact, as FHA maps uncovered by Jackson reveal, in one year, 1936, only 25 mortgages were approved in Newark, a major city, as opposed to 50 in Bloomfield, a small, neighboring white suburb about a fifth of Newark's physical size (1985, 201, 212).

After World War II, the GI Bill and Veterans Administration programs, which helped 16 million veterans buy homes, followed the same FHA procedures for mortgages, until as late as 1971. Thus, FHA procedures between 1934 and 1971 fostered the decay of inner city neighborhoods by stripping them of their middle-class residents—by favoring construction and purchase of single-frame homes in suburban areas over modernization of city neighborhoods. As Jackson has observed, the FHA redlining policies, later utilized by realtors and banks, enshrined segregation as public policy (1985, 213). This policy fostered the creation of black ghettos in America's cities, and hastened the deterioration of city homes.

Newark's black residents were increasingly isolated politically as well as by residence in the thirties, due to the commission form of government. All the commissioner elections were "at large" (all candidates ran on a city-wide basis); none was ward based. Most blacks were concentrated in the Central Ward, their numbers in the city were small, and no blacks were elected.

With the near bankruptcy of the city government, organized crime stepped in to offer residents—especially in the ghetto areas—soup kitchens and financial, funeral, and other services. According to Cook, in 1931 the Jewish organization predominated, although they and the Italian group ceased fighting over Newark, and ceremoniously divided up the city amongst themselves, "with the law as a bystander" (1974, 77).

THE SCHOOLS

During the first three decades of the twentieth century, hundreds of surveys were done of state and local school systems—"so many, in fact, that it seemed there was hardly a state or local school system in America which was not surveyed" (Callahan 1962, 112). At first, surveys were typically initiated by muckrakers or outsiders to the educational system to uncover graft. These surveys were resented and resisted by superintendents. One educator, describing the situation in 1919, wrote that it was "quite the fashion for the schools to be 'surveyed,' and many hundreds of systems have been through the operation." But, he added sarcastically, the result of this work was contained in volumes of "findings" which, he said, laymen "cannot interpret and which no one with the least grain of sense would attempt to read" (in Callahan 1962, 112).

Gradually, however, under the leadership of "efficiency experts" like George Strayer at Teachers College, the surveys became focused on methods through which school systems could improve and economize. Intended as an impetus to educational reform, the surveys applied "scientific research" to education; the goal was to assist districts in becoming more professional and efficient (Tyack and Hansot 1982).

In 1935, the Newark Board of Education, under severe pressure from the local chamber of commerce to economize, invited Teachers College to study the school system (at a cost of $35,000) (*Newark Evening News* December 28, 1950). The survey was headed by George Strayer, N. J. Engelhardt, and Hollis L. Caswell. A staff of 53 and an additional 71 "field workers" conducted an exhaustive assessment of administration, finance, and educational programs in the Newark schools. In this chapter I base my analysis of education in Newark during the decade of the 1930s largely on the results of the Teachers College survey.

Results of the Depression

In the face of a severely weakened local economy, uncollected taxes, and state and federal policies that penalized the city treasury and its population, the resources of the Newark schools declined during the thirties. Although many states aided their city systems financially during this period, New Jersey was one of the most laggard in providing aid to local school districts. In the United States as a whole in 1938, approximately 30% of school revenue came from the states, whereas in New Jersey the state provided only 4.8% in 1938 and 5.7% in 1940. In that year New Jersey relied more heavily on the property tax for the support of education than did any other state (Strayer 1942, 218).

By 1935, not only had the amount Newark could raise from local business fallen, but a survey showed that a majority of the city's families were poor and not a fruitful source of municipal income. According to the Teachers College team, 50% of the school neighborhoods in the city were considered poor, very poor, or inferior. Almost half (49.2%) of all students lived in these neighborhoods. "The entire central section of the city is served by poor and inferior buildings," and "only 16.7% of the students live in superior or good neighborhoods of the city, in several favored residential sections" (Strayer 1942, 250).

Patronage and Its Consequences

In response to the eroded job base in the city during the depression, the amount of patronage dispensed by the board of education increased to the point that the board became the city's largest public employer (Strayer 1942, 193). The research team from Teachers College found extensive evidence of this patronage and of its consequences for the schools. For example, the board members—rather than the professional superintendent—named persons for service in the schools, leading to "inefficiency, if not disaster" in the placement of unskilled people (Strayer 1942, 9). The team reported that "the obstacles in the way of locating and appointing the best qualified persons to teaching positions have . . . not been surmounted" in Newark, which limited its applicants to those living in Newark or in neighboring communities (171–172). A board of examiners conducted written and oral exams. Of this process the research team remarked, "The written exams differ greatly in difficulty from year to year. They are not objective (but useful if you have candidates you want to keep out or include)" (173–174). The team found that the instructional personnel in Newark were more highly paid and had a higher rate of absences and more paid sick days than those of many other city systems (177, 181, 185, 188).

Moreover, teachers in Newark were less educationally qualified than those in many other cities. During the thirties, in the face of a national surplus of teachers, educational qualifications for teaching in most states had risen rapidly (Warren 1989). By 1938, 60% of teachers in American city systems had completed 4 or more years of college. Only 47% of Newark teachers had this training. Nationally, in cities of comparable size, 40% of elementary teachers had 4 or more years of college. Only 26.5% of Newark elementary school teachers had this amount of training in 1938. In fact, 45.2% had less than 3 years of preparation (National Education Association Bulletin 1938, in Strayer 1942, 177; 188). In the late 1930s, New Jersey was one of 11 states that did not require a bachelor's degree for elementary teaching (Warren 1989, 282). Although state requirements for the job of principal included a master's degree or equivalent, 30% of Newark's 44 principals had not completed college (Strayer 1942, 337, 338).

Evidence of patronage appointments was apparent in the noninstructional staff, as well. The custodial and cafeteria staffs were overlarge, unskilled, with "liberal allotments of non-working time," and on wage scales at least 15% higher than the norm (166–167). A Teachers College survey of Chicago in the late 1920s concluded that that city had at least 502 more janitors than were needed. The janitors' connections with the political machine gave them such influence that many received salaries higher than those of the school principals (Wrigley 1982, 222). Noninstructional employees in Newark were added to the civil service in 1932, thus locking in unqualified personnel, and blocking out new applicants, for years to come.

Finances

The Teachers College researchers found that the business administration of the Newark district was of questionable accuracy and thoroughness. For example, they discovered that "no one has complete responsibility for all aspects of income management" in the Newark schools (Strayer 1942, 61). The board secretary had control of preparing the budget (through his assistant, the "budget director"). The figures of cost reported to the state and national governments varied from figures for similar purposes reported locally (66). No one person in the district was responsible for personnel administration and payroll. There was not enough bidding on supply and equipment purchases (71). The survey team found that there was no uniform policy with respect to funds lodged in the individual school. There were no definite rules and regulations in the hands of principals concerning the safeguarding, accounting, and auditing of funds (78). In the 5 years prior to the Teachers College survey, the city's newspapers publicized a series of probes of dual holdings of school jobs and financial graft involving school personnel (see, for example, *Newark Evening News* February 3, 1930, August 30, 1932, September 29, 1932, June 29, 1933 or *Newark Ledger* May 18, 1933).

Perhaps because of chamber of commerce pressure, or lack of knowledge or official concern, the city of Newark did not apply for, and did not receive, any of the hundreds of thousands of dollars of federal Public Works Administration aid that many other cities of its size received during the 1933–1940 period. Other federal aid, WPA projects, provided to the board of education was used for school lunch programs and by the building department, but for some of the projects the school system forfeited or did not secure the maximum available grant because of failure to set up the projects in accordance with specifications for federal aid (Strayer 1942, 78).

The extensive number of employees, and their higher than average salaries, made the Newark school system an expensive one. A survey by the U.S. Office of Education of 68 cities with populations of 100,000 or more found that "general control" costs of the Newark schools were $5.11 per pupil against an average of $3.48. Newark's instructional costs were also higher than average, $108 per pupil, compared with an average of $87.03 in the other cities. These costs included salaries and expenses of supervisors, principals, and teachers, and costs for textbooks and other educational supplies (*Newark Ledger* July 4, 1938). Yearly audits by Price Waterhouse lamented the fact that the board had unexplained balances of over $500,000 in many years, and urged that the school system "install a scientific budget system to replace the antiquated methods in vogue" (*Newark Ledger* August 29, 1932).

During the decade of the thirties, for the first time, the Newark newspapers publicly noted a decline in the schools. An editorial in the *Call* for example, stated that "education is a field in which Newark has long been a leader. . . . But in the last few years, retrenchment rather than experimentation has been the watchword in so far as the public school system is concerned" (March 29, 1936). An editorial in the *Newark Ledger* a year later stated that

Newark has been lavish in appropriating public funds to advance the commercial and industrial development of the city but it has shown less regard for the educational and social needs of the community.

Chamber of Commerce opposition has been especially bitter against
improvement in hospitalization and educational facilities. (November
2, 1937)

The Newark board reported in 1933 that salaries and special services (health service, special supervisors, visiting teachers and psychol-
ogists) had been cut by 15% between 1930 and 1933 (Newark Board of
Education 1933). Twelve of Newark's 56 principals were put in charge
of two schools each (Strayer 1942, 334; 356). Although the Teachers
College report was to make many recommendations for reforming the
school system as a result of their assessment, the authors remarked that
"new educational ideas are not considered [by the board of education],
because it is assumed they will cost money" (53).

The retrenchment in Newark schools was occurring in other cities
as well. In Chicago, the 1930s brought financial collapse to the board of
education, and the schools became the target of a business-sponsored
cost-cutting drive, which resulted in sweeping cutbacks in the public
schools.

In one 20-minute meeting, the Board of Education abolished all vocational education, all athletics, 50% of kindergartens, all bands and
orchestras . . . dismissed 1,400 teachers and [made] elementary school
principals responsible for two schools instead of the usual one. [The
board protected the janitors, however; not one was fired.] (Wrigley
1982, 218)

Mirel (1993) also shows that Detroit schools suffered severe retrenchment in the thirties. (For financial retrenchment in other city districts,
see R. Cohen 1990; Katznelson and Weir 1985; Tyack, Lowe, and Hansot, 1984.)

Physical Facilities

The Teachers College survey team found evidence of "significant decline" in Newark district's physical plant, and noted that this characterized school systems in New York (Manhattan), Philadelphia, Pittsburgh, Cleveland, and St. Louis (Strayer 1942, 105). The team stated
that "Newark has not maintained its school plant over the past decades" (98). The survey team found deterioration of school buildings
built in 1880, 1890, and 1910. Only four schools had been built since
1930. Some special schools were still in buildings from the 1840s and
1850s. Eighty percent of the buildings in use were rated in fair, poor, or

inferior condition (109). Almost half (46.6%) were poor or inferior. Only 21.6% were superior or good. Forty percent of the children were in school buildings rated as inferior or poor (110).

The survey team found that "many buildings present major fire hazards," and complained of "cheap, shoddy construction of new buildings," citing, for example, extensive leakage in the new Weequahic High School and Chancellor Avenue School, which, the report stated, "points toward the need for more careful checking of specifications and supervision in planning" (115). In 1935, Newark's 81,542 schoolchildren, almost double the enrollment of 44,605 in 1908, were attending facilities 70% of which were originally built before the turn of the century and intended for approximately half that number. All high schools but one were on double shift (*Newark Star-Eagle* September 9, 1935).

The Teachers College team found "a most conspicuous general weakness of custodial care" concerning toilet rooms (Strayer 1942, 155). "At present in many schools, toilets are insanitary [sic] and in some cases indescribably unclean. . . . these areas are filthy and foul-smelling. There is no hot water for washing in many buildings, and soap, towel, and toilet paper provisions were lacking" (155). "[Nor is there] evidence in the schools of Newark of an awareness of the tremendous change that improved plumbing has made in the building structures which mankind uses" (113).

Instruction

Members of the survey team made on-site assessments of curriculum and instruction in the Newark schools. In the elementary classrooms, visiting team members complained that there was "an overemphasis on achievement testing." They reported that

> in the majority of elementary classrooms visited, the greatest amount of energy and concern in the program was directed toward the teaching of skills, as opposed to thematic concepts or activities. Especially reading and arithmetic is taught in an exceedingly formal and isolated manner. (Strayer 1942, 248)

Reading instruction involved "a rather rigid program of drill," which principals thought of "as necessitated by the reading tests given by the district" (250). There was "too much drill in math" (248). Nor were there enough teaching materials in the elementary classes (51).

Elementary schools were "uniform in program throughout the city, despite the differences in class and ethnicity in populations" (47).

> There is no adaptation of curriculum to the varied ethnic and socioeco-
> nomic communities. . . . Children in the Third Ward [poor, black chil-
> dren] are studying the same things about Newark and New Jersey and
> making the same kind of notebooks as the children of the most favored
> residential [sections]. (270)

In 1930, similar retention rates existed in Newark elementary schools as at the turn of the century, with a cumulative effect of 60% having repeated at least one grade by fifth grade (in 1909, 59.3% of the students had been held back by fifth grade). According to the *Newark Evening News*, "this retardation [repeating] runs as high as four terms in many instances. More than 10% of repeaters in grades 5 and 6 are at least 4 terms behind" (September 30, 1930). In tests of elementary reading achievement reported by Strayer in 1942, Newark pupils scored at slightly better than or equal to national averages in grades 3 to 5, were somewhat behind nationwide achievement in grade 7, and still further behind in grade 8. In arithmetic, Newark pupils beginning the eighth grade were more than one school year below national standards. Strayer commented, "It is quite possible that this lag in achievement of upper elementary students reflects the influence of such factors as foreign language difficulty, widespread unfavorable living conditions, and the transiency of the school population" (333).

Examining the high schools, the Teachers College team found that at several there were high failure rates in required subjects: 34% failed physics and Spanish and 38% failed general science (Strayer 1942, 449). "In many science classes there is no laboratory work . . . workbooks and standardized direction sheets are used continuously" (398, 449).

There were also inadequate vocational offerings. Outmoded "vocational civics" was required, and technical and industrial equipment was not up to date and often not functioning. Only Weequahic High School, serving middle-class Jewish neighborhoods (where more students— 35.5%—went to college than from any other high school) "has a rich and varied . . . industrial arts program" (391). The team found that "the general high schools of the city are almost without industrial arts offerings. These schools are predominantly academic high schools in a city in which the academic careers of most students will be terminated with high school graduation" (391). As a result, "the great majority of young people graduate from Newark high schools almost totally unprepared to make a living" (428).

Comparison of Quality by School

According to a board of education survey, in 1936 a large majority (85.7%) of Newark's elementary pupils were white, 14.2% were "Negro," and 0.1% were "yellow." Most of the white parents (64.3%) were born in other countries, the majority of those (52.4%), in Italy (Newark Board of Education 1936). Although the survey did not so state, we can assume that, given the fact that 90,000 Jews lived in Newark making up 20.3% of the population, a good percentage of the rest of the white parents were Jewish (Newark Public Library 1995, 10). The children of these parents aside, the remainder of the white students were Irish, Romanian, Lithuanian, and so forth. As noted above, Newark neighborhoods by the 1930s were ethnic and racial enclaves, and most white neighborhoods, with the exception of several that were middle class Jewish and Italian, were working poor.

The Teachers College research team rated all the schools in Newark on a scale that they called an "Index of Educational Need." This index took into account the condition of the school building and playground, the number of additions, the date of the last addition, cases of truancy, the percentage of classrooms above the second floor, the number of grades housed, the percentage of classrooms in the basement, the number of vacant rooms, and the total population. An estimate of student ethnicity and race (native white, foreign-born white, "Negro," and other) was also included, based on estimates by the principals. A rating of "inferior" indicated relatively greater need; a rating of "highly superior," relatively less (Strayer 1942, 122).

The report presented the data and indexes for each school by city section (e.g., Ironbound, Weequahic, Central Ward, Forest Hill). My analysis of their data reveals extreme contrasts between the schools in the black, poor ghetto area of the Central Ward, and the schools in the white, more affluent areas. There are also contrasts, although less stark, between schools in predominantly middle-class areas and those in which poorer white immigrant working-class families lived.

Of the 48 schools reporting race data, 62%, or 30 schools, enrolled 70% or more native-born white students; the remaining students were foreign-born white. Of these schools, 73% were rated as superior or good (one was "very superior"); 27% as fair. None was rated as poor or inferior. The team found that "the Weequahic [Jewish middle-class] section is the most favored section of the city with respect to school facilities" (this despite the fact that even these schools were vastly overcrowded) (131). All of the schools rated as very superior or superior were in the more affluent white sections.

The survey team found that the school libraries at Weequahic High School and its recently built addition contained over 50,000 books, double the number at any other high school (553). The research team found "an extremely wide range in the number of texts, as well as their use, in the various elementary schools of Newark. Some classrooms, such as those in Weequahic, were well equipped, [while some classes in other schools] have no texts—only workbooks" (282).

The Teachers College survey staff found that the only school receiving "excellent custodial service" was in the Weequahic section. In the rest of Newark, custodial care was "good" in 3 buildings, "fair" in 7, and "poor" in 1 of the 12 buildings they rated. In general, they found custodial work to be "careless," and of "low standards" (152, 154). "The distribution of custodial employees among the . . . buildings varies so widely that some buildings are overstaffed while others are understaffed" (160).

A high quality activity at Weequahic can perhaps be inferred from local news reports; the following are representative: "Pulitzer poetry prize winner Robert P. Tristram Coffin addressed Weequahic High School students at yesterday morning's assembly. He also read some of his poetry" (*Newark Evening News* February 22, 1939). "Benny Goodman gave his contribution to funds for uniforms for the school band at Weequahic High School" (*Newark Ledger* February 22, 1939). "The WPA federal art project murals done by Michael Lenson for Weequahic High School will be dedicated in the auditorium there next Tuesday at 10 AM" (*Newark Star-Eagle* March 3, 1939).

Of the 48 schools reporting race data on students, 21%, or 10 schools, had more than 15% black enrollment. Most of these schools, however, were in the Central Ward, and had much higher black enrollments. None of the schools with black enrollment was rated as good or superior. Eighty percent were rated as poor or inferior, and 20%, fair. In the city as a whole, 63% of the schools rated as poor and inferior were in the black ghetto—the Central Ward and downtown district. These percentages suggest that in the late 1930s, the vast majority of the children of Newark's 45,000 black residents were receiving an education that was inferior to that of white students in other sections of the city.

Marcy School, outside the downtown business area, enrolled 8.2% black students, and was rated as fair. Seventy-three percent of the students were white native-born children of immigrants, and 18% were foreign-born white, mostly Italian and Irish (Strayer 1942, 138). None of the eight schools in the Ironbound section, where students were white, but incomes were lower, was rated as superior. Of these eight schools, 62.5% were rated as fair, and 25%, poor or inferior. Only 12.5% of these schools were rated as good. Thirty-seven percent of the poor and inferior schools in the city were in the Ironbound.

The comparisons of schools in different social class and racial contexts suggest that available resources in this financially strapped city were funneled by the Jewish, Italian, and Irish commissioners to the white, middle-class sections of the city at the expense of the sections predominantly inhabited by the black, or to a somewhat lesser degree, the immigrant, poor. Studies of Chicago and Detroit schools show similar discrepancies among resources in neighborhood schools in the thirties. Homel (1985) and Mirel (1993), for example, found that boards of education in Chicago and Detroit actively promoted the segregation of black students during these years, by gerrymandering the outlines of school attendance areas and by unequal distribution of finances and instructional materials (see also Katznelson and Weir 1985; but see Peterson 1985, for the view that in Chicago resources were distributed rather equally among neighborhoods).

CONCLUSION

In the thirties, a decline in economic resources led to a decline in city services and in the maintenance of infrastructure. Lack of resources had a dampening effect on education as well: There were no educational reforms undertaken during the Great Depression, and in all but the white middle-class areas of the city, educational offerings and facilities suffered. Local business leaders fought educational and other social spending—as if the orgy of corporate expansion (much at public expense) and profit taking during the 1920s had not contributed to the stock market crash or its consequent societal distress.

The bias against cities in the state's reliance on local property taxes to fund education became apparent in this decade, as dwindling "ratables" led to impoverishment of the city government and no meaningful state or federal support for education existed. The problem of patronage in the schools persisted, as corruption among the commissioners increased, contributing to the forfeiture of federal funds, questionable business practices in the school system, and political appointments of people without relevant skills. Although distinguished historian David Tyack and colleagues have argued that the decade of the thirties was not a watershed in American education (Tyack, Lowe, and Hansot 1984), histories of Newark, Detroit, and Chicago have shown, as Mirel argued for Detroit, that "the thirties began the gradual but unmistakable decline in the quality of public education" in these cities (1993, 90; see also Katznelson and Weir 1985; Carnoy and Levin 1985). Of great significance is the fact that this decline has yet to be reversed.

It is also important to note that changes in city fortunes during the thirties were attributable in large part to economics and politics of social class, rather than of race. Only 10% of Newark residents were African American. The city population was primarily white and working-class, as were the majority of students. The actions of political and corporate elites fostered the decline of the city when it was a white "working-class town," and the schools suffered as part of that.

Racial segregation, however, was also a powerful force for discrimination during the period. Segregation became federal policy, and was subsequently enacted by financial institutions and real estate boards. The redlining initiated by the government fostered not only disinvestment of the city as a whole, but also the ghettoization of black residents. In Newark, this ghettoization had unfortunate consequences for the education of black children and, as we shall see, would continue to do so for generations to come.

CHAPTER 5

Pauperization of the City and Its Schools: 1945-1960

By 1960 the economic and political isolation of the city of Newark from the more affluent and mostly Caucasian suburbs was a demographic and social fact. Once African Americans, and increasingly, Hispanics, in U.S. cities became segregated from surrounding towns, the segregation of their children in urban schools followed. In this chapter I describe how the isolation of city residents that characterizes most urban areas today took root and grew in Newark between 1945 and 1960, and the consequences of that isolation for Newark schools and their students.

THE CITY

A number of social, economic, and political developments contributed to the segregation of American cities. The first of these was the Great Migration of southern blacks to urban areas in the North and the Midwest during the 20 years following World War II.

Demographic Changes

Until the 1940s in the American South, cotton and tobacco crops—the economic mainstay of most southern states—were grown and harvested much as they had been in the nineteenth century. Then, in the 1940s and 1950s, tractors and picking machines mechanized the cotton industry, replacing animal-drawn plows and agricultural workers; approximately 40% of former cotton acreage was converted to timber and pasture—uses that did not require labor. The mechanization of tobacco growing followed in the 1960s (Groh 1972, 64–65).

This industrialization of southern agriculture left most of the South's 12.5 million rural poor blacks and whites without work. Nine of the 10 poorest states in the Union were southern, and federal unemployment and welfare laws passed in the 1930s did not require them to offer unemployment insurance or financial sustenance to their unemployed laborers. Facing hunger, legal segregation, and southern, black educational systems in which 40% of the schools could not afford desks because per capita pupil spending was less than $15 per year (compared with a national average of more than $80), approximately 5 million rural black Americans moved from the south to northeastern and midwestern cities in the post–World War II period (Groh 1972, 66, 69–70, 72; Tyack, Lowe, and Hansot 1984, 32; Wilkerson 1939). Between 1940 and 1960, over 92,000 members of this Great Migration arrived in Newark (analysis of U.S. Census data in Curvin 1975, 14). During this period 1.6 million Appalachian whites and 700,000 Mexicans also moved to America's inner cities (Judd and Swanstrom 1994, 152).

By 1959 the Central Ward in Newark, which had been 63% black in 1940, was 85% African American. Almost every neighborhood in the city had undergone rapid transformation during the previous 6 or 7 years. The core ghetto expanded southward, as the percentage of blacks in the neighborhoods immediately to the south of the Central Ward grew from 20% to 61% (Kaplan 1963, 149; Office of the Mayor, 1959, 17).

As the black population increased in Newark after World War II, middle- and working-class white families bought homes in the suburbs, aided by federally subsidized (FHA) mortgages. The federal government also subsidized the development of suburbs in other ways: Suburban builders received federal subsidies of cheap land in outlying areas; states received federal funds to build highways to the land, and townships were given federal subsidies to develop sewage and other systems that would make the land suitable for homes (Judd and Swanstrom 1994, 200–211; Jackson 1985).

In the late 1940s and early 1950s, many white lawyers, realtors, and educators left Newark (Kaplan 1963, 61). By 1956, half of Newark's teachers and administrators lived outside the city (*Star Ledger* August 8, 1956). The majority of Jewish families moved, as did most working-class Irish (Curvin 1975, 40). According to Newark historian Charles Cummings, Jewish families gave as a major reason for leaving the city the decline in the schools. "We left when they shortened the school day after the War," was a typical response of former residents interviewed by Cummings (personal communication, July 12, 1995). Using figures from a 1961 booklet on urban renewal published by the Newark Central Planning Board for the U.S. Urban Renewal Administration, I estimate that over 115,000 whites left the city in the 10 years between 1950 and

1960. Only one outlying section gained in white population during the decade (71–114).

In 1940, blacks were 10.7% of Newark's population, by 1950, they were 17%, and by 1960 this figure had doubled to 34.5%; an additional 5% of the population was Spanish speaking (Curvin 1975, 13). A year later, board of education figures revealed that the schools were majority black (54.9%), with Puerto Ricans making up an additional 3.7% (Newark Board of Education 1961). Only two other cities changed racial composition as fast as Newark—Washington, DC, and Gary, Indiana (Curvin 1975, 13).

Economics

Southern blacks arriving in Newark in the 1950s came to a city with very few entry-level jobs available to them. The low- and midskill manufacturing jobs which had provided the uneducated European immigrant with employment and—in many cases with sufficient wages to ultimately buy entry into the middle class—had either departed for the suburbs, or were closed to the black newcomers because of racial discrimination.

The dispersal of manufacturing jobs from American cities accelerated after World War II, spurred not only by technological innovations that freed factories from a dependence on rail connections (e.g., trucks and nationally subsidized highways), and single-story plants (e.g., electrification) but also by federal policies regarding depreciation of assets. These policies allowed manufacturers to take tax deductions when they abandoned inner city factories. Later, investment tax credits, introduced in 1962 by President John Kennedy, allowed manufacturers to take dollar-for-dollar tax credits for new plant and equipment—though not for renovation of old plants. Between 1954 and 1981, these federal subsidies of manufacturing flight to the suburbs were worth $120 billion (Judd and Swanstrom 1994, 258).

In Newark, a city in which almost all jobs had been in manufacturing but 30 years before, by 1948—after a war-induced industrial surge had abated—only 44% of the city's jobs were in manufacturing (Newark Central Planning Board 1949, 84). By 1960, 24.5% of the manufacturing establishments present in Newark in 1940 had departed for the suburbs. According to information supplied by a State of New Jersey Department of Labor analyst, in 1947 there were 1,874 manufacturing establishments employing 73,605 workers in the city. By 1967 there were only 1,413, employing 47,500 workers. These figures show a decline of 461 establishments, or 24.5%, and of 26,105 workers (personal communication, June 5, 1995, based on Newark City Census of Manufacturers data).

Many office and service jobs remained, but employers typically required a high school education or clerical skills, which most southern migrants did not have (Tyack, Lowe, and Hansot 1984, 173). Adolph Holmes, secretary of industrial relations for the Urban League of Essex County, testified before the U.S. Commission on Civil Rights in Newark in 1962 that

> most companies in the Newark area do not hire Negroes . . . Of the approximately 4,000 employees in the Essex County banks, for example, only 150 are Negroes and all of these except three or so who are tellers . . . either hold custodial, messenger, or menial task jobs. . . . [Moreover,] most unions do not admit Negroes . . . few, if any, Negroes ever have the opportunity to apply for apprentice training. (11–12)

Holmes testified further that in the vocational schools in the county nonwhites pursued various trades, but local unions and employers seemingly failed to find "qualified" applicants. The result, he stated, was that

> the Negro youngster who is attending school in the local area . . . fails to see his senior citizens employed and, as a consequence, is somewhat stymied in his motivation as to: Why should I train for something that I will not get? (13)

Taxable business property in Newark declined by 26.4% between 1935 and 1952. Net taxable property declined from $943 million to $694 million between those years (Decter 1959, 9; see also Newark Teachers Union 1953, 14). Major corporations that remained in Newark were able to have their taxes lowered. The 1945 Barton Reiffer Act passed by the New Jersey legislature gave insurance companies, including major ones headquartered in Newark, substantial relief from property tax (Eiger 1976, 12). In order to raise revenue, Newark politicians increased property taxes to almost double between 1930 and 1952 (from 3.94 to 7.56%) (Decter 1959, 10, 15–17). By 1951, the assessment ratios (that is, the assessed valuation of a property as a proportion of its market value) in eight of New Jersey's 13 largest municipalities were at least 50% above the state average (Salmore and Salmore 1993, 246).

Housing

By 1945 in Newark, "blight in varying degree [had] spread over almost the entire city area. Only a few tracts in Weequahic, Vailsburg, and Forest Hill [were] relatively free from houses in bad repair and lacking sanitary facilities. These [were] the exceptions" (Bartholomew 1945, 23). The U.S. Housing Act of 1937 had enabled states to allow municipalities to build low-rent housing with federal loans and grants. The Newark Housing Authority (NHA), established in 1937 and the first such agency in the nation, soon built "two Irish, one Negro, two Italian, and two Jewish" projects, in ethnic enclaves in the city (Kaplan 1963, 40). Only two projects of the seven were racially integrated (Newark Central Planning Board 1951, 72).

In Newark, the self-professed goals of the NHA in the 1950s were business development in the downtown business district, and "middle-income housing on cleared slum sites" (Kaplan 1963, 15).

> The business block in Newark argued that sites should be cleared for new firms, [and that] the immediate emphasis should be on increased access for suburban shoppers to and from the business district. The city should clear sites for downtown parking lots, not for more tax-exempt public housing projects that use up good commercial real estate and seal off the central business district. (94)

City plans formulated in the 1950s by NHA successfully secured federal urban renewal funds for institutional building in the downtown area (for expansion of three colleges, and for two hospitals and hotels and shops in Penn Plaza) and for low-income housing in the Central Ward ghetto (184). Yet Newark's important banks and insurance companies reiterated (as they had in the 1930s) their refusal to spark local NHA redevelopment or housing with their own capital (24, 97–98, 103, 110).

The low-income projects that were built sometimes destroyed white ethnic neighborhoods contiguous to the black ghettoes, as "blighted" neighborhoods were torn down. Referring to the destruction of an Italian neighborhood and the construction of the high-rise Columbus Homes projects that opened in 1955 with 300 white (mostly Italian) families, a former Italian resident of Newark told me,

> those Italian neighborhoods had three- and four-family
> houses, and they may have been blighted on the outside, but
> they were okay inside. The neighborhoods had many busi-
> nesses that employed lots and lots of people. When they tore

down those neighborhoods, those middle-class people left,
and they never came back. The projects also destroyed all
those businesses and took away lots of jobs. (Interview, July
25, 1996)

The next three decades of urban renewal activity (1937–1967), however,
were not going to remove the blight from, or supply modest-rent living
quarters in, the majority of Newark's neighborhoods. As Judd and
Swanstrom point out,

> from the beginning [of urban development in the United States], half
> or more of all [government] funds were diverted away from low-
> income housing to commercial development. [Nationally] urban re-
> newal was turned into a pawn of the local downtown business elites.
> There was slum clearance, but not much low-cost housing. (1994, 138)

Nationally, only 5% of new housing units were for low-income families
between 1949 and 1964. Less than one quarter of homes demolished
were replaced, and less than one percent of urban renewal funds were
used for relocation assistance (146). As in Newark, slum dwellers had to
pay to move, and, at least in Newark, usually ended up paying higher
rent (and higher rent than that of whites remaining in the area) (Office
of the Mayor, 1959, 35).

In another development, as a result of the National Defense Highway Act of 1956, the federal government and state highway departments could now force private homeowners to sell, and local governments could not refuse to participate. City governments and business
leaders concurred, in the belief that the new highways would revitalize
the central cities by giving suburban dwellers a direct route to city shop-
ping in the downtown business districts. Yet in most cities the downtowns were not revitalized: In Boston, the Fitzgerald Expressway reduced surrounding property values by about $300 million; in New York
City the South Bronx—which would become one of the nation's worst
ghettos—was created in part by being cut off from the rest of the city
by the Cross-Bronx Expressway (Judd and Swanstrom 1994, 210–211;
Jackson 1985).

In Newark, highways were built westward to the suburbs through
the Jewish section of Weequahic in the late fifties, and the neighborhood
around the highway began to deteriorate as homes and businesses were
destroyed. Highways were built, radiating out from the center of Newark in every direction, destroying neighborhoods in almost all wards of
the city (see Newark Central Planning Board 1961; Kaplan 1963).

In the postwar period, highway building nationwide received huge subsidies year in and year out, but urban mass transit was starved. Estimates are that 75% of government expenditures for transportation in the United States in the postwar period went for highways and only 1% for urban mass transit (Judd and Swanstrom 1994, 212). Thus, cars became necessary for the commute to the entry-level manufacturing jobs, many of which had moved to the suburbs. Since most of the urban poor did not have automobiles, the absence of federal transportation subsidies for buses and trains increased the economic isolation of city residents. (For case studies and discussions of this "spatial mismatch" dimension of inner city residents isolation from jobs, see Kain 1968, Kasarda 1989, and Wilson 1987).

Politics

Nearly 100,000 blacks lived in Newark by the mid-1950s, but due to their concentration in one ward, and the city's at-large elections, required by the commission form of government, blacks could not affect the city-wide vote sufficiently to gain representation in city government. In 1945, Italians and Jews made up the majority of the voting public. (Irish politicians, however, continued to hold power out of proportion to the number of Irish voters remaining in the city.) By 1960, with most Irish and Jews having left the city, between 40 and 45% of the electorate was Italian, with Jews less than 10% of voters (Pomper 1966, 79–97).

The politically appointed whites in city agencies and in the schools had been given job security by the civil service laws of the 1930s. So, for those newcomers from the South who were qualified for the jobs in government or education, there were few if any openings. Organized crime in the ghetto, however, did provide some opportunity for political training of black leaders. Black political leaders in the Central Ward in the 1930s and 1940s were connected with the city politicians who had the support of the Zwillman forces. They were, it could even be said, a part of the Zwillman organization. Black men worked as numbers runners, getting these jobs through the Underworld system, which also aided in the survival of many of the black social clubs, where Prohibition liquor was sold. Of the black men working in this system, one of the few offering them opportunities, some emerged as the political leaders of the ward (Curvin 1975, 18). According to Curvin,

> The direct and indirect control by underworld forces over the emer-
> gence of black political leadership had several destructive conse-
> quences. First, the underworld needed black leaders who were cor-

rupt or corruptible; it obviously would not tolerate leaders who might criticize or expose the damage and exploitation bestowed on the black community through organized crime's illicit activities. In addition, the underworld encouraged the kind of social behavior that was profitable to their businesses but damaging to black community life. (19)

The political arena in Newark during this period was characterized not only by the active participation of organized crime in ghetto and city affairs, but also, in 1953, by the overthrow of the commission form of government by a political reform movement. By 1950, Newark was the only major city still utilizing the commission form of government. In part because of mismanagement and graft by commissioners, Newark had (with the possible exception of Jersey City) the most expensive government of almost any of 24 cities studied with populations of between 300,000 and 600,000 (Decter 1959, 16). In 1951, Newark's costs were $102.42 per capita, compared to $54.8 for the other cities (and $67 for other commission-run cities). Because of the extensive patronage over the years, Newark had more municipal employees per 1,000 population than had most other cities its size (15.32 vs. 10.6; and vs. 11 for other commission cities) (National Municipal League 1949 in Decter 1959, 16–17).

The late 1940s and early 1950s saw an increase in the pace of scandal and corruption that had characterized the commission government since 1917. Commissioner Ralph A. Villani and several others, for example, when indicted for extortion and kickbacks, protested that they had done nothing wrong: Kickbacks and extortion were "part and parcel of government," Villani argued (*Newark Evening News* May 4, 1958, in Douglas 1972, 25). The commissioner was indicted on the same day on which the FBI announced a probe of police brutality and on which the police released its findings of widespread corruption in the Department of Parks and Public Programs, including the systematic shakedown of employees, and kickbacks. A grand jury found in 1953 that the men on the zoning board were personal representatives of the commissioners and had neither the educational background nor the understanding of zoning laws to do their jobs (*Newark Evening News* April 10, 1953, in Decter 1959, 31).

In 1950, faced with the city's persistent financial straits, seen in its declining tax base, high taxes, an increased demand for city services, and a crumbling infrastructure, two major corporations threatened to leave: the Mutual Benefit and Prudential Insurance companies. "In 1953, community morale was at a low ebb. In the face of national prosperity, Newark was rapidly deteriorating, as were many other old industrial cities. Almost every segment of Newark's population was affected by the government's inability to cope with its basic problems" (Decter 1959, 136).

A multiyear effort of several labor groups and a citizens committee to reform the city charter was successful in 1953 when a referendum passed that converted the commission government to a "strong mayor-weak council" form, with nonpartisan ward-based as well as at-large elections of a city council (Douglas 1972, 47, 50). Opposed by business and some labor organizations as "placating certain groups," the ward-based elections were thought by the citizens committee to be important for providing political recognition to the city's black residents (51).

The ward-based elections in 1954 did yield Italian and black councilmembers (Mario Farco and Irvine Turner) and a reform mayor (Leo Carlin). The reform mayor kept tighter control over payroll at city hall, centralized tax collection, and provided the first tax rate decrease in 10 years (Douglas 1972, 68). He eliminated payroll padding, no-show jobs, and the political machines of the former commissioners. He talked of business efficiency, civil service exams, integrity and impartiality in city government. Significantly, he halted the dispensing of patronage and, to save money, decreased city services. These last two initiatives would soon alienate blacks and Italians—the ethnic groups that were just beginning to demand their share of patronage and city services.

Only months after Mayor Carlin's election, Mutual Benefit and Prudential announced that they would stay in the city, but Prudential soon moved its regional operations out. A building boom began downtown, with a YM-YWCA, a new hospital, new chemical plants, and plans for a $40 million board of education capital program. In 1955, the business community publicized Newark as an "All-American City," and as a "New Newark"—to attract business and encourage building. In attempts to revitalize the downtown, the business groups built an underground garage under a small park in central city for suburban shoppers (72). But there were no corporate contributions to slum clearance, neighborhood rehabilitation, or low- or middle-income housing. Neighborhoods and city services continued to deteriorate (70–72; see also Sternlieb 1966, 231).

The 1950s saw the transfer of hegemony from the Jewish crime organization to the Mafia. According to Robert Curvin, members of the Italian group worked in the black ghetto with elected official Irvine Turner, to run gambling and prostitution operations, and to "keep the peace" (Curvin 1975, 30, 31, 37). In 1962, the Mafia, which the reform mayor had aggressively pursued, bankrolled Italian congressman Hugh Addonizio's run for mayor (*Newark Evening News* April 9, 1970). Addonizio's Italian heritage and liberal civil rights voting record in Washington also helped make him Newark's first Italian mayor ever elected. When Addonizio was inaugurated, there were no blacks in appointed jobs of note at city hall (one judge, Harry Hazlewood, had been appointed by the reform mayor). Many of Newark's black citizens were hopeful that the liberal Addonizio would provide much needed jobs and services in the city's neighborhoods.

THE STATE

Between 1940 and 1960, the population of New Jersey grew by almost half. Practically all the net population increase was in the suburbs. Newark's population had peaked in 1930 at 442,337. In 1940, the state's large cities' share of the population would begin to decline dramatically, until by 1980, fewer than 1 million of the state's 7 million residents, or only 13%, lived in the six largest cities; by 1970 the voting share of these big six would drop to 11% of the statewide vote (Pomper 1986, 39; Salmore and Salmore 1993, 47; U.S. Census, in Sternlieb and Barry 1967, 12).

In the immediate postwar period, a coalition of Hudson County Democrats (the infamous machine and organized crime connections of Jersey City's Mayor Frank Hague) and rural Republicans continued to rule New Jersey's legislature (Cook 1974). The state's urban Democrats were concentrated in a few counties. With few exceptions, among them Mayor Hague, they focused their attention on the local governments. To have any influence at the state capital, these Democrats had to make common cause with rural Republicans (Salmore and Salmore 1993, 114).

It was the case in 1950 that four Republican senators representing 3% of the state's population had the power to hold a proposal hostage. By 1960, the Republicans had controlled the upper house for all but 3 years of the entire century, and the assembly for all but 13, despite frequent statewide election of Democratic governors, whose powers were limited by the state constitution (Salmore and Salmore 1993, 46, 145). This stranglehold by the rural elites prevented the passage of legislation that would benefit the cities. Moreover, throughout most of the postwar period, either four of the five, or all five, legislators on the New Jersey Commission on School Aid were from rural counties (see, e.g., *Star Ledger* May 13, 1952; also Salmore and Salmore 1993). In 1945, Newark was still considered by the state to be a wealthy city, and received no educational state aid at all. Rather, the city paid about a quarter of a million dollars a year to rural counties for their educational costs (*Newark Evening News* May 13, 1948). In 1946, the formula for state education aid was finally redrawn so that no community lost funds. By 1951, Newark was receiving approximately $900,000 a year in state education aid (*Star Ledger*, September 20, 1951).

In 1956, the Newark Board estimated that it would take a minimum of $50 million to get the school system into a "reasonable condition" (Schotland 1956, 27). But the board could only borrow $15 million more under the debt limit fixed by the state. All the cities needed more money, but the state legislature would not revise the debt limit to permit more borrowing (*Newark Evening News* September 5, 1957). The rural legislators' antipathy to urban problems during these years may be intimated from the following anecdote: In 1948, the state refused to reimburse Newark for $5,000 it had spent on state-supported vocational schools, because officials in Newark had completed the state form incorrectly (*Newark Evening News* June 23, 1948, November 26, 1948).

Although the cities were in financial straits, affluent towns spent heavily on education. School spending in New Jersey was second only to Montana in the postwar decades. Yet New Jersey ranked 37th among the then 48 states in aid to education. New Jersey furnished only 16% of school budgets, as opposed to 40% in some other states. Only two states contributed less (Salmore and Salmore 1993, 259–260).

THE SCHOOLS

How did the influence of corruption and organized crime, the continued financial distress of the city, and the increasing percentages, and ghetto-ization, of black citizens affect the city schools?

Patronage and Corruption

In 1941, Newark Mayor Vincent Murphy and a political aide, Arnold Hess, without public justification but quite obviously to more directly control patronage and finances, put the board of education directly under the mayor's control, as part of the city's revenue and finance department, which the mayor, who was also a commissioner, directed (*Star Ledger* August 14, 1941). The state board of the Civil Service Commission wrote to the city that this was illegal, and that even though the mayor appointed board of education members, and several city officials and board members constituted an oversight board of school estimate, the commissioners "must deal with the school [board] as a separate government." Three months later, Mayor Murphy placed aide Arnold Hess on the board, and in 1945 made Hess board secretary, with wide powers

(*Star Ledger* November 1, 1945). Hess would remain in control of budgeting, personnel, payroll, accounting, and auditing for the Newark school district through four successive mayors, until 1972, when he retired.

Soon after Hess had been appointed, his office was criticized for loose business practices. An audit of the board in February 1946, found "total disregard for control of financial and other records." Although Hess nominally headed up the department, the audit claimed that there was actually "no one in charge of financial accounts" in the district and the "Board keeps no records of actual expenditures." The audit charged that there was "no inventory control" and "no control over work orders." The "Board of Education makes transfers of [large sums] of money in major accounts that are neither authorized or approved by the School Estimate Board, and the State says this is illegal" (*Newark Call* February 17, 1946). Hess was also criticized for attempting to force 900 teachers to buy tickets to his testimonial dinner (June 30, 1946; December 2, 1946).

Indeed, teachers were affected in other ways by this corruuption. In 1943, the Newark Board of Education changed the city exam requirements for kindergarten and elementary teachers from 50% written and 50% oral to 30% written and 70% oral and were immediately charged with attempting to make it easier for "friends" to get appointed. Applicants from outside Newark were required to have 4 years of college to teach in Newark, whereas residents only needed 3; most teachers were still Newark residents (*Newark Evening News* April 11, 1943).

The patronage in the schools was also noticed by the press. The *Call* editorialized that,

> Board personnel used to be "pretty good." In the last two decades [1926–46] it [sic] has deteriorated, reflecting the declining standards of successive mayors. The [reason] may be found in the administrative and so-called special services that have mushroomed in the [school] system. Some . . . feel that the system is top heavy, with too many supervisors and assistant supervisors, directors and assistant directors, and too many newly created jobs. (January 27, 1946)

The Civil Service Commission informed the Newark school system that there were too many temporary workers (more than a third) and too many job categories and titles. The commission complained about the status of "teacher-clerks" who, although not teaching, were getting the higher salary of teachers: "There are 74 of these persons employed at the Board of Education, and that number would seem to be very much out of proportion" (*Star Ledger* December 20, 1945).

Just before the overthrow of the commission government in 1953, Mayor Ralph Villani (the first Italian mayor chosen by the commissioners) was criticized for his control of the board of education. He was charged with holding "weekly meetings" in his office with the board members he had selected, to "tell them how to vote, where to spend money, and where to build new classrooms" (*Newark Evening News* October 25, 1950; for other charges of corruption at the board of education in the early 1950s see, among others, *Newark Evening News* March 29, 1950, May 12, 1952, July 3, 1952, June 16, 1953, June 20, 1953, April 30, 1954).

During a search for a new superintendent in 1953, several candidates, whom the press called "outsiders," said that "they wouldn't come to Newark if offered the job because the city had the reputation of having 'too much politics in the public school system'" (*Star Ledger* June 10, 1953). Although the politics and graft in Newark may have been more extensive than in other cities, boards of education were tainted by corruption and influenced by politics to varying degrees in any number of cities in the postwar years—as studies of Gary, Detroit, Boston, New York, and Chicago reveal (R. Cohen 1990; Katznelson and Weir 1985; Mirel 1993; Strayer 1944, 1951). George Strayer and a Teachers College team studied the Boston schools in 1944. They reported that

> politics has dealt a paralyzing blow to progress in the Boston schools. 'Politics' is given as the cause of relatively incompetent persons holding responsible positions, of decisions being made that are contrary to the best judgement of those most concerned with the result, of staff members failing to deal with problems courageously and frankly, and of a pervading fear which survey members found existent among school personnel. (11)

As we have seen, for several years after Newark's reform mayor was elected (in 1954), he was successful at stopping the patronage appointments and corruption at city hall. One unfortunate result of the unavailability of patronage jobs at city hall, however, was that, because the mayor had less control over Arnold Hess and the quasi-independent board of education, patronage appointments continued to be available at the board. During the fifties, the board became "the largest and most penetrable patronage pool in town." Council members, unable to get their supporters (most often uneducated people from the neighborhood) city hall jobs, obtained jobs for them at the board of education (Conforti 1974, 25). As we shall see, one result would be a continual lowering of educational standards and staff skill levels in the following years.

Several audits of financial operations at the Newark board in the early 1950s found "failure to comply with established uniform cash control procedures, failure to remit to the board periodical surpluses in internal accounts," and other questionable practices (*Newark Evening News* January 5, 1951, March 6, 1953). As a result of these audits, and perhaps strongly encouraged by the reform mayor and the chamber of commerce, in 1955 the board hired the Survey Institute, Inc., a consulting firm recommended by the superintendent of the nearby New York City school system. This group was paid $13,500 to study the board's financial and business operations, to determine how they could be made more efficient (*Newark Evening News* March 28, 1956). The report, delivered in March 1956, was not scrutinized by the Newark Board of Education until a year after it was completed (*Newark Evening News* March 10, 1957). According to the press, the report found "cancerous mismanagement" by the school system and "waste of $350,000 a year. . . . The report places the responsibility for the mismanagement on a decade of neglect and indecisiveness on the part of the policy makers and operating officials" and "imprudent administrative spending by Secretary Hess" (*Newark Evening News* May 16, 1956).

The survey also cited Joseph Schotland, assistant superintendent of schools in charge of business administration, and complained that "many hundreds of repair requests have been waiting seven or more years." The report declared that the board was "drowning in a sea of paper." It stated that a 44-cent purchase generated 31 pieces of paper and a $6.95 repair generated 32 pieces of paper" (*Newark Evening News* May 16, 1956).

Assistant Superintendent Schotland responded to the charges by cataloging what appears to be an accurate assessment of the situation: a severe decline in the number and quality of persons available to his department, and decreased resources for operations and maintenance. He wrote that the number of repairmen was reduced from 96 to 50 in 1950 (Schotland 1956, 6; see also *Newark Evening News* February 6, 1951). He stated that there was an "extreme shortage of permanent skilled personnel below the executive level" (Schotland 1956, 20) and a "lack of first-class 2nd level executives to whom broad responsibilities can be delegated." "There are no departments for planning, or for administration; there is no director of plant and not enough personnel to carry out these functions" (30–31). He said that he had been unable to fill executive positions due to salary and other budget limitations (21; also *Newark Evening News* February 6, 1951, in which it was reported that to save money, the education budget for repairs was decreased). Moreover, other areas of his department (e.g., division of supplies) "have lost key skilled personnel, due to retirement (after 20 and 30 years of service). . . . New replacements did not have the same qualifications" (Schotland 1956, 23). "Civil service exams have not been held for several years, and part-time people have been hired without the skills" (23). The department has experienced a recent "frequent turnover of skilled personnel" and "extensive use of temporary employees without the necessary skills," especially in repair and maintenance (23).

Deterioration of Physical Facilities

As if to corroborate the charge that building maintenance and repairs were inadequate, the *Star Ledger* announced that "parts of brick posts and concrete slabs weighing 1,000 pounds fell off Central High School [in the Central Ward] near pedestrians walking . . . past the school. . . . A 15-foot long tile partition in a school built the previous year collapsed in the cafeteria of a school in the Central Ward injuring three students" (August 8, 1956; August 9, 1956).

A decade before Schotland was forced to reply to charges that the school buildings were in dire need of repair, *Newark Call* headlines declared that "Newark Schools [are] the 'Worst.' . . . Buildings [are] Decaying Rapidly, Repairs Are Neglected" (March 31, 1946). Schools built in the 1840s and 1850s were still in use, and with no capital improvements made since the 1920s, in the 1940s the physical decay of the school plant proceeded rapidly, and for the first time became an issue in the press. Since the majority of the city's schools were built before 1912, when the New Jersey Department of Public Instruction adopted a fire code governing school construction (*Newark Evening News* December 27, 1946), most of the schools did not have fire safety features or alarms. Newspapers reported at least 10 fires in which classrooms were gutted or the school building otherwise seriously damaged between 1950 and 1960 (*Star Ledger* March 1, 1955, March 20, 1957, January 14, 1959, January 24, 1959; *Newark Evening News* July 14, 1956, August 27, 1957, February 4, 1958; January 30, 1959, April 12, 1960, February 5, 1959).

During the postwar decades, the decay of school buildings built in the nineteenth and early twentieth centuries plagued most older cities. For example, Strayer reported in 1944 that in Boston, "repair projects are initiated on a chance day-by-day basis rather than as a result of comprehensive planning." Most Boston schools "are extremely old, and have not been maintained." Strayer reported that there were 90 fires in Boston schools in the previous decade (222–224). Mirel (1993) found that in Detroit, because of a lack of finances, ''the material condition of the schools'' was ''unquestionably . . . far worse in 1949 than it had been in 1929'' (200).

Finances

The deterioration of the physical plant was but one example of the decline of the school system during the 1940s and 1950s. As the fifties progressed, the city spent fewer of its resources on education. The decline in spending was documented in hearings before the U.S. Commission on Civil Rights in Newark during September 11–12, 1962. According to the testimony of Newark National Association of Colored People (NAACP) attorney George D. Jeter,

> The board of education . . . has repeatedly told the public that it is not sparing any expense for education. The figures, however, do not bear this out. In 1955–56, Newark was 6th in the county in per capita spending on instruction. By 1959–60, Newark ranked next to last. On spending for textbooks and supplies, according to the annual reports of the N.J. State Commissioner for Education, Newark ranked fourth in the county in the 1951–52 school year. By the 1955–56 school year, it had dropped to 7th out of 16 systems, and by the year 1959–60 had plummeted down to 13th of the 16. (1962, 11)

Attorney Jeter further testified that in 1960 Newark's tax rate was the highest in the county, yet it ranked 11th in the portion of its tax rate which went to education. By 1961, the city had the second highest tax rate, and its school tax rate [had fallen] to 13th of 21 communities in the county. Its school tax rate as a percentage of total tax ranked it 21st, in last place (12). ''These figures are even worse than they appear,'' Jeter concluded, ''when one considers that the Newark Board of Education historically manages to have a 5 to 10% surplus to be entered into the next year's budget revenue'' (12).

Boards of education in other cities were also experiencing diminishing financial support. In a study of 12 metropolitan areas (Baltimore, Birmingham, Boston, Buffalo, Chattanooga, Chicago, Cincinnatti, Cleveland, Detroit, New Orleans, St. Louis, and San Francisco), the U.S. Civil Rights Commission found that, in 1950, 10 of the 12 central cities spent considerably more per pupil than did the surrounding suburbs; by 1964, in 7 of the 12, the average suburb spent more per pupil than did the central city.

This reversal reflects the declining or stagnant city tax base, and increasing competition [from police, fire, and welfare] for a share of the municipal tax dollar. The suburbs, where nonschool needs are less demanding, allocate almost twice the proportion of their total budgets to education as the cities. (1967, 1:27)

Teacher Attitudes

During the 1940s and 1950s Newark's teachers, most of whom were Irish, Italian, or Jewish, began to face students with backgrounds very different from their own, as black children and youth from the rural South entered the schools. A retired, long-time Newark teacher told me that teachers often perceived these new students as "more difficult to teach" and "unruly" or "unmotivated" (personal communication June 20, 1996). In 1945 Bruce Robinson, director of the Bureau of Child Guidance of the Newark public schools, publicized a survey of teacher attitudes toward students. The *Sunday Call* printed the following statements made by Newark teachers to their students, which the director had recorded, which he said were "common," and which, he alleged, showed disrespect: "You're a disgrace to your family." "You're filthy." "Get out! I'm tired of looking at you." "Did you ever hear of soap?" (September 30, 1945).

The survey, criticized in the same article by the teachers union as unfair "due to the new pressures on teachers, with the many numbers of 'difficult students,' and fewer materials" caused somewhat of an uproar, and represented the difficult time many teachers were experiencing as they dealt with cultural backgrounds to which they were unaccustomed. Kenneth Clark later argued, however, that this "clash of cultures in the classroom" was "essentially a class war, a socioeconomic and racial warfare being waged on the battleground of our schools, with middle-class and middle-class-aspiring teachers . . . arrayed against hopelessly outclassed working-class youngsters" (1965, 129).

The potential collision of racial and class cultures may have made teaching in the city unattractive to new college graduates. Moreover, long-time teachers were experiencing the reduction of revenue in cities available for teacher salaries and instructional materials, and many left for better jobs in other professions, or in the suburbs (Newark Teachers Union 1953). In Newark, as in New York, because of a lack of applicants, experienced teachers were often replaced with unqualified long-term substitutes (Clark, 1965). In 1947, 10% of Newark's teachers were substitutes (*Newark Evening News* March 16, 1947). In 1956, one of six, or 16.6%, were substitutes. By 1958, almost one quarter of the teachers in

Newark were long-term substitutes (November 30, 1958). Although some substitutes were qualified, most either did not have the educational credentials or had failed the city exam. In February of 1958, Newark lowered its examination standards to try to attract more teachers (February 7, 1958).

Schools in the Black Neighborhoods

Having few resources to use on the educational system in Newark, the city council members and members of the board of education, most of whom, in both groups, were Jewish or Italian, distributed these resources according to the interests of the voters in their own neighborhoods and according to the political power held by each group, and by officials and mayors. Consequently, the schools in the black ghetto received very little.

As blacks arrived from the South to the housing projects in the Central Ward, the neighborhood schools became swamped with students (*Newark Evening News* September 21, 1958). Hayes Homes, a project in the Central Ward that housed 5,000 people, provides an example. "Hayes Homes Children Pose School Problem," declared the *News* in 1954:

> Enrollment [in one neighborhood school] is now 1,653. A year ago it was 907 [a 746-pupil increase in one year]. At a nearby school, administrators increased the kindergarten entrance age to five to limit enrollment, and classes are being held in the basement of the project. (October 17, 1954)

The situation in the Third Ward also came to light, as many complaints came from members of the black community about schools there. William Jackson, with a master's degree from the University of Illinois, and, in 1942 the first black appointed to the board of education, said that Third Ward schools were a "teachers' Siberia." He alleged that "teachers in Third Ward schools were unsympathetic and unprepared" and that there were far too many substitutes in those schools (*Star Ledger* April 17, 1943).

A black pastor asked the board for "Negro teachers in Robert Treat Elementary School," which was 80% black, and was denied. He then asked the board that "two Negro substitute teachers there who were fully qualified to be certified be appointed permanently." The board of education told him that it "can't bend the rules" (*Newark Evening News*, April 27, 1944).

Irvine Turner, the city's first black city councilmember, elected in 1954 after the reform of the commission government, stated that although Central Ward schools were more than 90% black there were no black principals, although there were black teachers with Ph.D.s. Turner cited "teacher neglect and lethargy" as far as Central Ward children were concerned. "The substitutes are only getting practice," he said, "and the regular teachers, not all, of course, only seem interested in pushing the child through the eighth grade (and out)." Turner said that he was "alarmed and amazed" when several Central Ward teachers told him, "Most of these kids aren't going through high school anyway. They'll quit at 16 and get a job in a factory somewhere. The parents aren't concerned with them and our job is only to see they remain in school until the compulsory age" (*Herald News* July 14, 1956).

The board of education was not responsive to complaints from the African American community. Rather, they responded instead to the fears of white parents who wanted their children to transfer from majority black schools. The board gave permission for schools to transfer white pupils out of Third Ward schools where the enrollment was predominantly black (*Star Ledger* March 26, 1947). By 1950, 4,300 white pupils had been transferred from schools with majority black enrollment (*Newark Evening News*, May 12, 1950, June 16, 1950). A number of white non-Italian students transferred from schools with majority Italian students, in addition (May 12, 1950). During school year 1960–61, the board adopted a plan which redistricted feeder elementary schools in order to maintain an all-white high school in an Italian section (which was heavily populated by city workers) but at the edge of an area experiencing an influx of blacks (U.S. Commission on Civil Rights 1962, 11).

Alarmed by what they perceived to be the rapidly increasing segregation of black children in schools with inferior resources and teaching, the Newark NAACP undertook a study of the city schools in the late 1950s, and in 1961 presented to the board of education the following findings:

> Examination of the data supplied by the Board of Education reveals that 25.8% of the elementary school teachers are long-term substitutes. Moreover, as a school district [neighborhood within the Newark system] becomes more nonwhite, the percentage of substitute teachers increases. Conversely, the fewer Negroes in the school district, the smaller the percentage of substitute teachers. (NAACP 1961, 391–392)

The *Newark Evening News* had reported in 1958 that 6 of the 63 Newark schools had 24% of all the substitutes, and all but one of these schools were in the black Central Ward (November 30, 1958).

The NAACP discovered that schools of high white composition had class sizes well below the city average. All but 1 of the 47 unused classrooms were in schools with lower than average black enrollments. On the other hand, all but 14 of the 128 double-session classrooms were in schools with high black enrollments (NAACP 1961, 397). Moreover,

> almost without exception there has been a deplorable shortage of text-books available to elementary school children in districts with high Negro enrollments. . . . In schools with high Negro enrollments, text-books were either not available or so outmoded and in such poor condition as to be of virtually no value as texts. Workbooks are not available in many of the schools. Many of the textbooks available in the Negro schools are stamped 'Discarded' from other schools in the city. While the supply situation has been far from flawless in the primarily white-enrollment schools, there is a marked difference in the supply situation between high white enrollment schools and high Negro enrollment schools. We found that some class libraries consist of nothing but comic books. In one reading class, since no "reader" books were available, the teacher spent the time reading to the children from a book of his own. How the children were expected to learn to read by this process was never explained. (402–403)

The NAACP charged that schools in districts with high black enrollments were far behind schools with high white enrollments. "Many Negro children are being promoted out of the elementary schools without being able to read well or without having a grasp of the rudiments of math and other basic subjects" (404).

Nationally, between 1920 and 1950, black teachers who had graduated from some of the best colleges and universities, some with master's and doctorates, applied for, and often received, positions in northern city schools. However, they were typically hired as nonpermanent teachers and permitted to teach only in schools with black students (Warren 1989, 359). The NAACP research in Newark also revealed a further form of discrimination against black teachers. No African American had ever been promoted to a supervisory or administrative position in the Newark school system (1961, 405).

> In the 1958–59 examinations . . . six Negroes passed all portions of the exam for vice principal. However, their placement on the list was such that it was almost guaranteed that the first Negro would not be reached for the life of the list. Of the Negro candidates, several scored superior in the written portions of the exam and finished at the top of the list of that portion of the exam. However, in the oral portion of the exam, all the Negro candidates were scored at about the same posi-

tion—in the mediocre range of the list. High scores on the oral exam lifted many white candidates above their Negro competitors on the placement list, in spite of poorer showings on the written tests. In background vocationally and educationally as well as from the standpoint of civic, community, and related activity, at least two of the Negro candidates stood far above candidates who were lifted above them by virtue of grades on the oral portion of the examination. (406)

After the NAACP presented their findings, a special committee of the board was formed and upon investigation found the following irregularities: Some white candidates had been permitted to take the oral exam in spite of the fact that they had not passed the written exam. The superintendent illegally put comments on 22 of 52 exam papers, and each candidate who had received favorable comments from the superintendent scored exceedingly well on the oral exams. Those candidates receiving adverse or no comments from the superintendent scored poorly on the orals (*Newark Evening News* October 30, 1959, June 13, 1960, August 31, 1960, September 28, 1960; *Star Ledger* June 29, 1960). However, the board of education later decided in a unanimous ruling that the NAACP report did not warrant any further action or investigation (U.S. Commission 1962, 391).

As noted earlier, by school year 1960–61, a majority of the city's public school students were black. Each of the high schools was predominantly of one race of students. Board of education figures showed that "Negroes [were] 54.9% of public school students, and Puerto Ricans [were] 3.7%. Negroes [were] 66.9% of special schools [for the 'mentally deficient' or otherwise disabled], 58.3% of elementary schools . . . and only 34.3% of high schools." Two high schools, Central and South Side [were] 89.1% and 86.3% black. The other high schools [were] 67, 93.5, 98.9, 80.7, and 65.1% white. Puerto Ricans made up only 1.3% of the total high school enrollment (Newark Board of Education 1961).

Residential, economic, and educational policies during the previous decades had produced segregated school systems by 1960 in many other northern cities as well (as earlier in the South). Accompanying this segregation was the allocation of fewer resources to the nonwhite schools. Chicago schools, for example, were segregated by the 1930s, with 85% of Chicago's blacks living in the city's "black belt" (Drake and Cayton 1945, 204). A survey of the Chicago schools found in 1931 that 39.2% of the black schools were "so inferior . . . that it is not advisable to expend any considerable amount of money on them." By 1940, Chicago's black schoolchildren attended part-time sessions (although whites did not) because there were insufficient facilities for them (Katznelson and Weir 1985, 244). In Boston by 1944, the "24,000 Negroes [were] largely concentrated in relatively few elementary school districts in the South End and Roxbury" (Strayer 1944, 416). In Detroit by the mid-thirties most black students were in segregated schools (Mirel 1993, 188). By the 1950s, "Detroit was operating a separate and unequal school system for black children" (251). The Detroit Board of Education gerrymandered attendance boundaries along racial lines, segregated black teachers in black schools, placed higher numbers of emergency substitutes in black schools, and offered an inferior curriculum to black students in which blacks were funneled into "general tracks" in the high schools and denied apprenticeship opportunities in the most promising vocational programs (188, 252, 275). The U.S. Commission on Civil Rights found that studies showed "purposeful segregation by administrative action" of boards of education in numerous cities in the forties and fifties outside the South, among them Cincinnati; Chicago; Detroit; Gary; Hillsboro, Ohio; New Rochelle, New York; Orange, New Jersey; and Portland, Oregon. Numerous states outside of the South maintained separate and inferior schools for blacks well into the postwar period—among them Illinois, New Jersey, New Mexico, New York, Ohio, and Wyoming (1967, 1:43; see also Wright 1941).

Education in the White Middle-Class Areas

Despite the decline of most of the Newark system, in the white middle-class areas of the city educational quality remained high. The best example is the middle-class Jewish section of Weequahic, traditionally an area with one of the two academic high schools in the city. The other is Barringer High School, which served Italian neighborhoods. In 1950, Weequahic High School received a "very superior" overall rating by Middle States Association of Colleges and Schools, and in 1951 Barringer was rated "superior" and its academic courses "extraordinarily fine" (*Newark Evening News* June 27, 1951).

According to a pamphlet devised by the Weequahic High School's head counselor for students to submit with their applications to college, the high school curriculum included college-level courses in math and science taught by Weequahic teachers who had studied at the Massachusetts Institute of Technology and Bell Labs: "'a much more extensive program than anything offered before in any of the high schools,' stated the superintendent for secondary schools" (*Newark Evening News* December 7, 1958). Special language courses were regularly offered in Hebrew, Russian, and Greek, with voluntary, after-school classes held in Chinese and Swahili (19.3% of Weequahic High School students were black in 1960–61). According to the curriculum pamphlet, 70% of the school's students attended college (*Newark Evening News* January 13, 1962). The *News* had earlier reported that at a recent "career parlay," Weequahic High School students had heard from representatives of 54 different careers—business, professional and scientific leaders had spoken at the school (*Star Ledger* December 8, 1958). In 1957, Governor Robert Meyner had addressed the students in the Weequahic auditorium (*Newark Evening News* February 27, 1957).

During the fifties, as in many other cities, Newark schools were overcrowded. However, only schools in the middle-class Jewish and Italian neighborhoods had additions built. For example, Weequahic High School was newly built in 1933, and in 1957 a 16-room addition was added. Plans to build additions to schools in other areas of the city were not carried through. In contrast to the neglect in poor neighborhoods, one elementary school in the Jewish and one in the Italian area were provided with "gifted education" programs (*Newark Evening News* June 12, 1957).

The board of education tested third-, sixth-, and seventh-grade Newark students in reading and math every 6 months. The scores as reported in the press were not disaggregated by school, so we cannot compare the performance on these tests of students in Weequahic with those in the Central Ward. On the whole, however, in 1957 the city pupils were reported "deficient in reading and math, [and were] at least a year and a half behind" by seventh grade (*Newark Evening News* February 8, 1957).

In this discussion of Newark education in the postwar period, I have attempted to demonstrate the decline of the majority of the city's schools. It is important to remind readers that despite this decline there was never a clear "golden age" of schooling in Newark. Even during the latter half of the nineteenth century when Newark schools were models and held in high esteem, and at the turn of the century when they were leaders in Progressive administrative reform, the schools failed the children of the poor—who were often taught in dirty, overcrowded classrooms, with uninspiring teaching methods; and the system itself was fraught with corruption. During the Great Depression, as fewer middle-class and affluent children attended the city public schools, finances evaporated, corruption increased, and the quality of education for most children declined. In the postwar period the decline accelerated, and in these years was produced not only by lack of finances and lack of concern for "lower-class" whites, but by pervasive racism. In Newark, at least two more generations of children in the ghettoes received an education that was inferior to that of their middle-class peers and that would disadvantage them in the new white-collar economy.

CONCLUSION

In the years between 1945 and 1960, a number of developments coincided to lay the foundation for the isolation and alienation of the urban poor that characterize our cities—and our city schools—today: the migration to cities of southern blacks fleeing poverty, segregation, and inadequate education; federally subsidized suburbanization of white families and manufacturing firms leaving these same cities; federal and state policies that did not adequately address the problems festering in urban neighborhoods; corporate disinterest; and local political patronage and corruption.

In Newark during the 1960s, rapid economic disinvestment of the city, the conversion of the U.S. economy to a service base, the indifference of powerful state politicians, the limited reach of federal educational reform, and a culmination of local corruption and greed built ghetto walls around the city—and its schools—that to this day appear to be insurmountable.

CHAPTER 6

Organized Crime and Municipal and Educational Chaos: The 1960s

It is often assumed that the sixties inaugurated a period of substantive educational change in urban America: the beginning of a long slide in the quality of urban schools and the "deconstruction" of the old but reasonably effective educational world (Grant 1988, 45; see also Hampel 1986; Murphy 1990; Ravitch 1983). Previous chapters in this book have shown that this was not the case for Newark; the decline had begun thirty years before and was a direct result of economic and political decisions on the part of federal, state, and local groups. I want to demonstrate in this chapter that the continued deterioration of education in Newark in the 1960s was a result of the culmination of these trends. In this decade, perhaps more blatantly than before, the confluence of social class and race determined the resources made available for a child's schooling. The decade also demonstrates the continued, mutually reinforcing relationship between a declining urban school system and the flight of business and the middle class.

THE CITY

During this last decade of mass migration of black rural agricultural workers to northern cities, 69,000 arrived in Newark (for a total of 161,000 blacks settling there between 1940 and 1970). During the 1960s, over one quarter of Newark's census tracts changed from white majority to black majority. The flight of whites added up to an out-migration of 106,500, or the departure of 4 of every 10 whites who had been living in the city at the beginning of the decade (*New York Times* February 20, 1972, in Curvin 1975, 14). The 1970 U.S. Census showed that African Americans were a majority of city residents (54.2%), Puerto Ricans were 9%, and whites were 36.6% of the population (Curvin 1975, 13). The majority of whites remaining in Newark were either elderly European immigrants, or children of immigrants (Pomper 1966). As noted earlier, by 1969 there were fewer than 10,000 Jews living in the city (Newark Public Library 1995, 10). Nationally, by 1968 the 12 largest central cities contained more than two thirds of America's black population outside the South, and one third of all American blacks (National Advisory Commission on Civil Disorders [National Advisory Commission] 1968, 243).

By 1969, between 50 and 100% of the Central, West Central, and Southern wards of Newark were populated by blacks, and 33% of the remaining wards were between 20 and 50% black. With 17,710 inhabitants per square mile, Newark was the second most dense of all major cities. The population density in the core ghetto, of course, was higher than this overall average, with 14 housing units per acre, against 9 in the city as a whole, and 16% of units overcrowded as opposed to 13% for the city. My estimate, based on data provided by Newark's 1967 application to the federal Model Cities program, is that by the end of the decade almost one quarter of the city's 405,000 residents lived in the newly expanded ghetto areas (larger than but following the same contour and expanding the core area described in the application) (Model Cities Application [MCA] 1967, 1B:14; 2A:2; 2B:table 1).

Poverty and Housing

In 1967, 32% of families in the core ghetto had incomes at or below the poverty level of $3,000; more than half of ghetto families were earning annual incomes of $5,000 or less. In Newark as a whole, 23% were living below the poverty level, and 38% had incomes of $5,000 or less. Although 30% of persons under 21 in the core were receiving Aid to Financially Dependent Children (AFDC) payments (and 23% of those under 21 in the city), less than half (47.8%) of the families in the city of Newark who were living below the poverty level were actually receiving public assistance (MCA 1967, 2B:table 1; Model Cities Program [MCP] 1969, 134; U.S. Census 1970).

By 1965 Newark was fifth in the nation in the amount it had received for urban renewal, and first in amount per capita (MCA 1967, IA: 9). The city's urban renewal plans, published by the Newark Central Planning Board in a report in 1961, called for the removal of an estimated 31,400 families, or about 25% of Newark's population, to make way for clearance of blighted areas and for proposed expressways to run through the city. Of the estimated 95,000 people whose homes were to be destroyed, 67.6% were to be removed from the Central Ward (39).

Approximately "88 percent of the families to be relocated will be Negro" and "most, though not all, of the families to be relocated are in the low income groups" (40–42). Black tenants in homes in the Central Ward were thus forced to move, typically into adjoining areas or to public housing built on cleared land in the slums, thus increasing the concentration of the poor in ghettoes, and increasing the acreage covered by ghettoes.

By the late sixties, five large housing projects, three of them highrise, had been built in the Central Ward, all within a radius of three miles. These huge structures housed almost 5,500 families (Curvin 1975, 15). More than 95% of the residents were low-income and African American or Hispanic. An official of the city's Human Rights Commission concluded in 1968 that the concentration of public housing in Newark's Central Ward helped to create "one of the most volatile [ghettoes] anywhere on the eastern seaboard" (New Jersey Advisory Committee to the U.S. Commission on Civil Rights 1968, in Curvin 1975, 15).

Despite the fact that by 1970 1 of 10 Newark residents was living in a housing project, "the major share of funds for many years had gone to middle and moderate income people," to downtown business district development, and to college and other institutional building in the city's downtown business district (Governor's Select Commission on Civil Disorder State of New Jersey [Governor's Commission] 1968, 55). One result was that by the mid-sixties Newark was highest among major cities in amount of substandard housing (MCA 1967, IA:1). Thirty percent of the city's housing units remained substandard or dilapidated, with 80% built before 1929. In the core ghetto, 77% of the land area was blighted, and of the 21,000 dwelling units, more than 50% were structurally substandard (MCP 1969, 2).

One result of residents' living in poverty in overcrowded, substandard housing was that they suffered the highest rate of new cases of tuberculosis in the nation. The 100,000 ghetto inhabitants in the core area were served by two aging hospitals and one city clinic. There were fewer than 80 doctors practicing in the entire city, and Newark had the second highest infant mortality and highest maternal mortality rates of major cities. During the decade, 57% of women with live births in the core had not received prenatal care, and there was an almost one in five premature birth rate (of a sample of 4,250 births), presenting a potential for high risk of neurological and physiological damage in children, and later, learning problems. Infant deaths per 1,000 live births a year were high: 47 in the core and 39 in the city against a state rate of 23.3, and a national rate of 24.8 (MCA 1967, 1A:1–2; 2A:24; 2B:table 1; 3E:2).

By the end of the decade, most of Newark was home to low-income

black families. The ravishment and poverty that had formerly characterized only the city's center had expanded to cover substantial portions of
the city. It is only a slight exaggeration to state that Newark was a city
that had become a ghetto.

Economics

Between 1960 and 1980, New Jersey's six largest cities lost more than
27% of their total jobs, while employment elsewhere in the state increased by more than 96% (Seneca 1990, 79–80). Between 1960 and 1970,
Newark lost 24.2% of its manufacturing jobs, and 1,300 manufacturers
(Curvin 1975, 21). Groh (1972, 187) calculated that more than 300 acres
of industrial tract and some 125 acres of floor space, essentially abandoned factories, were unused in Newark.

The economy of the city had not only diminished, it had changed:
The city's growth areas in the 1960s were architecture, engineering,
industrial research, computing, and white-collar jobs in insurance and
banking. As manufacturing—and the unskilled and semiskilled jobs it
offered—had declined, there had been an increase in the number of jobs
that required a high school or college education (MCP 1969, 138).

In the mid-1960s, however, of Newark residents 25 years and older,
only 27.8% in the city as a whole and 25.3% in the core ghetto had a
high school education (MCP 1969, 122). Thirty-seven percent in the city,
and 47% in the core had less than 8 years of schooling. The percentage
of adults 25 years and older with 6 years of school or less was almost
double the state percentage (MCA 1967, 2B:table 1; 2A:20).

The failure of Newark schools to educate residents in the 1940s and
1950s—and the failure of southern schools to have educated the rural
poor who migrated north—as well as the recent departure of white
skilled workers to the suburbs, meant that by the 1960s, a largely unskilled workforce remained in the city. According to a longtime resident,
some businesses and self-employed professionals—attorneys, for example, unable to find qualified local workers or unwilling to hire them if
they were black—moved their offices from the city, shrinking the job
base further.

Seventy percent of Newark's employed black males had unskilled
or semi-skilled blue-collar jobs, and 17.9% had white-collar jobs (MCP
1969, 132); only 2.6% of the blacks who lived and worked in Newark
were employed in some of the city's leading economic sectors—insurance, banking and real estate; and only 10% of whites who lived and
worked in Newark were employed in these businesses (Governor's
Commission 1968, 70). Approximately half the ghetto labor force was

employed outside the city (as black domestics, and in suburban factory and service jobs) (MCP 1969, 138). More than half the jobs in the city were held by white commuters (Curvin 1975, 3).

During the late sixties there were many federal and state job training programs in Newark, but their leaders complained that the business community would not hire graduates (Governor's Commission 1968, 72). Moreover, many applicants had literacy and numeracy skills too low for them to be accepted at the job training programs. The county superintendent alleged in 1964 that most of the 14,000 unemployed youths who registered for a federally sponsored job training program were from the "inferior schools of the Southeastern U.S." and "don't have enough education to begin a job training program. We are being asked to make up for what Alabama and Georgia haven't done for the students," he said (*Newark Evening News*, March 15, 1964; see also July 1, 1964). The three vocational high schools in the city were run by the county. Relatively high academic entrance requirements kept out the less academically qualified and the school dropout. Further, city businessmen reported that the course offerings were outmoded (MCA 1967, 2A:22).

Even though there was a shortage of skilled workers in the city, most unions would not admit blacks. Of 1,787 union apprentices registered in late 1967 with the Bureau of Apprenticeship and Training in Essex County, only 150 were African American (Governor's Commission 1968, 72).

As a consequence of the changed economy, low education levels, the lack of jobs for blacks in Newark, and employer and labor union bias, black unemployment in the city was almost twice that of whites during the decade. Thirty-three percent of black males and 44.3% of black females aged 16 to 19 were unemployed. A study of eight major ghettoes (Bedford-Stuyvesant, Central Harlem, and East Harlem, in New York; Boston; New Orleans; Philadelphia; and St. Louis) showed that many people who were working in these central cities were actually *underemployed*—doing part-time or intermittent work. (MCA 1967, 2A:6). In Newark, a full 44.6% of the ghetto labor force was in this category. The average underemployment of workers in the other central cities was 34.55%. (MCP 1969, 132–133).

STATE POLICIES

The U.S. Supreme Court case *Baker v. Carr* in 1962, brought by urban voters in Tennessee, and a series of U.S. Supreme Court cases collectively known as *Reynolds v. Sims* in 1964 overturned apportionment plans in most states that allocated the bulk of legislative power to rural elites. By the 1966–1967 state elections, 46 states had reapportioned with districts based substantially on population. The 1970 census created another wave of reapportionments, favoring the suburbs in most states (Wilkinson 1976). In response to these one-man-one-vote rulings, the New Jersey state constitution was redrawn in 1966 to expand the legislature and base both senate and house on population, rather than on number of counties. By 1970, most New Jersey residents lived in the suburbs. Thus, dominance in the legislature bypassed the cities and was allocated to the suburban representatives (Salmore and Salmore 1993, 125).

By the mid-1970s, for the first time, more Americans lived in suburbs than lived either in cities or in small towns and rural areas (Judd and Swanstrom 1944, 179; also Wilkinson 1976). In the U.S. Congress, therefore, although inner city seats had risen slightly between 1962 and 1973, they fell thereafter (Dolce 1976, 67) until a short-lived effort to create minority-dominant districts in the 1980s. By the mid 1970s, although suburban voters did not yet vote as a block, they controlled their share of votes in every state (Wilkinson 1976, 70). Nationally, as well as in New Jersey, the suburbs were overwhelmingly Caucasian. In 1967, in the four suburban areas forming an arc about Newark, of a total population of more than 150,000, only 1,000 residents were black (National Advisory Commission 1968, 70).

One result of the cities' political isolation from state power in this decade of shrinking city tax bases and increasing demand for services was continued dependence on local property taxes for educational and other municipal spending. As a result of Newark's diminishing tax base, the property tax rate in 1971 was twice as high as the suburban average—7.22% compared to 3.73%. The school tax rate in a nearby wealthy town, Milburn, for example, was $1.43 while Newark's was $3.69; yet Milburn could afford more teachers per pupil than Newark, spend more for teachers' salaries, and have more professional staff per pupil (*Robinson v. Cahill* 1972, 240).

According to the office of Newark's mayor, the city's property tax base decreased by 21% between 1959 and 1974—a decline amounting to $319 million (City of Newark, Office of the Mayor, "1974 Proposed Budget," January 16, 1974 in Curvin 1975, 124). Yet Newark was receiving substantially less in state and federal aid (and spending more from local property taxes) than other cities of comparable size (U.S. Department of Commerce 1972, in Curvin 1975, 122). Although New Jersey had the seventh highest per capita income in the United States, the state ranked last in direct aid to education (the national median was $41.53

per capita and New Jersey's rate was $18.88 per capita) (Governor's Commission 1968, 48).

The tax base declined for several reasons. The departure from the city of businesses and homeowners lowered the tax base. There were 61,416 fires in Newark between 1961 and 1976, and between 1972 and 1976, 1,015 foreclosures annually. Moreover, looking ahead to the next decades, we see that a considerably higher proportion of property in the cities than in the suburbs would be removed from the tax rolls. In Newark in 1968, 5.3% of Newark properties were tax exempt; in 1976, the figure rose to 16.5%, and by 1988 almost 70% of Newark properties were in this category (due to the presence of a relatively large number of federal, state, and university and college buildings, abandoned buildings and lots, and the Pennsylvania Railroad Station) (Cunningham 1988, 364; Winters 1977, 6). In American suburbs in 1988, an average of only 10% of properties were tax exempt; the proportion of tax-exempt property in most central cities was about twice what it was in the suburbs (Judd and Swanstrom 1994, 222, 442).

Finally, state tax legislation passed in 1960 (Chapter 51) kept city business taxes at almost the same rate throughout the decade. As a result of this legislation, businesses in New Jersey's cities were paying the same rate in 1967 that they had paid in 1963. However, homeowner property tax climbed throughout the decade. Newark homeowners in 1967 received a tax increase of 171 points—to $7.76 per $100 of assessed value—the largest 1-year increase in the history of the city (Curvin 1975, 125).

FEDERAL POLICIES

Cities across the nation in the sixties were severely distressed; moreover, the national poverty rate had risen to a full 22% by 1960 (Judd and Swanstrom 1994, 174). Attempting to address problems in the cities, between 1964 and 1966 Congress authorized 219 new programs, including Medicare and Medicaid; the Elementary and Secondary Education Act (which included Titles I and III, and Head Start); food stamps; education and job training for the disabled; expanded public housing and urban renewal programs; initiation of Model Cities; and the creation of a cabinet-level department of housing and urban development to administer the urban programs. Aid to urban areas shot up by 590% between 1961 and 1972, while aid to nonurban areas rose by only 182%. Total federal aid spending increased by 405% (Judd and Swanstrom 1994, 167).

The War on Poverty (Head Start, food stamps, Medicare and Med-icaid) and Model Cities attracted the most attention and were controver-sial because they both required the participation of the poor. Many funds were given directly to community agencies, bypassing elected officials (Judd and Swanstrom 1994, 172). In some cities, antipoverty programs provided the political base for the first black mayors or elected representatives (Edsall and Edsall 1991, 67). This was true in Newark: Whereas in the 1940s and 1950s, organized crime provided a training ground for the early black politicians, in the 1960s the War on Poverty gave black leaders—such as Newark's future first black mayor and a number of black educational leaders—political resources, skills, and a degree of financial and political independence (Curvin 1975, 59; see also Piven and Cloward 1970).

By 1968, the issue of race—in busing and affirmative action, for example—was tearing apart the Democratic coalition which had given Lyndon Johnson a landslide in 1964. In 1966, due to a white backlash vote, Johnson lost his liberal majority in Congress (Edsall and Edsall 1991, 59). In 1968 Richard Nixon, a Republican, won the White House, and the national government began to withdraw from the cities, al-though the continuance of programs mandated in the sixties meant that direct federal aid to cities did not actually peak until 1978, after which it declined, with the decline accelerating in the 1980s (Ladd and Yinger 1989, 270; Judd and Swanstrom 1994, 254, 320). Nixon did not drasti-cally cut federal spending, but his New Federalism shifted resources from the Frostbelt (the 14 states of the Northeast and the Upper Mid-west) to the Sunbelt and suburban jurisdictions (the Sunbelt defined as the southern and southwestern portions of the U.S. below the 37th parallel, extending across the country from North Carolina to the West Coast) (Bernard and Rice 1985, 7; Judd and Swanstrom 1994, 245, 254, 320).

The War on Poverty reduced the poverty rate in America from 22.2% in 1960 to an all-time low of 11.1% in 1973. However, another consequence of the assistance provided the cities was the dependence of America's aging industrial centers on federal funds. Most of these funds during the late sixties and early seventies were spent by mayors on the day-to-day operation of running their cities in the absence of other money, rather than on building an economic base for future development (Judd and Swanstrom 1994, 56, 174, 277–278). Thus, de-spite large infusions of federal funds, city services, infrastructure, and local economies continued to decay. In Newark, this decline was aided and abetted by the brazen consort of organized crime and elected offi-cials.

LOCAL POLITICS

After his election in 1962, Mayor Hugh Addonizio was asked why he had wanted to leave the U.S. Congress to be mayor of Newark, a declining city. Perhaps intimating what would later be revealed as his close alliance with organized crime, Addonizio is reported to have replied, "It's simple. There's no money in Washington, but you can make a million bucks as mayor of Newark" (*Newark Evening News* June 24, 1970).

Harold Kaplan described the radical changeover in government personnel that followed Addonizio's election. Almost all of the leading city hall officials, including civil servants with tenure, who had worked for the reform—antipatronage—mayor during the 1950s resigned, and their positions were filled with a crop of Addonizio's appointees. At city hall 532 additional jobs were created, many of them in the "temporary" category, thereby skirting the civil service reforms designed to discourage such activities. The increase was due in part to expansion of governmental services, but most jobs were patronage positions—some were even of the "no show" variety. Although in his first term Addonizio appointed some blacks to positions at city hall, the housing authority, and the board of education, Italian Americans tended to head departments and hold other influential positions (Kaplan 1963, 189; Barbaro 1972, 44).

According to critical observers, 90% of the new jobs that Addonizio created were filled with unqualified personnel (Douglas 1972, 126; *Newark Evening News* May 5, 1966; April 27, 1966). George Washnis, author of a study of Model Cities in eight major metropolitan areas in 1974, alleged that a primary reason that Model Cities was judged to be a failure in Newark in the late 1960s was that Addonizio "filled Model Cities programs from the start, from top to bottom, with patronage and incompetence" (184). During Addonizio's first year, the city spent less than half the money allocated to it for the programs (151).

During Addonizio's reign, the police became autonomous, as they had been before the 1950s reform mayoralty, and accountable primarily to organized crime (Douglas 1972, 121); gambling became a "very large business" in Newark, especially in the Central Ward, with the Mafia and police chief Dominick Spina in charge (Spina's alleged encouragement of police brutality toward blacks was reviled by the community) (*Newark Evening News* November 8, 1970). In 1969, of 1,300 police officers, 145 were black, and 1 was Puerto Rican. All but 9 of the blacks were at the lowest rank of patrol officer (Governor's Commission 1968, 24).

Forced to live in dilapidated housing or packed in projects, denied jobs, basic city services, and a decent education, black residents rebelled in civil disorders in 128 cities nationwide during the first 9 months of 1967 (National Advisory Commission 1968, 113). The Newark ghetto exploded on Wednesday, July 12, 1967, after the arrest and alleged beating of a black taxi driver. Black citizens in Newark vented their anger at the police and the power structure in 4 days of rioting and looting. On August 8, 1967, New Jersey governor Richard Hughes asked a commission of prestigious citizens, led by Robert Lilley, president of NJ Bell Telephone Company, to examine the causes, incidents, and remedies of the civil disorders in Newark and 13 other New Jersey communities. The report produced by the Governor's Select Commission on Civil Disorder (cited above as the Governor's Commission) included a thorough assessment of the riots in Newark and of economic and political conditions in the city. The commission found that only 20% of Newark residents arrested during the rioting had prior convictions. Almost half (49.7%) had been part of the vast migration from southern states of people seeking jobs and freedom and had been born in Georgia, North or South Carolina (1968, 131).

The riots in Newark and the approaching demographic majority of blacks induced Addonizio to increase the pace of corruption. City parks were mysteriously ripped down to become parking lots for Italian restaurants. The mayor tried to destroy a large section of the Central Ward for a hospital. He attempted to repay a political debt by giving away a 64-square-mile watershed, a main source of Newark's drinking water. In order to make up for huge deficits caused by graft, such as huge pay increases for 500 employees, many of whom did not show up for work, Addonizio consigned the Newark airport to the Port Authority of New York and New Jersey for cash (and a pittance in future rent) (Douglas 1972, 146; Washnis 1974, 138). According to the Governor's Commission, there were no resources left to provide city services (1968, 19). In 1969, Addonizio, several councilmembers, the city's director of public works, the corporation counsel, and several underworld figures were indicted for extortion and bribery (Curvin 1975, 65).

As a result of the assessment of Newark by the Governor's Commission, during which multiple witnesses testified that there was a "pervasive feeling" of corruption in city hall, a grand jury was impaneled on May 27, 1968, to investigate the possibility of corruption in the Newark government. The jury met over 100 times during the next two and a half years, listened to 280 witnesses, and compiled 5,805 pages of testimony (Newark Evening News November 7, 1970). Judge James Giuliano, who impaneled the jury, stated at the end of its work,

Mr. Addonizio, and the other defendants here, have been convicted on one count of conspiring to extort and 63 substantive counts of extorting hundreds of thousands of dollars from persons doing business with the city of Newark. . . . These were no ordinary criminal acts; these crimes were not the product of a moment of weakness. . . . The crimes for which Mr. Addonizio and the other defendants have been convicted represent a pattern of continuous, highly organized, systematic criminal extortion over a period of many years, claiming many victims and touching many more lives. . . . The corruption disclosed here is compounded by the frightening alliance of criminal elements and public officials, and it is this very kind of destructive conspiracy that was conceived, organized and executed by these defendants. (*Newark Evening News* September 23, 1970).

Interestingly, Samuel Klein, auditor for the Mafia for 24 years, had also audited the Newark books during the Addonizio years, and had found no irregularity in the city's finances (Douglas 1972, 197). Addonizio and the four other defendants were convicted in 1970 in a federal court trial in the state capital. Addonizio was fined $25,000 and sentenced to 10 years in jail (he served 5 years at the Lewisburg Federal Penitentiary).

In 1970, Kenneth Gibson, whose family emigrated from Enterprise, Alabama, in 1940, was elected the first black mayor of Newark. According to Robert Curvin, at the time of Gibson's inauguration in 1971,

Newark's government was virtually at a standstill. City departments were disorganized; some personnel did not even show up for work. The City Health Department was forfeiting state funds because the director under Addonizio failed to make several simple organizational changes requested by the State. Another department was bypassing federal assistance because the Addonizio administration feared federal auditors would uncover widespread graft in the agency. (Curvin 1975, 96)

The deterioration and corruption in the city could be seen quite dramatically in the public school system. Despite huge increases in numbers of students (see below), Addonizio did not build any new schools in his first 4 years, yet increased the board of education budget by 75% and raised taxes by more than 200 points. By 1970, however, he had decreased the school budget by $17 million while maintaining the same level of spending. As a result, one of the crises facing Mayor Gibson was a 60-million-dollar deficit in the school budget for the year of 1970, and the prospect of insufficient funds to keep the schools open (Curvin 1975, 128).

THE SCHOOLS

By 1967, public school enrollment in Newark was 76,993 (an all-time high), having increased by 22,116 students in 17 years. Sixty percent of the increase (13,196) had been in the preceding 7 years. By 1967, Newark had a shortage of 10,000 pupil stations, half of which were in the core ghetto. Seventy-one percent of the city's public school students were African American, and 7% were Puerto Rican (Newark Board of Education 1968, 2; Newark Board of Education Minutes [Minutes] August 24, 1967, 298).

Despite an integration plan hammered out by the NAACP and a reluctant board in the early sixties, by 1967, as in 75 other American cities studied in 1964–1965, racial segregation was a dominant feature of the Newark schools (U.S. Commission 1967, 1:3–4). Of the 49 Newark elementary schools, 35 (71%) were majority black, and 1 was 55% Puerto Rican. Three of five junior high schools were majority black. Five of eight senior high schools were majority black and two others were majority white; one senior high school (Barringer) was approaching the halfway mark (it was 40% black). Earlier, in 1954, as blacks moved into the city, Marcy School had counted an enrollment of 1,060—an increase of almost 200% over 1950 (*Newark Evening News* September 22, 1954). By 1961, the school was 79.8% black, 9.8% Puerto Rican, and 9.2% white; in 1967, it was a Title I school, and 82% black, 15% Puerto Rican, and 3% white. It was considered a school with a "high" Puerto Rican enrollment.

Weequahic High School, the formerly all-white college-preparatory school that had been predominantly Jewish, had 19% black enrollment in 1961, 70% in 1966, and 82% in 1968. When a nearby town, Hillside, canceled the 32-year-old Thanksgiving Day football game with Weequahic High School in 1968, a member of the Newark board of education expressed the opinion that it was cancelled because Weequahic was now predominantly nonwhite (Minutes May 29, 1967, 1362). In the school year 1959–60, the highly regarded principal of Weequahic High School left to become principal of the high school in Livingston, a wealthy New Jersey suburb. In 1964, several teachers and the counselor from Weequahic, along with five city principals and "many other" administrators, also left Newark to work in the suburbs (*Newark Evening News* May 14, 1964, also May 26, 1964). In 1967, the next principal of the school left also, for an appointment at the board of education offices (*Newark Evening News* July 1, 1967).

Inside the Schools

Several books written about schools in northern urban ghettos in the 1960s described the overcrowding; the majority black student populations; the ill-prepared, frustrated, and sometimes unsympathetic teachers; and classrooms without teaching materials (see Clark 1965; Kohl 1967; Kozol 1967; and Rosenfeld 1971). The available evidence suggests that similar conditions characterized the Newark schools.

A 1959 curriculum study reported by the *New York Times* found that there had been no substantial curriculum revision in the Newark schools since the 1930s, except in the Weequahic section (May 28, 1961). In 1973 the accrediting agency, Middle States Association of Colleges and Schools, evaluated Central High School, in which 96% of the students were black and two thirds lived in nearby housing projects. The visiting evaluators complained about a "20-year-old course of study," "out-of-date curriculum," and "watered-down content" in four disciplines. The "watered-down" curriculum was an effort, the evaluators stated, to adapt to what they called "the low ability" and "limited talent" of the students (Middle States 1973, 5, 6, 11, 12, 17).

The Middle States evaluation of Central High also found severely restricted use of instructional materials by most staff, and outmoded or nonfunctioning equipment in art, home economics, science, foreign language, shop, and music classes. There were no science labs (6, 9, 12, 15, 17). According to minutes of the board of education, there were 100 girls in each gym class, and only 15 lockers at Central (May 24, 1966, 1144, 1187).

A self-study written by the principal, vice principal, and chair of the Planning Committee at Webster Junior High in 1968 provides another glimpse inside a Newark school. Webster was located in a formerly Italian neighborhood. Many homes and stores had been demolished in the late 1950s for Columbus Homes, a high-rise housing project. According to the self-study, the student population had completely changed in the previous 5 years (Webster Junior High School [Webster] 1968, 38). By 1968 the student population was almost 50% minority— 39% black and 10% Puerto Rican. Some of the black students were bused from the city core to alleviate overcrowding there.

According to informants, the majority of teachers in Newark in the sixties were from the older ethnic groups—Italians and Jews. At Webster Junior High the self-study states that teachers were "unprepared" to handle the new type of student (22). "There is a lack of motivation of teachers to understand and sympathize with their new students. . . . Too often teachers express frustration at their students' lack of aspirations and motivation. . . . The boredom, apathy, and indifference of pupils continually challenges teachers" (43). Moreover, teachers are often "unwilling to depart from traditional recitation methods, and experience low morale at large classes and no instructional materials" (26, 42).

The federal Title I money that was received was considered to be a "savior": "Some teachers have plenty of materials and trips as well—because of Title I" (63). Yet, continued the self-study, "there are no science labs" (70); "There are no doors on the bathrooms; no tissue, paper towels or soap" (137). "Equipment new in 1947 when the school opened needs replacing all over the building" (84). "[The school] had been an elementary school. Desks and chairs, and the seats in the auditorium, are all too small for adolescent boys" (148).

The Webster self-study remarked that high student absenteeism made sequential teaching impossible, and that high student turnover made it "difficult to plan" (51, 103). The evaluation of Central High had also stated that "sporadic student attendance" at Central made "continuous and sequential teaching very difficult" (Middle States 1973, 2).

The Webster document complained that a "major problem" had arisen because "teachers are late, and absent too much, and there is a constant teacher turnover as teachers leave" (28, 47, 51, 77). The self-study team also remarked, however, that "despite the difficulties, we make a great effort to arouse interest in school work [in the students] . . . then economic and social and cultural forces sweep it away" (Webster 1968, 50).

In the Newark system as a whole during the sixties there was more than 50% turnover of students every year. Approximately 28% of the students transferred out of the schools every year, and one third of the school population transferred in, primarily from North and South Carolina, Virginia, Florida, Georgia, and Puerto Rico. In some schools in the core area there was an 89.2 to 100% turnover each year (MCA 1967, 2A:16, 51). The official cumulative drop-out rate for grades 9 through 12 between 1962 and 1966 was 35%, but community groups charged that in the ghetto the drop-out rate exceeded 68% (*Star Ledger* February 27, 1963).

There was a high (15%) yearly turnover of teachers, as almost one of six teachers left each year (MCP 1969, 119). There was a 10% daily absentee rate for teachers, which was high, given a national 2 to 4% absence rate in schools (Greater Newark Chamber of Commerce 1971, 7: 55). According to the Organization of Negro Educators, in some schools teacher aides (women from the community without college degrees) were being used as substitutes when teachers quit or were absent (Minutes March 25, 1969, 1291).

Student achievement was low. In reading, as measured on the 1966 Revised Stanford Achievement test, in grade 3, 6% percent of pupils were at or above the norm and 94% were below the norm; 72% were one year or more below the norm. In grade 6, 9% were at or above the norm and 91% were below the norm; 82% were one year or more below the norm. Pupils in predominantly white schools scored almost a full grade higher than those in nonwhite schools on the standardized tests. Yet none of the elementary schools in the city had an average achievement (median) at or above the national norm (Newark Board of Education 1968, 3).

During the sixties, the segregation of American schools and the bleak record of public education for ghetto children came to national attention, and in 1965 Congress passed the Elementary and Secondary Education Act (ESEA) to attempt to redress the problems of urban schools.

Educational Reform

The 1960s provide another example, as did the decades surrounding the turn of the 20th century, of a period of extensive efforts to improve public school systems in America's cities. Mostly federal in origin, numerous programs and projects were begun in city schools in the mid-sixties. One of the major programs was Title I of the ESEA, which provided assistance to schools having concentrations of educationally disadvantaged children, defined as children from families having annual incomes of less than $3,000 or supported by AFDC. Title I provided funds for remedial reading, career guidance for potential dropouts, reduced pupil-teacher ratios, special teacher training, educational television and other teaching equipment, and specialized staff for social work, guidance and counseling, psychiatry and medicine (National Advisory Commission 1968, 141). In Newark, as in many other cities, Title I was also supplemented by programs provided by individual businesses, colleges, and foundations. In the following section of this chapter I argue that these attempts at reform did not make substantial improvements in the Newark school system, and offer some discussion of factors that worked against the success of the sixties' urban educational reforms.

There were over 40 educational improvement projects operating in Newark's 73 schools in the 1960s, in addition to the Title I programs that existed in 48 public and 10 Catholic schools (the Title I programs began in 12 schools in 1966). A perhaps overly enthusiastic evaluation of Newark's Title I programs in school year 1969–70 found that although the median reading scores remained below the national norms,

> The data clearly indicates [sic] that, although the pupils [in Title I programs] started below the national norm, they have been steadily improving in reading . . . The vast majority of the pupils make exceptional progress for the short period of time during which they are exposed to the climate of the reading laboratory. (Planners Associates 1970, 2)

However, despite the new programs in the schools, and the gains made by some students as a result of Title I, the majority of Newark students did not make achievement gains in the next few years. Between 1967 and 1972, Newark's third-grade reading standardized scores remained the same, a year below level, and below national norms; grade 6 reading scores fell steadily, as did grade 7 math scores, all of which continued below national norms (Tractenberg 1977, 239, in Winters 1977).

The Webster Junior High self-study had hinted at one problem: Educational efforts were overwhelmed by the community poverty, and the cultural differences between the students and the school and teachers—that is, the students' social class and racial backgrounds. However, there were other characteristics of the Newark situation that also mitigated against improvement of the schools.

The reform programs were small, and isolated one from another, with a minority of students who needed the attention receiving it. For example, at Webster less than a third of the eligible students were in Title I (1968, 91). Moreover, the funds were not constant, and planning became impossible. Again, at Webster in 1967–68, the school's Title I money was halved, despite the program almost tripling in size.

As we have seen, the city's ability to raise money for education had continually declined beginning in the early 1930s. Between 1960 and 1968, 80% of the Newark school budget came from Newark property taxes (*Star Ledger* October 24, 1993). By 1967, the city had reached its bonded indebtedness limit. On November 28, 1967, the board of education was notified by the city that—despite there being a $250 million shortfall in capital funds needed to bring the physical plant up to date— new school construction totaling $51 million would have to be delayed indefinitely (*Newark Evening News* December 5, 1967; Governor's Commission 1968, 48–49, 75.) Thus, there was little city money to augment and institutionalize individual reform projects. Federal aid was not sufficient to make up the difference. Nationally in 1965–66, federal aid was less than 8% of total educational expenditures. A survey of federal projects in Detroit, Newark, and New Haven during 1967–68 found that a median of approximately half of the eligible school population was receiving assistance under Title I (National Advisory Commission 1968, 436).

In addition to the poverty and cultural difference between residents and their children and the teachers, and the city's lack of resources, the following factors also worked against improvement of the schools: Inept and corrupt leadership at the board of education, disarray at board offices, difficulties in planning for the constantly changing situation, and finally, as the decade wore on, large—scale hiring of underprepared and unqualified teachers and administrators.

Inept and Corrupt Leadership

By 1963, Addonizio appointments to the board of education were a majority (*Newark Evening News* June 26, 1963). Verner Henry, appointed in 1954 by ex-mayor Leo Carlin, became the first black president of the board. Addonizio appointed Dr. Harold Ashby in 1962, and now for the first time there were two blacks on the board. Dr. Ashby became president of the board in 1963 (*Newark Evening News*, May 19, 1963). Addonizio's other appointments to board offices included an Italian former football official, as assistant superintendent of business administration who was hired without the position being advertised (*Newark Evening News* June 26, 1963), and an Italian attendance officer as director of the Bureau of Attendance, chosen over a long-time civil service acting director (March 21, 1963). The supervisor of school accounts who worked under Arnold Hess had been a campaign worker for Addonizio (*Star Ledger* September 5, 1963). Another campaigner for Addonizio was appointed budget analyst (*Newark Evening News* May 19, 1964).

There was no director of the 48 Title I programs in Newark. An administrative assistant at the board coordinated the Title I paperwork; no one in the city had responsibility for program development or control of quality (Minutes December 4, 1967, 903, 909; December 28, 1967, 801; August 24, 1967, 298). One result of the lack of leadership was that $1.9 million of Title I money was not expended by the deadline and had to be returned by the mayor in 1967, this in addition to earlier money that had to be returned—$100,000 for supplies, and $125,000 for a teacher aide project (*Newark Evening News*, May 28, 1967). Other cities also returned federal education funding during the 1960s, perhaps for similar reasons (Washnis 1974).

Board of education president Ashby stated at a board meeting that the $1.9 million was lost because of "lack of planning and imagination on the part of our professional staff—and the non-availability of personnel to staff Title I programs." Another speaker suggested that because of confused business practices, Secretary Hess "probably didn't even know that nearly $2 million was still in the till" (Minutes August 24, 1967, 909).

In September of 1969, the state commissioner of education charged that Newark filed the Title I and II reports late, and that $13 million was not accounted for. The state called Secretary Hess and the director of the board's federal aid program "inept" (*New York Times* September 18, 1969). The state commissioner required the secretary and the business office to begin maintaining separate books and records on the management of the Elementary and Secondary Education Act monies; and they were to make a list of all elementary and secondary school projects, and report progress every two weeks to the commissioner (*Newark Evening News* October 1, 1969).

A study several years later by the federal Department of Health, Education and Welfare ordered Newark to return $1.1 million of the $28.7 million given the Newark schools over a 3-year period because part of the money had been spent on ineligible schools. In 1970, for example—while the Addonizio board was still in office—13 schools, in two predominantly white, higher income areas of the city, were misclassed as eligible. "They were spreading the money around to their friends," an official alleged (*Star Ledger* July 31, 1975).

In 1972, superintendent of schools Franklyn Titus and Secretary Hess, as well as two other board officials appointed by Addonizio, were indicted for failing to investigate the existence of suspected and alleged criminal activity in the school system's night security force during the previous several years (December 7, 1972). They were also charged with "hiring substitute teachers who presented phony credentials, and other fraudulent practices." Twenty-four other persons were indicted on charges relating to the investigation of substitute teachers (December 12, 1972, December 21, 1972).

The overall investigation showed the school system to be "riddled with no-show jobs, payroll padding, falsification of records and fraud" (January 26, 1973). Despite almost 100 years of educational graft and corruption, this was only the second indictment of officials in the school system, and the first in the twentieth century. As a probable consequence of widely acknowledged corruption in the court system, the politically connected former superintendent, Secretary Hess (and two other board officials), were acquitted (October 24, 1973, see Cook 1974; also Governor's Commission 1968).

The inept and corrupt leadership at the board of education was challenged at every board meeting by representatives of parent groups, community organizations, unions, and teacher groups, as well as by individual parents and religious leaders: PTAs, the Civic Association, the Newark Committee for Better Schools, the Congress of Racial Equality, the Clinton Hill Neighborhood Council, Crusade for Learning, the Newark Human Rights Commission, the Organization of Negro Educators, Newark branches of the National Teachers Union and the National Teacher Association, as well as the area Ecumenical Council, among others, presented their views.

Common complaints had to do with hazardous conditions in the schools, overcrowding, the need for textbooks, the declining quality and number of teachers and principals, the number of "unqualified teachers," and the use of Title I funds. Of particular concern to members of the black community were the lack of Negro administrators, the abundance of substitutes in ghetto schools, and the use of city exams for promotion to administrative positions. (The exams, black representatives argued, "were discriminatory to Negroes") (Minutes August 24, 1965, December 29, 1966, February 24, 1966, March 28, 1967, April 27, 1967, August 24, 1967; *Newark Evening News* March 1, 1961, July 28, 1964, October 27, 1964; *New Jersey African American* February 24, 1962).

Disarray at Board Offices

In 1969 the business community, through the chamber of commerce, planned a study of the school board, in order to assist the board of education in revising "practices which may have been deemed acceptable in 1940 or 1950 [but] are no longer applicable to current needs" (Greater Newark Chamber of Commerce 1971, 1:1). Consultants supplied by local corporations (NJ Bell Telephone, Western Electric, the public utilities company, Fidelity Union Bank, Prudential Insurance Company, Englehard Minerals and Chemical, Firemen's Fund and Howard Savings Bank, Mutual Benefit Insurance Company, and National Newark and Essex Bank) completed a feasibility study in school year 1969–70. An 8-month assessment of data processing and communications, purchasing, personnel, record keeping, the departments of business administration, and "the entire Secretary's Organization" was completed during the 1970–71 school year. Despite the inauguration of a black mayor in 1971, the Addonizio board, 3 Italians and two blacks, was still in power, and the board of education personnel were those active in preceding years.

The chamber of commerce found extensive disarray at the board offices, and reported their findings in seven volumes. A few of the findings are summarized below:

- *Administrative organization* The study found numerous instances where the board of education inserted itself in the professional educators' job of running the schools. Individual board members were charged with usurping functions of the employment office (1:1-6).
- *Organizational structure* "There are three bosses—which is unsound administration—the superintendent, secretary, and business manager." (The Teachers College report in 1942 recommended that this be changed.) "The Secretary to the Board is responsible for accounting, financial operations, payroll administration, and data processing of records. He prepares the budget, prepares reports to the board, county, state, and the U.S. Department of Education . . . There is no meaningful budget control and no cost control procedures. . . . There are many unpaid bills from previous years" (1:23). "It takes 21 steps to pay an employee. . . . Modernization is needed—as everywhere else!" (1:30).
- *Payroll* "There are no controls. . . . It is not a secure system and much illegality would be very easy to accomplish" (1:51).
- *Division of Design and Construction* "There is no coordinated system for designing or constructing new buildings. There is no director and [there are] no job descriptions for engineers" (3:10). "Old files should be discarded—files have old plans for proposed construction from decades ago which never materialized" (3:27).
- *Division of Maintenance* "Delays in responding to requests for repairs and maintenance are common. . . . There is no preventive maintenance in the system" (4:6).
- *Supply Management* The chamber of commerce found a dramatic increase in "open orders" (purchase orders made without clear evidence that the item ordered had ever been delivered) in the few years before the study. "Last year, for example, the purchase department never knew whether 650 items had been delivered" (4:10). The *Star Ledger* reported that during the 1970–71 school year, the 'open orders' jumped to 2,050 (August 1, 1971).
- *Personnel* "The personnel office must clean house! We found the offices in deplorable condition. Personnel folders are piled on desks, chairs, and cabinets—active and inactive records are in cardboard boxes on the floor—active teacher records are in unlocked filing cabi-

nets and boxes of supplies stored in the lobby" (3:1). "Obsolete records are lying around, and should be destroyed. . . . The director of personnel position is vacant" (2:5).

"The Assistant Superintendent and Assistant Director of Personnel were both elevated from the . . . teacher ranks. They had no previous experience in personnel work, nor any formal training to adequately equip them to fully grasp the implications of personnel management. This is also evident at the supervisory level. . . . There are many individuals at all levels whose job titles and/or civil service classification do not correspond with their actual performed duties or the capabilities of the particular individual. . . . Many individuals do not have the skills necessary to perform their assigned job. . . . The personnel department is an outcast, orphaned department, tolerated as a necessary evil by the board of education" (2:14).

"The permanent teacher record cards in recent years have been poorly maintained with strike-overs, erasures, and ineligible handwriting. There is outdated information on many cards. We found teacher applications never acted upon dating back to the early 1900s; retired and terminated teacher jackets dating back to the 1800s; general correspondence from the 1940s. These are examples of records which must be destroyed" (2:48).

The chamber of commerce study also complained that teacher tenure seemed to be automatic, and that teachers in the system were not being evaluated. They recommended that a form be developed to evaluate teachers, and that principals be required to carry out evaluations (7:71).

The chaos into which board of education affairs seems to have descended mitigated against successful implementation of improvements in the city schools. However, there were additional factors which also contributed to the failure of sixties reforms.

Difficulty of Planning

Rapid turnover in neighborhoods as new population came in and previous residents left made planning at the board and in schools very difficult. Moreover, highway construction through the city and urban renewal policies also increased the difficulty.

For example, the board waited 7 years for notification, from the state Department of Highways, of which neighborhoods were to be demolished for the construction of Route 78. A survey found that 800 children were to be displaced from one Central Ward school and 500 from another. Altogether for highway construction, 6,000 students had been displaced as of July 13, 1967 (Minutes July 13, 1967, 1610). According to the board, the highway department also renegged on its promise not to take the Charleton Street School and land in the Central Ward for a new highway. Board minutes state that "the school will have to be vacated within the year," but they had been planning a new addition to that school, and "now we will have to find another place for those children" (March 21, 1966, 902).

The completion of housing projects also created havoc. Superintendent Titus complained that they could not plan where to build schools because "25% of the families in Newark had to be relocated" (July 13, 1967, 1610). The Newark Housing Authority did not inform the school board where or when projects would be built. When one of the largest projects was built in 1960 in the core ghetto, there was no available school. A new school was then planned, for two years hence, for 1,700 pupils. But the project was to house 1,700 *families* (*Star Ledger* October 26, 1960). An additional housing project was subsequently built nearby.

Because Newark had to bear the entire cost of school construction, the city had insufficient funds to build as many new schools as were needed (MCA 1967, 116). Instead, the board bought and installed 25 portable classrooms, which they admitted at a board meeting were illegal, being made of wood and therefore inflammable. The board also attempted to rent space for classrooms in alternative buildings (e.g., that housing the Young Men's Hebrew Association), but not until 1967 did the state lift its ban on using alternative buildings for classrooms (Minutes August 24, 1967, 298).

Hiring of Untrained Staff

A crucial problem in any school system—or reform effort—is the training and quality of teachers and administrators. Newark, like other large city systems, faced the problem of locating qualified staff.

A survey of teacher attitudes in 1960 revealed that many teachers were leaving the city because of what they said were "intolerable conditions." As reasons for leaving the Newark schools, teachers cited low pay (Newark salaries, in the first 4 decades of the century the highest in the state, had fallen by 1962 to 40th [*Newark Evening News* October 6, 1962]), overcrowded classrooms, inadequate instructional materials ("many classes sharing the same books") and "too many low IQ pupils in regular classrooms" (May 15, 1960, see also *Star Ledger* October 17, 1962; *New Jersey African American* November 10, 1962).

Although the schools swelled with newly appointed teacher aides from the federal programs, there was a "steady and drastic decline" in the number of applicants for teacher and administrator positions. An exam for elementary principal in 1962, for example, attracted only six persons—"not nearly enough," according to a board official. In contrast, in 1949, 120 applicants had taken the exam for an eligibility list that was limited to 15 (*Newark Evening News*, March 1, 1962).

Additionally, fewer applicants passed the city exams. For example, of 449 candidates who took the teacher test in May of 1960, only 172, or 38%, passed, leading the assistant superintendent of personnel to say, "This means a serious shortage of quality teachers in September, and a record number of substitutes." The city needed 250 elementary teachers, but only 73 of 221 candidates passed the exam (*Newark Evening News* May 15, 1960).

A parent from a Central Ward school told the board in 1967 that her school had more substitute teachers than any school in Newark, and no principal, and, she stated, "if [my school] is entitled to Title I money, then they should have a principal in the school too, to administer the money properly" (Minutes August 24, 1967, 300).

The board increasingly filled vacancies with untrained, unskilled staff. In 1960, the city tried unsuccessfully to lure back former Newark teachers by promising to waive new exams if they returned (*Newark Evening News* April 21, 1960) and, in 1961, by allowing non-college graduates to begin teaching under a provisional 2-year license (March 29, 1961); the state, through the counties, also issued "emergency" certificates, to people with 60 college credits.

Most new teachers hired, however, were long-term substitutes (who may have been college graduates but who had not passed the city's teacher exam). In 1961, the president of the teachers' union, the American Federation of Teachers (AFT), complained that "the shortage of teachers and the consequent hiring of unqualified teachers has changed the entire picture of education in Newark, causing uneven quality" (*Newark Evening News* October 31, 1961).

By 1963, The *Newark News* was charging that 900, or 36%, of the 2500 teachers were either unlicensed long-term substitutes or provisionals (December 5, 1963). In 1968, board president Ashby complained to the other board members of "the chipping away of qualifications and the lowering of standards" for teachers. But the board decided, against his wishes, to further lower the standards by giving regular, permanent (i.e., lifetime) licences to provisional and emergency teachers without the exam on the basis of their having a college degree and teaching experience. At one meeting alone in 1968, 160 emergency and provisional teachers were given regular appointments (Minutes April 23, 1968, 1323). (See also lists in February 28, 1968, 1065, 1066. A complete set of minutes for the board during the 1960s is not available, so a full count is not possible). In 1969 the board lowered the requirements again, deciding that long-term substitutes could also receive regular appointments without the teacher exam if they passed an oral exam and a health exam and if they had 3 years of experience and a satisfactory rating (Minutes November 25, 1969, 1104–1105).

By 1969, despite the numerous provisionals, emergency teachers, and substitutes who had recently been given lifetime appointments, almost 1 of 3 (1,005 of 3,500) teachers in Newark were still long-term substitutes, with only 30% of them having any sort of certificate. Only 14% of the 1,005 had had health exams (Governor's Commission 1968, 80; Greater Newark Chamber of Commerce 1971, 7:35). State supreme court testimony several years later revealed that in 1968–69 in Camden, another large city in New Jersey, a full 30% of teachers there were uncertified long-term substitutes as well (*Robinson v. Cahill*, 1972, 25). According to the National Advisory Commission on Civil Disorders (1968), in New York City, 40% of the teaching personnel did not have regular permanent licenses. The Advisory Commission stated, "in one inner city school in another large city, of 84 staff members, 41 were temporary teachers, 25 were probationaries, and 18 were tenure teachers. However, only one of the tenure teachers was licensed in an academic subject." In Chicago, in the 10 highest ranking, almost completely white schools, 90.3% of teachers were fully certified; in the 10 lowest ranking black schools, only 63.2% of all teachers were fully certified (428).

Looking ahead to the following decade, we see that the hiring of unqualified teachers continued in the 1970s. My estimate, based on figures in a 1979 district application for a federal grant, are that at least half of all teachers were, by the late 1970s, either provisionals, regular teachers without certificates, or long-term substitutes. During a city-state certification audit of all Newark instructional employees in 1977, certificates "could not be found" for nearly 50% of the city's teachers (*Star Ledger* July 27, 1977). On June 13, 1996, I asked an official of the board of education, who has been in senior positions since 1980, "What happened to all the provisionals and subs who were appointed in the sixties and seventies?" The informant replied that "most of them were 'regularized' in the early eighties. Permanent licenses were granted by the district."

Entangled in the problem of teacher shortages, qualifications, and hiring in the 1960s is the question of racial discrimination. According to NAACP testimony reported earlier, and to statements made to me in May of 1995 by a retired African American Newark school official, until the 1960s, black men and women who were substitutes were usually highly qualified, but were not appointed to regular positions because of discrimination (see also NAACP 1961). Even as late as 1968, of Newark's 3,500 teachers, approximately one quarter were blacks, and most of them were still substitutes—without tenure or benefits, and at lower pay (Governor's Commission 1968, 80).

In the 1960s, as the educational requirements were reduced to attempt to attract applicants to city schools, the degree of preparation, skills, and the educational background of most newly hired teachers—both black and white—decreased. Because the board appointed many black teachers during the decade, and, as we shall see, administrators as well, in an attempt to pacify an increasingly reactive black community outraged by the state of education in the city, large numbers of the blacks hired were unqualified (see also Mirel 1993, for similar developments in Detroit).

The relatively low standards, however, were viewed by some as a way of ending discrimination against black candidates. The two black board members felt, as did many community members, that the city's teacher exams discriminated against blacks. Dr. E. Wyman Garrett, a black dentist on the board, stated at a meeting in 1967 that "Between 70–80% of the subs are non-white" and "they are subs because they couldn't pass the exam—a high percentage failed it." Garret and board president Ashby stated in answer to a question that they had not actually seen the exam, but Dr. Ashby said, "It's highly discriminatory to Negroes and that's why we got rid of it for provisionals" (Minutes November 28, 1967, 705).

As we have seen, community groups had complained in the late fifties and early sixties because there were no black administrators in the system (*Newark Evening News* June 29, 1959, May 28, 1962; NAACP 1961). A black male teacher with advanced studies at Harvard University resigned from Newark to go to Philadelphia for an administrative post because, he said, "It's not possible for blacks [to get promoted] in Newark" (*Newark Evening News*, January 31, 1961).

Subsequently, in the early and mid-1960s, the Addonizio board appointed a number of blacks to acting-administrative and supervisory posts (*Newark Evening News* July 31, 1963). The Addonizio board also appointed the first African American acting vice principal in the city's history from an eligibility list—Mrs. Carrie E. Powel, a teacher in Newark since 1923 who had earned a master's degree from Teachers College in 1935, and who had been a qualified and active applicant for promotion for 27 years (she stated that she would always pass the written exam, but be "knocked down" in the oral interviews) (*Newark Evening News* August 5, 1962).

By 1967, however, it was clear that most blacks assigned to serve as acting administrators were not kept in administrative positions. The chairman of the Newark Human Rights Commission told the board that

> in many instances Negroes are appointed [as administrators] on a temporary basis without fringe benefits and remain in that status, while whites remain on a temporary basis only a short while and are then given full status and benefits. (Minutes January 24, 1967, 906)

The experience of Dr. Alma E. Flagg provides a further example of the problem. On April 18, 1964, she was appointed the first black principal since James Baxter of "the old colored school at the turn of the century" (*New York Times*, July 30, 1964). Her husband, like herself a Ph.D., who had earlier been appointed by Addonizio as director of the Neighborhood Youth Corps, was made acting principal of Broadway Junior High (*Newark Evening News* July 29, 1964). Significantly, however, just before the riots in July of 1967, all three black principals, the Doctors Flagg and Mrs. Gladys Frances, a third African American principal appointed a year later were given positions at the central office, and there were no black principals in the city (Minutes July 1, 1967, 7).

Moreover, "there were no Negroes in the Purchasing Department at the Board, in top level board jobs, none in the Superintendent's office, no Negro secretaries to any of the assistant superintendents, deputy superintendents, acting superintendents, or in Secretary Hess' organization" (Minutes, December 4, 1967, 906). And there were no black school secretaries, and only two black custodians in the entire school system (Minutes January 24, 1967, 909).

In an action that further enraged the black community, Mayor Addinizio in 1967 attempted to appoint an unqualified white—who had never completed high school but who, allegedly, would "go along" with the mayor's illegal activities—to the powerful position of secretary to the board of education, when Arnold Hess announced his retirement (Rich 1996, 194). There was an immediate uproar from the black community. The NAACP proposed on May 23 that Wilbur Parker, the first black to become a certified public accountant in New Jersey, be appointed to the position. Parker had been a scholarship winner from Newark's South Side High School in January of 1944, with a scholarship to the college of engineering at Cornell University. The *Newark Evening News* had reported in 1944 that Parker was "rated at South Side as one of the most brilliant students ever enrolled there. He majored in mathematics and science and was an outstanding athlete, starring in football and track" (February 25, 1944).

The board of education finally took up the matter of Secretary Hess' replacement on June 26. The meeting opened at 5PM. There were 70 speakers. It ended at 3:23 AM. The final decision by the board was, rather than to appoint Wilbur Parker, to keep Mr. Hess in his job for another year. This decision was a trigger for the Newark riots 2 weeks later (Governor's Commission 1968, 15).

The board of education responded very quickly to the Newark riots by abolishing the written and oral exams for promotion to administrative posts. Addonizio had earlier (illegally) changed for the district the state requirement that principals be "qualified" with a master's degree, to the requirement that they must be "qualifiable"—able to pursue a master's (Informant, longtime Newark teacher, July 24, 1996; confirmed by another longtime Newark teacher now in an executive position at the board, August 14, 1996). Thus, the only requirements for principal and vice principal during most of the decade were 10 years of experience teaching outside of Newark or 5 years in Newark. A screening committee chose applicants from a pool (*Newark Evening News* August 23, 1968).

On the day that it abolished the exams, the board appointed 10 blacks as principals and 13 black teachers as assistants to principals. None had taken the exam (*Newark Evening News* August 23, 1968). During the next two years, the board appointed 60 acting administrators, most of whom were African American, and none of whom had taken the written exam (February 8, 1970). The *Newark Evening News* reported later that, "Most of [those appointed] are black, and the school administration has readily acknowledged that they were appointed in part because of their color" (March 31, 1971).

Defending the appointments against charges that abolishing the exams had led to the hiring of unqualified people, Assistant Superintendent Edward Knopf said, "We have [black] acting principals in many schools, appointed without the exam. We can't tell them they can't be principal. We'd have a riot" (*Newark Evening News* March 31, 1971). Board president Ashby had stated, "If we abolish the exams we'll show the community we're going in their direction" (Minutes August 22, 1968, 90). (It will be argued in this book in chapter 8 that lowering the qualifications for administrators significantly lowered the quality of administration in the system.)

After a nearly 3-year delay caused by an unsuccessful lawsuit filed by 10 white teachers who had earlier passed the principals' exam, the Newark board made the 60 administrative appointments permanent. These positions were spread throughout the system: four high school principals and 12 high school vice principals in the eight city high schools; one junior high school principal and three junior high school vice principals in the five junior highs; 20 elementary principals and 18 elementary vice principals in the 49 elementary schools; and two special school principals (*Newark Evening News* March 31, 1971).

A retired black school administrator who worked in a supervisory capacity at the board of education in the late sixties and seventies told this author on July 19, 1995, "After the riots, the board said, 'We have to have 20 black principals right away!' So they abolished the exams." When I asked what the biggest problems in the district had been over the years, the informant replied, "It's all *people*—that's what makes a good system." After a moment's pause, the informant added, "When the board hired all those unqualified blacks in the sixties—to make up for all the years of discrimination—that's when the quality of personnel really went down."

In 1968, in testimony before the Governor's Commission, board president Ashby expressed his frustration:

> I think somewhere along the line someone has to say, "Stop." This is it. We are not doing a good job. . . . Until such time as these reading levels and arithmetic levels come up, there isn't anyone who can say in the city of Newark . . . we are doing a good job because these children just can't read and do arithmetic. . . . What I want to do is put the facts on the table without any cover-up because I think this is the time to do it. I think we are going to have to call a sharp halt to all of the camouflage that has gone on for the past 10, 15 and 20 years. (43–44)

After a thorough assessment of the Newark district following the riots, the Governor's Commission described the school system as being in a state of "crisis." The report stated that "This crisis demands that the State take over the administration of the Newark public schools." The commission report advised the state to take the following actions:

> Inject new resources—money and personnel—into the system; acquire suitable facilities; give special training to existing personnel and

launch a recruitment effort both inside and from without the city for teaching and supervisory personnel, making special efforts to attract individuals equipped for effective performance; and request all relevant State departments and agencies to provide immediate technical assistance to the Newark public schools; and take whatever measures the Governor, through the Commissioner of Education and with the advice of the Newark school authorities, deems necessary to resolve the crisis. (171)

Governor Richard Hughes, a Democrat, presented a proposal to the state legislature to take over the Newark schools and solve what he called the problem of "ghetto education." (The takeover would only be carried out with the consent of the mayor and the Board of Education.) However, in a year of intense national backlash to busing and civil rights gains by blacks, the Republican legislature—still controlled by rural elites in the powerful posts although suburban legislators were becoming the majority—was not interested in investing time, money, or personnel in the city of Newark. The bill was defeated (*New York Times* November 8, 1968).

CONCLUSION

Because there was no rescue of the Newark educational system in 1968, it would continue to limp along, and further generations of Newark children—the grandchildren, great-grandchildren and great-great-grandchildren of the southern rural migrants—would join their parents in the ranks of the uneducated and the undereducated. Many would therefore be unable to participate in the economic and political institutions of U.S. society.

When Newark's first black mayor was elected in July of 1970, he inherited a city and a school system that were both bankrupt and dysfunctional. He was heir—as black majorities and mayors in other cities would be—to a century of policies and actions that had robbed American cities of the glory that had been theirs. The process which produced urban decline was not one of inexorable logic; it was a process of long-term larceny—of the theft of almost every resource the cities possessed. The dismal state of many American cities by 1970 had not been inevitable. Indeed, in Europe, by contrast, most major cities have been well cared for, and are regarded as national treasures.

In the next chapter of this book I assess the following 25 years of state educational reform—as advocates of equal education, in New Jersey and in the vast majority of other states as well, attempted to compel state legislatures to redress the grievances of students in poorer districts. As we shall see for the state of New Jersey, however, the reforms turned out to be not only "too little too late" but also tragically misguided.

CHAPTER 7

Class, Race, Taxes, and State Educational Reform: 1970-1997

The vast majority of states fund their educational systems through the use of a local property tax. Historically, and until 1973–74, more than 50% of revenues for public elementary and secondary schools came from local sources. Since then, local funding has fluctuated between 47.4 and 48.8% of total revenues, with most other educational funds derived from state governments, whose average contribution is now 45%; the national federal share has never averaged more than 9.8% (U.S. Department of Education 1995). Large city school districts receive, on average, a slightly smaller percentage, 42.3%, of their revenues from local sources, with 46.9% from state governments, and a slightly higher average, 10.9%, from the federal government (Council of the Great City Schools 1994b, 89).

Property wealth has been distributed unequally within states, and as Elwood Cubberly first noted in 1905, overall educational spending patterns in most states have also been highly unequal (see also Carnoy 1982; Odden and Picus, 1992). Between 1970 and 1995, there were legal challenges to educational funding inequities in 42 states. By 1995, in 15 states the school finance system had been ruled unconstitutional by the state's highest court (or by a lower court and not appealed), and had been upheld in 17 states. In 1995, litigation was in process in 11 additional states (Education Commission of the States 1995a, 1995b).

New Jersey offers an important example of unequal funding as well as of court challenges to the school finance system. It was, in 1990, the first state in which a school finance case addressed the unique educational and fiscal needs of children living in poorer urban areas and the first in which a state supreme court mandated that because of their disadvantage, poorer urban students were entitled to *more* school aid than other students (Goertz 1991, 1). In this chapter I analyze New Jersey school finance and related educational reforms between 1970 and

1997, addressing the following questions: What considerations drove state decisions regarding school finance and related educational reform? and, What were the results of these reforms for New Jersey's urban poor school children? In order to contextualize developments, I begin with a brief synopsis of the economic and political environment in which New Jersey's state educational policies were formulated.

ECONOMIC AND POLITICAL TRENDS

Between 1975 and 1984, New Jersey cities were "arguably close to economic freefall," led by employment declines in Camden and Newark approaching 25% (Hughes and Seneca 1992a, 11). During the 1980s, New Jersey lost over 81,000 manufacturing jobs. The urban employment decline and hemorrhage of manufacturing in the state were part of two structural changes underway in the national economy: divestiture of low-skilled, labor-intensive, low value-added manufacturing jobs and their replacement with highly productive, highly skilled, and capital-intensive positions—a postindustrial, information-dependent, high-value-added manufacturing and service-based economy.

New jobs created by the changes were most often at the extremes of high or low pay with a "void of middle opportunities" (Hughes and Seneca, 1992b, 6). Almost all high-wage jobs in 1980 required a college degree—which only 16.2% of American adults, 6.3% of Newark adults, and 22% of the nonmilitary labor force had then attained (Mishel and Bernstein 1994, 109; U.S. Bureau of the Census 1994; U.S. Bureau of the Census, *Census of the Population* 1980). Nationally, the wages of non-college-educated workers fell drastically between 1979 and 1993. By the end of the 1980s, the only educational group exempt from falling real wages was the 8% of the workforce with advanced or professional degrees (Mishel and Bernstein 1994, 110).

Accompanying the declining economic position of many working- and middle-class white Americans was antagonism to efforts to improve the position of African Americans—a backlash to the busing of school-children to achieve integration, and to tax burdens that grew as federal money was spent on the Vietnam War and on minorities in the cities. In large part because of social investment during the late 1960s and early 1970s, black incomes rose, although they remained much lower than those of whites. During this period the rate of reduction of poverty among blacks was much faster than among whites, and the percentage of affluent intact black families nearly doubled, although the overall poverty rate of blacks was still higher than that of whites. But in the late 1970s the percentage of intact black families fell to 55%, and the number of black adults who were working also declined, beginning the bifurcation of the black community into poor and affluent (Edsall and Edsall 1991, 117–119).

A national polarization between whites and blacks developed during the 1970s and 1980s:

> Substantial segments of the white working- and lower-middle-class found common ground with business and with the well-to-do in support of an agenda that not only shifted government benefits from those at the bottom of the income distribution to those at the top . . . but, equally important, an agenda that addressed the concerns of the lower- and middle-income white voting majority, by slowing, and sometimes reversing, the "downward" redistribution of benefits to blacks. (Edsall and Edsall 1991, 155)

This national ideological polarization was supported by a racial suburban-urban split and a growing preponderance of suburban voting power. While blacks were the majority of inner city residents, they were less than 5% of the suburban population in 1975 and approximately 9% in 1990 (Dolce 1976, 71; Lake 1981, 3; Judd and Swanstrom 1994, 160). In 1984, only 12% of the national vote in the Mondale-Reagan contest was cast in large cities, whereas 55% was cast in suburbs and small cities. By 1992, an absolute majority of all votes cast in the presidential election were suburban. In that year 15 congressional seats were reapportioned to the South and West from the northern states (Judd and Swanstrom 1994, 304).

The election of Ronald Reagan in 1980 by a conservative coalition of the white working class, the middle class, and the more affluent inaugurated a period of substantial redistribution of income as tax burdens for the bottom grew, but declined for the top brackets; and as both wealth and income increased at the top and shrunk for the majority. The only group to increase its share of wealth during the eighties was the top 0.5%; the bottom 40% of families saw their share of wealth erode (Edsall and Edsall 1991; Mishel and Bernstein 1994, 244).

As a result of the economic shift to high-end jobs and a politically directed redistribution of income, there was a sharp rise in urban poverty between 1970 and 1990. The poverty population in the five largest cities increased 22% between 1970 and 1980, and the number of people living in "extreme-poverty areas" (areas with a poverty rate of at least 40%) or shelters increased by a full 161%. Newark was one of ten cities with the largest increase in the number of ghetto poor during 1970 to 1980 (Jencks and Peterson 1991, 255; Kasarda 1993, 89).

The intensified segregation of the poor interacted with the segregation of minorities and recent immigrants in cities to create a situation of hypersegregation in urban areas (Massey and Denton 1989, 1993; Wilson 1991). As the Reagan government removed federal housing supports, homelessness increased rapidly during the period, doubling in Newark between 1986 and 1988 (*Star Ledger* March 7, 1988).

As we have seen, by 1991, central cities housed 80% of low-income African Americans and racial minorities—blacks, Hispanics, and recent immigrants—composed the demographic majority in most of our largest cities. The national isolation of the minority poor in central cities would have substantial impact on educational funding remedies proposed by white suburban-dominated state legislatures throughout the period.

The New Jersey Context

The census classifies every New Jersey resident as an urban dweller. Average population density is 1,000 people per square mile, the highest in the United States. However, population density varies from less than 300 in some suburban counties to 12,000 people per square mile in the most crowded county (Hudson County). More than half of New Jersey's 567 municipalities are genuine "small towns" with fewer than 10,000 residents. Only about one quarter of the population lives in communities of more than 50,000. And less than 10% of the state's population lives in the six largest cities. Only two New Jersey cities have populations over 200,000 (Newark and Jersey City). Many workers now commute from homes in one fringe suburb to jobs in another and never need enter a city. They give New Jersey its distinctive character as the nation's most *suburban* state, and lend strength to its tradition of home rule (Pomper 1986, 39; Salmore and Salmore 1993, 55, 57, 204).

According to Salmore and Salmore, Bergen County, now the most populous county, home to more than 1 in 10 New Jerseyans, epitomizes the state. Its northern half is semirural, rich, and Republican; its southern portion bordering Hudson County is industrial, blue collar, and Democratic. With over 800,000 people—more than in Boston or San Francisco—Bergen County could qualify as one of the nation's larger cities. Instead, its residents live in 70 municipalities with an average population of under 12,000 (1993, 204).

As we have seen, New Jersey was at the time of the 1990 U.S. Census the second wealthiest state, following Connecticut. The average per capita income was 33% higher than the national average (*New York Times*, November 19, 1992). However, almost one third of its citizens are black or Hispanic, most live in the large cities, and most of these minority urban residents are poor (Association for Children of New Jersey, 1992; Council of the Great City Schools 1994b, 196; U.S. Census 1990).

As early as 1970, the six biggest cities contributed but 11% to the statewide vote (Salmore and Salmore 1993, 47). No African American was elected to the U.S. House from New Jersey until 1988 (53). As in every other state, suburban voters control the lion's share of state votes and, as with most other state legislatures, New Jersey's is almost entirely white. Of 120 members in 1992, 12 were African American, and two were Hispanic (140). The concentration of minorities in New Jersey's cities results in little political representation at the state level.

There are more school districts (626) than municipalities in New Jersey. Almost half of them serve fewer than 500 students and have three schools or less (Tractenberg 1995, 5; McLaughlin 1996, 8). In part because of the strong home rule tradition, there are only 17 regionalized K–12 districts in the state (New Jersey Department of Education 1995, 10). There are 56 districts classified by the state as urban, of which 30 are considered "special needs" districts because of the low-income levels of the students and the municipality; there are approximately 450 middle-class districts, and 120 wealthy districts. The majority (71) of the state's 120 wealthy districts are comprised of only one, two or three elementary schools (McLaughlin 1996, 8).

The concentration of blacks and Hispanics in New Jersey's cities is accompanied by the concentration of minority children in the poorer urban school districts. New Jersey, along with Illinois, New York, Massachusetts, and Michigan, is one of the most segregated states and has had one of the most segregated school systems in the nation for more than a decade (Orfield 1993, 20). New Jersey schools are the fourth most segregated in the country, with 54.6% of black students in 90 to 100% minority schools, and 73.5% of black students in 50 to 100% minority schools. New Jersey has the fourth *lowest* proportion of whites in the country in schools attended by blacks—another measure of segregation (Orfield 1993, 12).

In the mid-1970s, when New Jersey's legislature began to struggle with funding decisions for the urban districts, 71% of all minorities in the state were educated in the 29 poorest urban districts, and the "overwhelming majority" of students in districts with the lowest socio-economic ranking in the state were from these 29 poorest urban districts (*Abbot v. Burke 1990*, 342–343). In 1984–85, about 25% of the entire public school population of the state was in the 29 poorest districts (347). Estimates are that by the year 2000, one third of the state's children will be black and Latino and go to school in New Jersey's poorer cities. By 1979 New Jersey was said to have two school systems: "one for the affluent which works, and one for the poor—which doesn't" (Braun 1979, 69).

As in other states, in New Jersey the isolation in cities of the minority poor and their children would impact significantly on decisions made by legislators who appeared to feel that urban black and Latino students were "other people's children" for whom suburbanites had no responsibility.

NEW JERSEY SCHOOL FINANCE AND RELATED STATE EDUCATIONAL REFORMS

In New Jersey as elsewhere, courts played a significant role in educational reform as school finance struggles unfolded in the majority of states. The first wave of cases grounded the argument for equal funding for all children in the equal protection clause of the U.S. Constitution. Thus, in 1971, the California state courts in *Serranno v. Priest* ruled that the unequal funding of school districts in California was unconstitutional because "the quality of education may not be a function of wealth other than the wealth of the state as a whole" (Tractenberg 1974, 312). Then in 1973 the U.S. Supreme Court in *San Antonio Independent School District v. Rodriquez* halted this avenue to school finance reform, ruling that education was not a "fundamental right" of the U.S. Constitution, and that school finance law relying on districts with disparate tax capacity was not unconstitutional (313).

Challenges to unequal funding in the years following *Rodriquez* were based on clauses that had been inserted in state constitutions during nineteenth-century constitutional conventions, when states were creating and consolidating their systems of public schools (Odden and Picus 1992, 29). Such clauses called for "efficient," "thorough and efficient," "thorough and uniform," "general and uniform," "complete and uniform," "free quality," "adequate," or "general, suitable and efficient," education throughout a state (Odden and Picus 1992, 38–45; Tractenberg 1974). As I mentioned earlier, the clause in the New Jersey

Constitution, that the state must afford each child a "thorough and efficient education," was added in 1875 (New Jersey Constitution, article VIII, section 4, paragraph 1).

Robinson v. Cahill

There have been nine major court decisions related to school funding in New Jersey:

Robinson v. Cahill, 62 N.J. 473 (1973)
Robinson v. Cahill, 63 N.J. 196 (1973)
Robinson v. Cahill, 69 N.J. 133 (1975)
Robinson v. Cahill, 69 N.J. 449 (1976)
Robinson v. Cahill, 70 N.J. 155 (1976)
Abbott v. Burke, 100 N.J. 269 (1985)
Abbott v. Burke, 119 N.J. 287 (1990)
Abbott v. Burke, 136 N.J. 444 (1994)
Abbott v. Burke, M622, Slip Op., May 14, 1997

The first, in 1973, declared that New Jersey's system of financing public schools was unconstitutional because it violated the state constitutional mandate for a thorough and efficient education by basing school funding on local taxation (*Robinson v. Cahill* 1973). The court ruled that the system led to "great disparity in dollar input per pupil" between urban and suburban districts, yielding an inverse relation between property wealth and tax rates, and did not provide urban students an equal opportunity for a thorough and efficient education as required by the state constitution.

Emphasizing the importance of sufficient educational resources to urban districts, the supreme court required the state legislature to devise a "constitutionally sufficient" system of financing education (Tractenberg 1974, 329). Moreover, the court argued that the state constitution places ultimate financial responsibility on the state for a thorough and efficient education system. "If local government fails to provide [a thorough and efficient education] the state government must compel it to act, and if the local government cannot carry the burden, the State must itself meet its continuing obligation" (*Robinson v. Cahill* 1973, 513).

The New Jersey Supreme Court thus first defined unconstitutionality in dollar terms. Over the next 3 years, however, as further court decisions attempted to prod the New Jersey legislature to some action to meet the mandate, the court included in its purview not only funding disparity, but disparity in "substantive educational content." In a 1976 decision, the court required that "each pupil shall be offered an equal opportunity to receive an education of such excellence as will meet the constitutional standard" for a thorough and efficient education that would, as the constitution requires, equip students for their "role as a citizen and as a competitor in the labor market" (*Robinson v. Cahill* 1976, 459–460, in *Abbott v. Burke* 1990, 309).

In response to the court mandate, the state legislature passed the Public School Elementary and Secondary Education Act (PSEA) in 1975, but did not fund it. A year later the legislature still had not created a funding scheme, and to prod state action, the court closed the public schools to 100,000 summer school students on July 1. Legislators responded by passing the state's first income tax in several weeks. The proceeds would be dedicated to education, and would provide "equalization aid" to districts in carrying out the PSEA.

However, the act retained, with minor variations, the funding provisions from the system which the supreme court had found unconstitutional in 1973. Educational funding would still depend on local taxing and budgeting decisions and the abilities of districts to increase taxes, supplemented with a limited amount of equalization aid (*Abbott v. Burke* 1990, 288, 291). "Minimum aid" was provided to all districts, including the middle-class and the wealthy. The result was that districts containing more than three fourths of New Jersey's students would receive education aid (Goertz 1991, 2).

In this legislative response to the supreme court mandate for a thorough and efficient education, equalization between districts would be attained not by an infusion of funds into poor urban districts, but by placing caps on local school district expenditures, for example, in the more affluent communities, by managerial efficiency, and, importantly, by requiring a minimum curriculum of basic skills for all students (*Abbott v. Burke* 1990; Centolanza 1986, 524). A basic skills curriculum focused instruction on rote, skill-drill exercises which typically emphasized cognitive skills of recognition and recall. Such a curriculum, utilizing primarily workbooks and worksheets, was relatively inexpensive, and would not require that the state invest in computers, science equipment, or other curriculum materials for urban schools. During the next two decades, the cities, which were closely monitored by the state, did offer a basic skills curriculum to students, while the suburbs continued to offer sophisticated curriculum programs and a range of courses (*Abbott v. Burke* 1990, 364; Centolanza 1986, 540–542; Firestone, Goertz, and Natriello, 1997).

In 1976, state education commissioner Fred Burke expressed what seemed to be one factor in the reasoning behind the state's view that "pouring money" into the city districts was futile. He stated, "Urban children, even after years of remediation, will not be able to perform in school as well as their suburban counterparts. . . . We are just being honest" (*Star Ledger* April 2, 1976). (As everyone in New Jersey knew, "urban students" was a euphemism for "minority students".)

The state also argued to those—such as the New Jersey Education Association—who criticized its attempt to equalize education in terms of basic skills rather than an infusion of funds that

> The education [basic skills] currently offered in these poorer urban districts is tailored to the students' present need . . . these students simply cannot now benefit from the kind of vastly superior course offerings found in the richer districts (in *Abbott v. Burke* 1990, 364)

Basic skills instruction was also seen by the legislature as most amenable to statewide testing for the purpose of producing readily demonstrable results to the public (Centolanza 1986, 554). In line with a national trend toward minimum competency testing (there were such programs in 33 states by 1978), legislators' desire for standards would be satisfied by state minimum basic skills tests; districts in which students were not proficient would receive compensatory (remedial) funding. Until 1993, when a test requiring more complex cognitive skills was instituted, the state had in place a minimum competency, basic skills testing program (Firestone, Goertz, and Natriello 1997).

According to S. David Brandt, a member of the state board of education and former local school board member,

> Standards established under the basic skills compensatory ed program had nothing to do with educational quality. Instead these standards were set according to a reasonable estimate of how much state money would be available to provide remedial instruction to those students who failed the test, and not on educational assessment, theory or practice. Attaining a passing score on the test did not necessarily mean that the students had reached any reasonable level of educational achievement. The passing scores were based on the assumption that 25 percent would fail statewide and there would be adequate state money to back remedial efforts at the local level. (in Centolanza 1986, 556–557)

An additional feature of the state remedial program was that it withdrew funds, and therefore, in cities, money for teaching jobs, if district standardized scores improved. This strategy, not lost on educators whose jobs depended on compensatory funds, penalized success and rewarded failure. On March 5, 1980, New Jersey became the first state to classify its schools according to their compliance with law and code and their students' success in mastering basic skills. State board president Paul Ricci declared, "Public education can regain its reputation and recapture public trust" (in Centolanza 1986, 426).

The results of minimum basic skills testing in the late 1970s and early 1980s, however, revealed the failure of the 1975 act to provide a thorough and efficient education in the state's urban districts. In many cities, the majority of students failed the minimum basic skills tests. In Camden in 1978, for example, two thirds failed reading in sixth and ninth grade and math in third. In Newark, more than 75% failed the sixth-grade reading test and 75% failed the sixth-grade math test. More than 70% of ninth graders in Orange failed the ninth-grade reading test and about half of youngsters in Irvington could not pass the sixth-grade reading tests (554–555).

Moreover, financial disparities between districts had increased in the years of the PSEA. Prior to the 1975 act, in 1971–72, the spread between the lowest and the highest spending districts was $700 to $1,500 per pupil, a difference of $800. By 1984–85, districts at the 5th percentile spent $2,687, while districts at the 95th percentile spent $4,755, a disparity of $2,068 per pupil. When adjusted for inflation, in 1975 dollars the disparity grew from $898 per pupil in 1975–76 to $1,135 per pupil in 1984–85. The result was that a group of richer districts with 189,484 students spent 40% more per pupil than a group of poorer districts with 355,612 students (*Abbott v. Burke* 1990, 334). According to Goertz,

> More than $31 million *per pupil* in property wealth separated the poorest and wealthiest school districts in 1988. The 10 : 1 difference in per pupil property wealth between Trenton ($111,475) and Princeton ($1,128,051) was more typical of the disparities in property wealth across the state. (1992, 7)

The differences in property tax base were a major cause of education expenditure disparities, because of the heavy reliance on the local property tax to finance education across the state, despite the *Robinson v. Cahill* 1973 decision which ruled this method unconstitutional (*Abbott v. Burke* 1990, 477). Excluding federal aid and pension contributions, local revenues accounted for 60.4% of all educational expenditures in the state, while state aid accounted for 39.6% in fiscal year 1989 (Goertz 1992, 7). Despite the act's 1975 mandate that districts increase their school tax to make needed increased funds available, during the 10-year period of PSEA, "no substantially increased local funding through school tax increases" occurred (*Abbott v. Burke* 1990, 357). Moreover, the state legislature fully funded the education aid provisions of the PSEA in only 2 of the 10 years between 1975 and 1985 (1977–78 and 1978–79) (324).

Abbott v. Burke

In response to increasing inequalities, a second lawsuit was filed in 1981, by the Newark-based Education Law Center, on behalf of students in New Jersey's urban poor districts. The trial record was completed in 1987, and the state supreme court decision handed down in 1990 (*Abbott v. Burke* 1990).

During the trial, state documents were presented in defense of recent legislative approaches to school funding and educational reform. These documents argued that (as reported in the *Abbott v. Burke* 1990 decision):

1. Large infusions of state aid to the poorer urban districts were not necessary because "districts had unlimited power to raise funds to satisfy their constitutional obligation; and the state could take over the operation of any district that fails" (299).
2. There is not a strong relationship between property wealth and per pupil expenditures (297). The difference in education between poorer urban and affluent districts is not caused by amount of expenditures per pupil, but by district mismanagement (323). Funding should not be supplied to poorer urban districts, because it may be mismanaged and wasted (295). Beyond a minimum amount, "money is not a critical factor in the quality of education in the first place" (376). Further, the belief that greater funding was needed to assure a thorough and efficient education across the state "enthrones naiveté" (299).
3. Course offerings, experience and education of staff, and pupil per staff ratio cannot be considered reliable indicators of the quality of education (358). Rather, "thorough and efficient" should be measured against state education standards and mandates, which defined a thorough and efficient education in terms of minimum basic skills levels that all students in the state must meet (359).

The supreme court justices, however, disagreed. They compared education in the poorer urban districts with the educational finances, program offerings, and student achievement in affluent areas (*Abbott v.*

Burke 1990, 289). They noted that the 1975 act "relies so heavily on a local property base that [in the cities] is already over-taxed to exhaustion" (357). They ruled the system of financing and achieving a thorough and efficient education unconstitutional as applied to poorer urban districts in New Jersey (288). The justices found that, as a result of the disparities in finances and educational programming, "students [in the poorer urban districts] simply cannot possibly enter the same market or the same society as their peers educated in wealthier districts" (368).

In this groundbreaking 1990 decision, the supreme court declared that the 1975 act had to be amended to assure funding of education in poorer districts at the level of property-rich districts (i.e., financial parity had to be achieved); funding could not be allowed to depend on the ability of local school districts to tax, but had to be guaranteed by the state; and the level of funding of the poorer city districts by the state had to include sufficient additional funds to provide for the extraordinary educational needs of disadvantaged students (288). The state was required to assess what those needs were and provide programs to meet them. Other aid provisions of the 1975 act, "which had the sole function of enabling richer school districts to spend even more money, thereby increasing the disparity," were declared unconstitutional (291).

The supreme court made several additional points: Calling the cities social and economic "disaster areas," the court declared that "municipal overburden," the excessive tax levy that some municipalities had to impose to meet governmental needs other than education, effectively prevented districts from raising substantially more money for education despite statutory provisions increasing the districts' legal ability to raise taxes (289, 356).

Stating that the poorer urban districts were essentially "basic skills districts," while more affluent districts provided educational opportunities in areas such as exposure to computers, laboratory science, sophisticated math and science courses, foreign language programs, and art and music courses, the court declared that the constitutional requirement of a thorough and efficient education encompasses more than instruction in the basic communications and computational skills, but also requires that "students be given at least a modicum of variety and a chance to excel" (*Abbott v. Burke* 1990, 290). The court noted that it would not tell urban poor students that "they will get the minimum, because that is all they can benefit from" (375). Moreover, remarked the court,

> If . . . 'basic skills' were sufficient to achieve [the mandate of a thorough and efficient education] there would be little short of a revolution in the suburban districts when parents learned that basic skills is what their children were entitled to, limited to, and no more. (364)

The court added that if as the state argued sophisticated curriculum courses are not integral to a thorough and efficient education, "why do the richer districts invariably offer them?" (364). The justices also stated that

> We have decided this case on the premise that the children of poorer urban districts are as capable as all others; that their deficiencies stem from their socioeconomic status; and that through effective education and changes in that socioeconomic status, they can perform as well as others. Our constitutional mandate does not allow us to consign poorer children permanently to an inferior education on the theory that they cannot afford a better one or that they would not benefit from it. (340)

The court addressed the issue of district mismanagement. They said that the record supported the conclusion that although, as the state contended, there may have been "mismanagement, politics and worse" in urban districts, mismanagement was not a significant factor in the general failure to achieve a constitutionally required thorough and efficient education for students in poorer urban districts; and of great significance, the justices declared that "no amount of administrative skill" would redress the deficiency and disparity caused by insufficient funding (381; 290–291).

The material presented in historical chapters of this book suggest that there may have been incompetence, politics, "and worse" in urban districts—although one cannot conclude that this occurred only in urban districts. However, this history also provides a basis for understanding the politics and corruption as a reaction by local leaders to the lack of political access and economic resources experienced by urban governments in America for many decades. Just as poverty and lack of recourse make a fertile ground for youthful criminal activity in inner city neighborhoods, so do they in city and school governing circles. If and when adequate political and economic resources become available in cities— which to date they have not—the material need for money grabbing and power mongering will be weakened, and corruption may play a much smaller role.

The supreme court justices concluded their 1990 opinion by reminding citizens that New Jersey localities spend more dollars per student for education than those of almost any other state. They continued,

> the dilemma is that while we spend so much, there is absolutely no question that we are failing to provide the students in the poorer

urban districts with the kind of an education that anyone could call
thorough and efficient. . . . The need is great and the money is there.
New Jersey is the second richest state in the nation. (394)

Events of the following few years proved that the financial capacity did
indeed exist, but the state's overwhelmingly suburban voters did not
want to spend money on the urban poor.

In anticipation of the 1990 *Abbott v. Burke* decision, which was
widely expected to mandate significant increases in funding for urban
education, the Democratic state assembly on June 18, 1990, approved a
$2.8 billion tax package which doubled the highest income tax rate (for
the top 20% of tax payers), raised the sales tax from 6 to 7%, and extended it to paper goods and luxury items (Goertz 1992, 12). This package came to be called the Quality Education Act (or QEA). The act
increased state education aid by $1.15 billion. It guaranteed low-income
districts a foundational level of spending for each child that approached
parity with the wealthier districts.

In addition, 30 of the poorest urban "special needs" districts were
identified by the legislature, and the foundation amount increased by
5% to these districts. The foundation level of support statewide was
irrespective of local tax capacity, as long as each district raised its "fair
share." The act also phased out general aid to wealthy districts and
capped increases in district expenditures. To make more money available for education aid, the legislature made teacher pension and social
security costs the responsibility of local districts, instead of the state
(Goertz 1992, 12; Salmore and Salmore 1993, 275).

New Jersey homeowners had seen their property taxes almost double in the 1980s because of many state mandates that were either not
funded by the legislature, such as recycling; or underfunded, such as
the statute for school aid. The QEA would increase state taxes further.
For example, in wealthier Bergen County, state income taxes would
double to pay for the QEA. Three fourths of the new school aid, dispro-
portionally financed by Bergen residents, would go to the special needs
districts, and to five cities in the south with lower than average incomes
and property values. The Republican senate minority leader, John Dor-
sey of Morris County, another hard-hit wealthy northern county, enraged advocates of urban education but said aloud what many others
were thinking when he declared that QEA and *Abbott* required "working-class people in middle-class communities who drive around in Fords
to buy Mercedes for people in the poorest cities because they don't have
cars." A Monmouth County Democratic assemblyman called the cuts to
his wealthy district the act of "almost a socialist state," and proclaimed,

"This is New Jersey, this is not Moscow in 1950" (in Salmore and Salmore 1993, 252, 276).

Taxpayer opposition to the QEA tax increases was swift. A popular revolt swamped legislators before the act could go into effect, as taxpayers rallied at the state capital in protest (Goertz 1992, 13). With the entire legislature up for reelection the next year, legislators revised the QEA (to QEA II) in March 1991, before it would take effect in September. As a result of the revision, in many districts—even the poorest—revised budget caps meant that new money covered little more than contractual salary increases and higher insurance costs. QEA II reduced the increase in state education aid from $1.15 billion to $800 million; cut funds to support the education of students from low-income households; guaranteed that no district would get less state aid than it had received the previous year; restricted the annual growth of state aid to education; and set more restrictive caps on districts' total budgets (Firestone, Goertz, and Natriello 1997).

No actual funding had taken place under QEA, because of the timing of the revisions. Out of the $800 million increase in total state aid for 1991–92 (the first year of funding under QEA II), the 30 poorest urban districts received a net increase of $44 million for their regular education programs; however, this amount represented only 3% of their aggregate 1990–91 regular education budgets (Firestone, Natriello, and Goertz 1994, 28).

Firestone, Goertz, and Natriello studied the use of QEA II money by 12 wealthy, middle-class, and poor urban districts. They report that all six urban poor districts that they assessed made good use of the increased funds from QEA II. The districts spent the money primarily for three purposes: "catch up expenditures" (new buildings, extra teachers, more supplies), social support programs for disadvantaged students, and expenditures to improve the quality of instruction, for example, staff development (1997; see also Firestone, Goertz, and Natriello, 1994, 21).

However, the funding increases were relatively small. Indeed, in Camden, often cited as the state's educational worst case, the QEA II reduced new school aid from $50 million to $24.8 million. In Newark, when I asked how QEA II had affected the Newark school budget, a longtime executive at the Newark Board of Education told me that the additional funds were

> not really enough to do much with. . . . They [the state] made
> a big deal of it, but it was a game. Our costs went up two million, say, and we got two million from the QEA [II]. We used it

for things we thought we were going to have to cut. We
moved it around where we needed it. Some salary increases.
We did go from several to over 100 all-day kindergartens,
though, with QEA money. (Interview, July 10, 1996).

According to the director of school finance in the state education department, the net effect of the revisions of the original QEA was ''an outflow
of aid from the urban districts . . . to the middle- and upper-wealth
districts,'' as compared with the QEA's original provisions (in Salmore
and Salmore 1993, 278).

CONTINUING FINANCIAL AND EDUCATIONAL DISPARITY

The Quality Education Act II was found to be unconstitutional by the
state supreme court in 1994, based on its failure to assure parity of
regular education expenditures between the special needs districts and
the more affluent districts for the regular education program, and its
failure to provide for the additional, special needs of disadvantaged
children. Reiterating the opinions of *Robinson v. Cahill* decisions and
Abbott v. Burke in 1990, the court declared in 1994, ''It is the state and
only the state that is responsible for the present educational disparity,
and only the state can correct it'' (*Abbott v. Burke* 1994, 15).

A verdict on the results of almost two decades of school finance
litigation and legislative educational reform aimed at the poorer urban
districts was delivered by the state itself in 1989 and 1991 when it decer-
tified schools in two large cities and installed state personnel to administer them. Newark became the third district ''taken over,'' on July 12,
1995.

To determine whether or not to take over the Newark school system, the state in 1993–94 carried out a ''comprehensive compliance investigation'' (CCI) of the district. External consultants and state evaluators assessed finance, governance and management, education
programs, and facilities. Teams of evaluators made unannounced site
visits at 50 of the 82 Newark schools. The five-volume report was introduced by a summary, excerpted here.

Children in the Newark public schools . . . endure degrading school
environments that virtually ensure academic failure. . . . [In many
classrooms] there is nothing. . . . Science laboratories lack basic
equipment.

[Students] in the Newark Public Schools, with rare exceptions, sit dutifully in rows, filling in the blanks in workbooks with answers to items having to do with isolated skills, or listening to a teacher deliver facts or talk about skills, divorced from meaningful context. . . . In elementary classrooms the predominant instructional activity observed was the filling in of blanks in workbooks, skill sheets or worksheets. . . . When direct instruction took place, it involved a teacher asking fact-type questions and students giving answers.

Students in high school classes fared no better. For example, high school English classes, with few exceptions, focused on the learning of facts about literature rather than participation in activities designed to enable students to experience literature. Seldom in any class observed, no matter what the grade level or subject, were students being taught how to write, how to read for understanding, how to solve problems, or how to think critically.

Physical conditions in most of the schools observed by the comprehensive compliance team reveal . . . neglect and dereliction of duty. Holes in floors and walls; dirty classrooms with blackboards so worn as to be unusable; filthy lavatories without toilet paper, soap or paper towels; inoperable water fountains; . . . and foul-smelling effluent running from a school into the street, speak of disregard for the dignity, safety, basic comfort and sense of well-being of students and teachers.

In many schools an air of unreality pervades. Attendance taking is erratic, often dependent on the whim of individual teachers. Clocks are wildly inaccurate; classroom doors are unmarked or wrongly marked; the few lavatories equipped with appropriate supplies are barred to students and for teacher use only; fire exit doors are chained; fire doors marked "Keep Closed" are open, but closed is no better than open, because the glass panels are missing.

A virtual army of supervisors, administrators, and coordinators holds all this in place, passing various . . . forms from one layer of bureaucracy to the next, while schools go unpainted for as long as 14 years, and in classroom after classroom whole banks of lights are without fluorescent tubes or light shields.

These conditions tell of shocking neglect. Equally shocking, however, from the team's perspective, is the lack of indignation on the part of staff. One teacher interviewed explained it this way: "After a while," she said, looking around, "you lower your expectations." (New Jersey State Department of Education 1994b, 43–44, 66).

Arguing that conditions such as these were a result of continued unconstitutional funding disparities, and in the absence of a state plan responding to the 1994 *Abbott v. Burke* reiteration of its 1990 mandate, the Education Law Center returned to court in April of 1996. Under the 1994

Abbott decision, the state had been given 3 school years (1995–98) to eliminate the 16.05% relative disparity in regular educational expenditures between the wealthiest districts and the poorest urban districts. This indicated an average annual reduction of 5.35%. Instead of bringing about steady progress, however, the state reduced the disparity by only 2.69% in 1995–96, and proposed a mere 0.76% reduction for 1996–97, leaving a projected 12.6% in disparity to be eliminated in the 3rd and final year (Education Law Center 1996, 2). This 12.6% figure places New Jersey at about the middle (27th of the 50 states) in the size of its spending disparity between the richest and the poorest districts (Education Trust 1996, 229). The Newark Education Law Center calculated that $341 million would be necessary to close the gap between the spending by rich and poor districts in 1997–98. However, in 1993 a gubernatorial candidate who had promised to cut New Jersey taxes by a huge 30% had been elected. Governor Christine Todd Whitman's resulting 30% tax cut in 1994 removed $1.2 billion in prospective taxes from the state's treasury—an amount that would have been more than sufficient to reach the mandate of the state supreme court.

The New Jersey state government has spent billions of dollars on education since 1975. While the number of dollars spent over the years has grown, the share of the state's contribution to education spending in New Jersey has not: In 1976–77, during the first year of increased funding from the 1975 PSEA, state aid was 38% of total school expenditures (Reock 1996, table 32). The percentage rose to 44% in 1985–86 and 1986–87 but fell in subsequent years. By 1996–97, state aid had fallen to the 1976–77 level of 38% of total school expenditures (McLaughlin 1996, 13). Although the state, under QEA II, in 1991–92 supported from 24 to 87% of the budgets of poorer urban districts (and 79% of Newark's, with an average support of these districts' budgets at 38.5%), state support of education in New Jersey is, at 38%, below the national average of 46.4% (Reock 1993, table 20; 1996, table 32; U.S. Department of Education 1994, table 155). Between 1993 and 1995, the New Jersey legislature actually decreased K–12 education funding by 3.1%, but *increased* the funding of prisons and other corrections budgets by 25.2% (Education Trust 1996, 143).

The New Jersey legislature's long-awaited plan to meet the Supreme Court's 1994 decision was passed December 19, 1996, and signed the next day by the governor. This law, the Comprehensive Educational Improvement and Financing Act (CEIFA), returns to a mandated minimum curriculum—comparable to the use of basic skills minimums of the seventies and eighties. Core curriculum standards, predetermined by the state and to be used as a basis for instruction, are required for all students, and are the means for providing "a thorough and efficient education.'' As with the previous basic skills mandates of the seventies and eighties, the required curriculum standards are the means by which educational parity is to be achieved (Sciarra 1997, 85).

Basing its figure on a hypothetical model school district, the legislature decided that $6,720 would be the cost of supplying each elementary school student in 1997-98 with a curriculum that meets these standards. They arrived at $7,526 for middle school and $8,064 for high school students. The state will provide foundation aid to each district according to the difference between its local fair share of property taxes, based on community wealth, and this amount. The figures have been widely criticized as inadequate. They are below the 1996-97 statewide average per pupil expenditure for the regular education budget, far below spending in more affluent districts, and even below that in many poor districts (Sciarra 1997). In efforts to meet the demands of this criticism, the law permits districts to go beyond this minimum by increasing local property taxes. Wealthier districts have the tax base to do so. Poorer urban districts, however, will not be able to raise more educational revenue from their depleted local resources, and therefore are dependent on the foundation aid as a maximum for their regular education budgets. Thus, increased disparities as a result of the act are inevitable. As the governor stated on December 2, 1996, ''[In enacting this law], we very frankly said we are not looking for parity in spending'' (*Trenton Times* December 2, 1996, in Sciarra 1997, 37). This act, one more example of purposeful noncompliance with the New Jersey constitution, follows almost a quarter century of willful legislative defiance of constitutional requirements and the State Supreme Court.

On May 14, 1997, however, the Supreme Court delivered a decision that may have far-reaching consequences. The court determined that the regular education funding provisions of CEIFA are unconstitutional as applied to the special needs districts. Arguing that without adequate resources, content standards can have little actual impact on the quality of education, the judges ordered the legislature to assure by the commencement of the 1997-98 school year that per-pupil expenditures in the poor urban districts are equivalent to the average per-pupil expenditure in the wealthy suburban districts. Of great significance, the court also held that because the documented needs of children attending school in the poor urban districts vastly exceed the needs of other school children, and because the state failed to meet the mandate of earlier Abbott decisions to provide supplemental programs over and above the regular education program that would meet these needs, the case is remanded to the New Jersey Superior Court (*Abbott v. Burke* 1997, 2-4).

This provides the courts an important form of leverage. The remand empowers the Superior Court to direct the Commissioner of Education to assess the needs of urban children, specify what programs will be provided, determine the cost, and plan for state-assisted implementation of these supplemental programs (*Abbott v. Burke* 1997, 4–5). The Superior Court also has the authority to determine whether legislative responses satisfy the requirements of the 1997 order. Moreover, the Supreme Court has retained jurisdiction: should the legislature refuse to appropriate the money the Superior Court finds necessary for the extra programs, the Supreme Court could order the suspension of current education spending in the state. Such an order would close schools and cause "administrative chaos and public outrage" (McLaughlin 1997, 34). Such anger would very likely be directed at political incumbents.

The history of school finance and related educational reform in New Jersey illuminates three dilemmas we as a nation face concerning funding for ghetto schooling: First, although nationally we spend a great deal of money on urban education, we are still failing to educate inner city youngsters. We spend far less on city schools than we do on suburban schools—and given the relatively large percentages of city school budgets that are removed from the regular education program for special needs purposes, the disparity is even greater. I believe, and will argue in chapter 8, that we ought to spend considerably more.

Second, on what should money be spent? By isolating city schools from their urban context, and then aiming funding at only the educational institutions, are we not "missing one whole side of the barn?" I will argue that we need to broaden our sights and focus, in addition, on the problems of what the New Jersey Supreme Court called the "economic and social disaster areas" that are our nation's cities.

Third, who should pay for educational reform? Should the consequences of 100 years of federal, corporate, and state policies that starved and isolated the nation's cities (as demonstrated in previous chapters) be placed on the shoulders of a state's suburban taxpayers? The history provided in part II of this book demonstrates that it is not the state alone that is responsible for the financial disparity between suburban and urban schools: Federal and corporate culpability suggests a large role for these entities in financial reparations, as well.

These questions and others need to be addressed in order to reorient government authorities and taxpayers, as well as to replace the strategies that have driven many years of unsuccessful educational reform. Current visions of reform have been quite limited, and have unnecessarily narrowed our sights. In the concluding chapter, I will attempt a re-visioning, and to do that, I will first ask what the history of Newark and the Newark schools can teach us about the tasks that need to be accomplished, and how we should proceed.

PART III

LEARNING FROM THE PAST

CHAPTER 8

Revisiting Marcy School: Lessons from History and a New Vision of Reform

The morning of my first cooperative learning workshop at Marcy School arrived, and there were coffee and bagels provided by the principal. We sat in the library, its wooden shelves built 131 years ago, and began to discuss cooperative classroom techniques. Despite the noise in the halls, fire alarms being set off by the children, the intercom blaring, and students running outside the library door, the teachers were attentive and involved.

What they liked, they said, was that we took time to acknowledge the reality of what one called "the situation we have here!" Most workshops, they alleged, are "useless" because "they never get to the discipline part. They say, 'we'll come back to that,' but they never do." "The [workshop] presenters say, 'here it is – go do it.' But we can't! There's too much going on here." The teachers said that they were referring to violence (for example, recent experiences with a gun in the school, where third graders were "shaking down" younger children for money), ongoing tumult caused by caustic relations with the principal, and what teachers felt were excessive demands of the numerous reforms. (Field notes, March 2, 1992)

When I arrived for the fourth day of workshops, the air in the school smelled acrid and foul. There had been a fire in the basement woodshop 5 days before. The fire had spread because the fire department, used to false alarms from the building, had not responded at first. My field notes from that afternoon's workshop read:

I couldn't focus the teachers. They were preoccupied, anxious, and unfocused. There was a tension in the air that you could cut with a knife. When I expressed this to Susan, an eighth-grade teacher, she grimaced and said, "Yes, I feel it too." Twelve of the 25 class-room teachers (48%) were out, which is not unusual for a Monday, but five of the subs did not show up and did not call to say they weren't coming. The noise in the hall was overwhelming, with kids running, shouting, and doors slamming. Where we sat around a table with the doors closed we had trouble hearing each other. The intercom, which you could not turn off, was blaring, "Teachers – lock your doors! They're supposed to be locked! [to keep unauthorized children and adults from entering the rooms]."

I attempted to start the workshop. It was already a half-hour late. I was going to use a video, but I could not get the VCR to work; a teacher told me that it had broken late last week. I felt immobilized by the chaos in the school.

We began to talk about what was going on. Some teachers expressed despair and frustration: "You can't teach here! It's got to be better somewhere else." "You can't teach! Every day it's something [some problem or interruption]." "Mornings the kids come in, there's been a shooting or something, and that's all they're thinking about. It doesn't matter what techniques you use, it doesn't make any difference." "It's because the community is dysfunctional; the parents are dysfunctional, and so are their kids." "The kids have so many problems." "Nobody cares! The parents don't care, the kids don't care; and nobody does their job. People [teachers] 'get over,' and take off whenever they feel like it." "It's so much worse now – they're so poor!" An older black teacher said, "You can't blame it on poverty. When I was coming up we were poor, but we had rules. There are no rules now."

A white teacher said, "These kids have major problems! Incest, drugs, the girls go from boyfriend to boyfriend. You look at them and say 'what's the matter,' and they can't tell you. I have a little boy [in first grade] who's wondering where his mother went. No one knows. No wonder things go in one ear and out the other [when you're trying to teach them]." Another white teacher said with what appeared to be an embarrassed laugh, "We think, 'they're only going to sweep floors' – why teach them science?" A third concurred, adding, "When you realize who they [the students] are, you laugh, and you can't take it [teaching] seriously."

I persevered, and led the discussion back to teaching the children social skills that are required for cooperative student groups – for example, sharing ideas and praising each other's contributions. I felt somewhat ridiculous: with all the problems that the children and teachers had in this school, why was I even bothering with something so trivial as "cooperative learning." I felt that at times the teachers thought it was ridiculous too.

Later I expressed my frustration to a male teacher and he said to me, "You know, some of the kids in this school run drugs for the dealers in the evening. They're young, they're unprosecutable. They do it just to put food on the table for their families. *That's* co-operation!" (Field notes, March 9, 1992)

The following is from my field notes of the last workshop of the series:

While we were working today, the counselor came in to ask if Tom Russo, a white eighth-grade teacher, could be excused for a few minutes to talk to his class. I said yes, and asked why. The counselor stated that one of the seventh-grade girls had been raped the previous evening, and some of the boys in Tom's class had been circling and taunting her at lunchtime. The rapist's cousin was in the class, and he was threatening the girl. The teachers and I exchanged glances, and shook our heads. Tom left to talk to his class, and we continued the workshop without missing a beat. One more brutality, too many to react to.

We had been discussing the difficulties they were having using cooperative learning with special education students (children with learning or other disabilities who are either put in a special class or "mainstreamed" for part or all of the day into regular classes). One teacher with a special education class said, "Some kid in my class pulled down his pants to his knees, turned around and said 'kiss my ass!' They wouldn't suspend him, so I quit. The principal told me to take the rest of the day off. Finally, they suspended him." When trying to explain why the student did that to her, the teacher said, "I think he got beat up [by the non-special-education kids] once too often." We talked about how the special education children often get hit by the others, and about how some of the mainstreamed students have been running out of the building and leaving the area. "They don't want to be mainstreamed. It's too dangerous!" one teacher said.

We discussed on what bases the teachers had been pairing their students for cooperative groups. Several teachers discussed the problems they were having. They mentioned those of their children who had been "crack babies" and those who had been "alcohol babies," and the difficulties of pairing some of these children with other students. A third-grade teacher said Charles, a boy "born to crack," is supposed to have glasses, but he hasn't been wearing them this year and "won't do anything." The social worker told me later that last year, when he was in second grade, this boy attempted suicide twice. The teacher continued, "He lives in a garage with his father, and comes in dirty with grease and God, does he smell. Nobody will sit near him." The teacher keeps soap and a towel in her class, but "he won't use them, and anyway, he needs a shower! Besides – he's always falling asleep" [she thought Charles's father was giving him drugs]. We agreed she should start the cooperative groups without Charles.

I turned on the VCR (which was supposed to have been fixed) to show a last segment of tape, and there was no sound. We could not fix it. There was one other VCR in the school, on another floor, and it also was broken. We continued without the video, working on their activity plans for my classroom visit. At 2:00, I noticed one of the teachers begin to nod and close his eyes. It was clear he would fall asleep if we were quiet. One other teacher said, "I can't do this now. I can't think." We talked about what the fatigue was from. They said, "Don't take it personally, Jean!" They agreed that because they were sitting down, and relaxed, the fatigue hit them. They said they are tense and watchful all day, on alert every moment. They become exhausted from the constant tension. When they get out of the classroom like this and start to relax, "it's all over," as one teacher put it, "and I collapse."

I relinquished my attempts to get them to finish their lesson plans. This was the last session before I began going into their classrooms to help them practice the new pedagogical skill, and we chatted until it was time to dismiss their classes. (Field notes, March 18, 1992)

These vignettes demonstrate some of the difficulties encountered in my own attempt, as participant in the district reform effort in the early 1990s, to upgrade the skills of teachers at Marcy School. The discussion in chapter 2 demonstrated related difficulties encountered in the school reform efforts in this school and in the district. The present chapter takes an historically informed look at these impediments to educational change.

Among the questions posed are, How does history help explain the chaos in the school, the neighborhood violence, the lack of functioning equipment, the teachers' professed inability to counter the "situation," their consequent "getting over," and their low expectations for the children? And, What insight can history provide into the tragedies in the lives of Marcy School students that work against successful teaching and learning in the educational setting?

More generally, this chapter assesses what the history of a city and its schools offers in our search for ways to improve the education of urban poor students. How does the city's economic and political past help us understand current schooling and educational reform? What does this past suggest is needed now?

The chapter also completes the book by developing a new vision of educational reform that takes into account the destructive results of urban history—overwhelming destitution in city environments.

LESSONS FROM HISTORY

To provide a backdrop for my analysis, I will summarize four points developed within the political and economic history presented in part II:

1. The social class and racial status of overall city and neighborhood population has been closely correlated with the level of the city's investment in education and with the district's success in educating its student population. Thus, when Newark was a leading industrial city and many children of the middle and more affluent classes attended the schools, the system was a model for others in the state. As children of different cultural backgrounds who were poor—Eastern European Catholics and Jews—began to predominate in the public school population, the district was unable to adequately serve significant percentages of these students. Then, beginning in the thirties, as economic and other social changes were creating a school system in which most students were white working class, investment and quality in all but the middle-class neighborhoods declined. After World War II, as the city schools filled with rural black poor, spending and educational quality in most city schools plummeted. By 1961, when the Newark schools were majority black poor, relative funding of the educational system reached its nadir. Continued ghettoization of the city's minority population—and educational inadequacy since then—has prevented further generations of Newark students from acquiring a worthwhile education.
2. The contours and fortunes of Newark's schools in the twentieth century have also been intimately linked to the economic transforma-

tions of the city—and to federal and state policy as well as to local
and national corporate decision making. Numerous policies and decisions contributed to the economic decimation of Newark, as the city's
middle-class population and jobs were supported in their move to
the suburbs and beyond. Among these policies are the following:
the federal redlining of city mortgage and renovation applications
beginning in the 1930s, and continuing until almost all of Newark
was redlined; federal tax regulations making corporate dispersion
to outside the cities cheaper than renovation in city locations; state
property tax laws that penalized the cities with shrinking amounts of
property to tax; and decisions by local industry, banks, and insurance companies whose investment in Newark was for most of the
century limited to the downtown business district. The transformation of the urban manufacturing economy to a white-collar clerical,
then to a service and sophisticated information base, also contributed
to the decimation of community jobs and city resources. As Newark's
economy changed and declined, the quality of the city's schools declined apace.

3. The political isolation of cities both before and after reapportionment
   in the sixties and seventies led to a century of tax and other financial
   policies that penalized cities—and therefore their schools. Unequal
   funding of city schools has, in the last 25 years, been challenged in
   more than half the states by advocates of poor school districts. Resulting reform efforts in most states, to date, however, have been
   too little and too late to reverse the decline of aged, decrepit school
   buildings, school personnel set in ways of teaching that have
   changed little in the last 60–70 years, and classrooms devoid of quality curriculum materials and programs. As Chapter 7 demonstrates,
   reforms of the last several decades in New Jersey have also been
   guided more certainly by class, race, and suburban personal income
   tax considerations than by educational best practice.

4. In part because of the absence of sufficient economic resources (entry-level jobs, for example, and political representation in state and
   federal legislatures), for most of the last 100 years the city's schools
   have been enmeshed in local networks of corruption and patronage
   run by white ethnic—and more recently, African American—minorities. Over a century of political appointments in the city schools of
   Newark has contributed to a staff that has over the years been less
   qualified than that in surrounding suburban districts.

Having reviewed these developments I intend to show how they
contributed to the situation I encountered in Marcy School.

Political Patronage

A fundamental but publicly unacknowledged problem in urban school reform today is the quality and commitment of inner city administrators and teachers—and the questionable ability or desire of some to participate in the rescue of the schools in which they work.

The principal at Marcy School had been a shop teacher at a Newark high school. He was appointed principal at Marcy without the benefit of additional course work or administrative training. By his own admission, he was "not the greatest principal in the world." The history of patronage in the district reveals that most probably he had not been appointed to provide leadership in a troubled school, but rather to do (or to return) a favor.

It is well known in Newark that most of the principals have for many years been appointed because they "knew someone" or because they paid someone a sum of money (New Jersey State Department of Education 1993; 1994b, 46). Echoing concerns of the Teachers College survey team in 1942 that political appointments had led to lower quality administration, a report by a state-mandated special investigation of Newark school administrative functions in 1975 stated that

> most of the problems [at the Board] seem to stem from a complete lack of competence on the part of the administrative staff. There appears to be an excess of school employees on the administrative payroll, . . . but more importantly there are people in middle and upper management positions who are totally unqualified to handle the positions they hold. (*Star Ledger*, February 9, 1975)

An article that appeared 14 years later in the same newspaper, on January 23, 1989, indicates that the problems continued:

> [Malcom George] the second Vice President of the Newark Board of Education pleaded guilty . . . to charges he solicited a $3,000 bribe from a teacher who sought to become a vice principal. . . . [The teacher] said others were purchasing vice principalships for up to $5,000, but he could purchase [the position] for $3,000.*

---

*For examples of articles charging or reporting patronage (including sale of jobs) in the Newark school district in the 1970s and the 1980s, see the following, among others: *Star Ledger* April 16, 1972; February 2, 1974; May 2, 1974; January 28, 1975; February 6, 1975; June 25, 1975; July 6, 1975; November 2, 1975; February 22, 1977; July 27, 1977; January 12, 1979; October 23, 1982; April 14, 1983; April 21, 1983; June 13, 1983; June 17, 1984; June 27, 1984; July 17, 1984; July 26, 1984; September 5, 1984; September 26, 1984; December 10, 1984; March 20, 1985; June 16, 1985; June 29, 1985. For summaries of corruption, patronage, and conditions in the Newark schools during the early 1990s, see the articles by veteran education reporter Robert Braun in the *Star Ledger* October 25, 1993; October 26, 1993; October 27, 1993; October 28, 1993.

Although there are also very fine administrators in the system, most were not appointed for their administrative skills. A longtime Newark teacher told me during my months at Marcy School, "In my opinion, the really talented teachers never get promoted—they're not [politically] connected." The central importance of the principal in creating and maintaining a good school climate and educational program is undeniable. The school change literature documents this at every turn. Yet the patronage system in large cities has been responsible for the appointment of many unskilled, educationally marginal school administrators, like the principal at Marcy School.

The history of patronage has also been partly responsible for those inner city teachers who are ineffective. One result of the sale of teaching jobs and patronage appointments in Newark was that, as noted in chapter 6, by the late 1970s at least half of all teachers were without professional preparation—they were uncertified, or on irregular (provisional, emergency, substitute) appointments. Most of these teachers are still working in the system. Moreover, evidence suggests that the process of political appointments continued throughout the 1980s and early nineties (New Jersey State Department of Education 1993; 1994b).

The following incident demonstrates one way in which political patronage works to retain ineffective teachers. One night during my months at Marcy School, a member of the board of education called the coordinator of the reform effort at home to inquire, "What the hell happened to Mr. Martin's papers?" Mr. Martin was a Marcy School teacher whose application for tenure had recently been denied by the principal, at the urging of the reform coordinator. This teacher, a former unsuccessful rookie police officer, had been hired without having had any education courses or other preparation. He was recognized and discussed by Marcy staff as "a disaster," as someone who "hated the kids and let them know it." (Perhaps the most offensive comment made to a child of those quoted in chapter 2—that a "fishy" odor on a child originated with her mother because the mother was a prostitute—was a statement from Mr. Martin.) His classes were more rowdy and louder than most, and many of his students roamed the halls during the day. Parents routinely protested when their children were assigned to him. Mr. Martin was politically connected, however. That night on the phone the official told the coordinator to redo the paperwork; Mr. Martin was subsequently tenured.

Ill-prepared when hired, under state mandate to teach rote, low-level skills, with little staff development to show them otherwise, and with too few quality curriculum materials (and often not even texts), many of the city's teachers are ineffective (New Jersey State Department of Education 1993, 10; 1994b, 66). As Linda Darling-Hammond points out,

> Studies have consistently found that, with little knowledge of learning or child development to guide them, teachers who lack preparation are more reliant on rote methods of learning, more autocratic in the ways they manage their classrooms, less skilled at managing complex forms of instruction aimed at deeper levels of understanding, less capable of identifying children's learning styles and needs, and less likely to see it as their job to do so. . . . (1996a, 6; see also 1992, 1996b)

Thus, the fact that teachers are appointed or retained on the basis of who rather than what they know and are able to do is of major consequence to the education of students in their classes, and to educational reform.

In this book, the history of patronage as a method by which city residents without access to other political and economic resources have taken care of themselves and their friends, is not offered as an excuse for such activities, but, rather, leads to a suggestion for a course of action that might weaken it as a system. If we were to provide political and economic resources in cities, especially sufficient numbers of decent jobs, so that patronage would not have to compensate for political and economic exclusion of city residents from other opportunities, we would lessen the material need for political appointments, and a meritocratic system might have a chance of taking hold.

As will be argued below, successful educational reform will require the political courage to remove and replace uncommitted and dysfunctional principals and teachers. It is not certain that even massive amounts of staff development can overcome years of habit, and state mandates of poor teaching. Moreover, effective performance in schools by teachers and principals requires, among other things, strong leadership at the district level, a good school climate, and adequate resources in students' lives and at teachers' work sites—all of which will need to accompany staff development.

Ghettoization of Minority Residents

The history of Newark and its schools reveals that many generations of African Americans have suffered from inadequate education there. It also indicates that the difficulty of teaching in and administering ghetto schools today is increased not only by the current tragic circumstances of students' lives, but by the compounded, familially transmitted effects of many generations of undereducation.

The concentration effects of poverty and racial isolation in urban ghettoes—the many generations of inadequate education and employment opportunities, and a long-term lack of resources for healthy and productive living for adults—results in malnutrition, prenatal and childhood disease, emotional trauma, a lack of material resources, neglect and sometimes abuse in children's' lives. This traumatic environment may produce daily acts of heroism in children as they negotiate a treacherous ghetto terrain (Kotlowitz 1991). However, the traumatic environment also leads to relatively high percentages of inner city students needing special services—neurological and psychological repair, remedial instruction, and other programs to address their many educational needs.

In 1992 in Newark, for example, 70% of the students were defined by the state as at-risk (low-income students at risk of educational failure and entitled to "at-risk aid"); 66.8% were remedial, between 7.1 and 15% were categorized as special education (depending on whose statistics one uses), and 11.4% were bilingual (Association for Children of New Jersey 1992, 65). In the city of Camden, New Jersey's poorest city, 73.5% were defined as at-risk, 78.7% as remedial, 9.3% were special education, and 8.3% were bilingual (39). By contrast, in typical middle-class districts in New Jersey, the percentages of children with special needs are considerably lower.

Natriello and Collins studied eleven New Jersey school districts in 1991–92. Five were poor urban districts, two were moderate-wealth districts, and four were high-wealth districts. The researchers found that percentages of students participating in free or reduced lunch programs, with limited English proficiency, and in special education in the *poorer* urban districts were 77.9%, 8.2%, and 9.1%, respectively. In the moderate and wealthy districts combined, the percentages of students in the same categories were 2%, 2.6%, and .01%, respectively (Natriello and Collins 1994, 2–3; see also Firestone, Goertz, and Natriello, 1997, Figs. 2.1, 3.1, and 3.2). In attempts to deal with these social effects, poorer urban districts in New Jersey spend up to one quarter of their budgets on special programming, which reduces the money that is available for the regular educational program (Firestone, Goertz, and Natriello 1994, 5).

Educational effects of the concentration of minority poor in urban ghettoes, and of the consequent low social status of the students and their families, can include a lack of accountability on the part of school staff. At Marcy School, for example, many teachers did not teach, the principal did not lead, and no sanctions were applied. Concentration effects of ghettoization can also include the stigmatization and consequent disrespectful, abusive treatment of students by white and black staff, as also occurred at Marcy School. Parents may complain to the school about the treatment their children receive, but they do not have the clout to prevent it. Neither state nor city government moved against child abuse in the Newark system, which, as noted in chapter 2, reported extremely high levels of child abuse by educational employees (New Jersey State Department of Education 1993, 68). This negligence—and the abuse itself, of course—indicate that state officials as well as school staff may regard ghetto children to be at best expendable, and at worst, appropriate targets.

Some local residents working in the school also took advantage of the children at Marcy by stealing their food. On five occasions that came to my attention during my work at the school, custodians or cafeteria workers stole, or left doors open for others to come in and steal, the food for the children's hot lunch. (Although there was no investigation, everybody "knew" this was what was happening.) During the few days following each theft, there was no lunch for the 497 free lunch students. To my knowledge no one was prosecuted or fired.

The refusal of New Jersey voters and of the legislature to adequately fund urban districts may express similar attitudes toward ghetto students as "uneducable" or "incorrigible," and certainly as unworthy of support. A 20-year mandate for a rote, low-level curriculum hints at ingrained racism. Local administrators, as well, may be revealing their own disdain for the students when they divert money from classroom instruction to jobs for local adults—for an overabundance of administrative positions, bus drivers, and cafeteria workers (New Jersey State Department of Education 1993, 9–10).

As shown in chapter 2, even the Marcy School curriculum—and the curricular reforms—which do not address the children's own heritage, suggest a lack of respect on the part of both black and white administrators and teachers for African American and other minority cultures. The isolation of the ghetto children from the mainstream of American life makes the middle-class curriculum, and language, alien to them; it can be confusing and debilitating.

The historical isolation of cities, and the concentration of minority poor in city neighborhoods, has contributed to the extreme separation in U.S. society between black and white, poor and more affluent, that has been noted by Hacker (1992), among others. This cultural gulf made cooperation and trust between parents and teachers in Marcy School and white professional and executive reformers unlikely. One of the more difficult tasks for reformers will be to overcome this tension and distrust. For indeed, the interpretations and activities of reformers may conflict with the current perceived needs or even jobs of teachers, administrators, and community aides, among others.

The history of Newark demonstrates the culpability of federal, state, national and local business and political groups in the development of minority ghettos. When, in the late nineteenth and early twentieth century, during the industrialization of the American economy, poor people in the city were needed as workers, they were wooed by the schools. Now, however, the poor, immigrant and native, do not seem to be valued as part of the economy—despite corporate protestations to the contrary. New Jersey public policy expert James Hughes and economist Joseph Seneca report, for example, that data confirm that the state has concentrated its economic development resources on strategies for high-skilled workers, research-based industry linked to higher education, and the diffusion of computer-based technology to the state's businesses in both the manufacturing and service sectors (Hughes and Seneca 1995, 19).

On the other hand, there has been little if any attempt in New Jersey to develop jobs with low- and middle-range manufacturing or service skills that would suit inner city residents (or others) lacking educational qualifications. In fact, many economists refer to these kinds of jobs as "dumbing down" the economy (4). It should be pointed out, however, that low- and middle-skill jobs were created or supported by the federal government in the 1930s—WPA jobs, for example—when white unemployment approached levels that have existed for over a decade in minority ghettoes today. Although the economy was certainly less sophisticated then, such jobs were not viewed by governments as "dumb," but as an important response to an emergency.

Municipal Overburden

In the late 19th and early 20th century, when cities were obviously central to the economy, and city students perceived to have an important future economic role, school buildings were erected that were often beautiful, enduring structures. Now that cities and their students are less highly valued, the cities' physical capital is left to decay (see Piccigallo, 1989; *New York Times* December 26, 1995). Marcy School, as noted in chapter 2, was built in 1861 for Irish and German workers in Newark's most prestigious and successful industries. The school had impressive woodwork throughout the building and a graceful Grecian frieze above the auditorium stage.

Most of Newark's school structures are now old: Thirty percent were built before 1890, 40% were built between 1900 and 1950, and only 30% have been built since 1950 (New Jersey State Department of Education 1993, 4). Marcy School's exterior walls are sufficiently deteriorated that, in the summer of 1993, burglars were able to scale one outer wall, to enter the window of a third floor computer room, by scraping indentations in the masonry as footholds. As in other cities, the buildings are in disrepair, and many are dangerous to inhabit. The Council of the Great City Schools in 1987 put a $5 billion price tag on upgrading the school buildings in its 50 districts.

The heightened municipal tax burdens of cities overwhelm the ability of local governments to meet, unaided, the educational and other social needs of residents. Of course, insufficiency of funding affects almost everything in schools—from lack of toilet paper and soap, to a lack of working equipment and insufficient numbers of computers and quality programs, to a lack of personnel adequately trained to enact reforms.

For example, Newark boasted two "Comer schools," named after James Comer, in the early 1990s. Comer schools are an attempt to improve student learning through the creation of a positive school environment, intensive psychological counseling of youth, integration of parents into school planning, and the establishment of a quality curriculum. Parents are paid for extensive participation. According to James Comer's prescription, mental health teams trained in "systems management" are intended to be an integral part of the school, are supposed to meet regularly to jointly plan school development and child development intervention strategies, and are to consistently and regularly intervene in classroom and school environments to foster psychologically healthy student responses. Arts and athletics programs in which the parents actively participate and which are integrated with the academic program, and a social skills curriculum to help children deal with adversity in social situations, as well as a "discovery room" containing interesting, hands-on curriculum items for children who need a psychologically safe place to spend time, are also part of the Comer model (Comer 1980). When the plan was implemented in the late 1960s in New Haven, Connecticut, costs were approximately $255,000 per year per school (58).

According to the principal of one of the two Newark Comer schools, Newark district did not make available sufficient funding or personnel to carry out the program. The number of trained staff for psychological intervention was insufficient to aid more than a handful of students; the mental health team that was available was not trained in systems management and did not assist in school planning. The district did not make money available to pay parents to participate; no external grants were obtained, and there were no district funds to develop arts or athletics or social skills programs; the school had no money to buy interesting curriculum materials for a discovery room. Because of duties at other schools, the mental health team met irregularly. While there were other reasons for the watered-down version of a Comer School, many of the deficiencies were attributable to a lack of district and school resources (Interview with principal of one of the Comer schools, May 9, 1993; principal's assessment confirmed by a longtime administrator at the Newark Public Schools Central Office, interviewed August 20, 1996).

The educational consequences of patronage appointments, of state mandates of rote teaching and educational underfunding, of ghettoization, and of longstanding municipal overburden are all to a significant degree themselves results of the protracted political and economic isolation of cities and their residents from legislative power and economic opportunity. Traditional types of educational reform, which do not attempt to repair or prevent these casualties, need to be augmented by a fuller, more comprehensive vision of social change.

A NEW VISION OF REFORM

Given the deep-structural diagnosis of educational problems presented in this book, what remedies can be suggested to rescue central city students and schools? Can we prevent the ghetto-death of another generation of schoolchildren? What vision could guide our activity?

Not only the diagnosis, but our prescriptions also must be deep-structural. The ultimate goals ought to be to redress the effects of destructive ghettoization of cities and their poorer residents, and to reduce or eliminate the political and economic isolation that produces such ghettoization. Indeed, we are aware—and over 30 years of research has consistently demonstrated—that academic achievement in U.S. schools is closely correlated with student socioeconomic status. To really improve ghetto children's chances, then, in school and out, we must (in addition to pursuing school-based reforms) increase their social and economic well-being and status before and while they are students. We must ultimately, therefore, eliminate poverty; we must eliminate the ghetto school by eliminating the underlying causes of ghettoization.

These long-range goals are likely to be criticized by some readers as "pie-in-the-sky." In the face of this charge I would respond with the following: To believe that fundamental social change is impossible, is to be overly oppressed by the parameters of the present. Are we unwilling to reach beyond the surface structure of our lives for new ideas?

Visionaries have long maintained that in order to make fundamental change we have to believe that such changes are possible; in addition, we need long-term plans for eliminating underlying causes. Unfortunately, educational "small victories" such as the restructuring of a school or the introduction of a new classroom pedagogical technique, no matter how satisfying to the individuals involved, without a long-range strategy to eradicate underlying causes of poverty and racial isolation, cannot add up to large victories in our inner cities with effects that are sustainable over time. Although vital and sometimes heroic, such achievements are often idiosyncratic and unconnected, and their existence in education typically subject to administrative or political whim. Moreover, the benefits of educational reform are nullified when the graduates of a restructured inner city high school have no more decent economic prospects greeting them than do graduates of unreformed schools.

In the hopes of providing a much-needed vision, then, and despite vulnerability to charges of idealism, I will lay out strategies for cities and for schools that, I believe, will produce changes ultimately leading to successful, enduring reform in our urban centers.

Revitalizing the Cities

Municipal overburden and the departure of manufacturing from cities may suggest the death of cities as sources of economic profit and importance. However, the cities have not died, they have changed—from manufacturing centers to centers of information technology and professional and other producer services (Sassen 1991). These changes need to be strengthened and some of the profits from these sources redirected into the neighborhoods which host them. A concerted national effort is needed to revitalize America's urban economies and to allow inner city residents to share in the prosperity.

In 1992 the U.S. Conference of Mayors in conjunction with the Economic Policy Institute sponsored a research and policy paper, "Does America Need Cities? An Urban Investment Strategy for National Prosperity." The authors of this report demonstrate that investment in urban areas in fact promises highest returns to the nation's economy, because such investment would be targeted where the greatest potential for growth exists. Where, the report asks, are the most underutilized people (particularly those who involuntarily work part-time or part of the year for lack of full-time jobs [Tilly 1990])? Where is the largest stock of usable or reparable infrastructure, and the biggest supply of conveniently located land? The answer, of course, is in America's cities (Persky, Sklar, and Wiewel 1992, 4).

The report notes that the cities of the nation, for all of their social problems, host the country's most productive economic activities (8). Despite the recent dispersion of small "edge" cities along state highways (Garreau 1991), economic and high-finance coordination (corporate headquarters), a good deal of high-level information processing, and technological and organizational innovation in the global economy are concentrated in our major cities (see Sassen 1991 for the most important of these cities and activities). Moreover, high-paying service jobs in the new information economy are attracted to secondary-tier cities like Newark (Sassen 1991). For example, Newark has recently completed the building of an impressive, high-tech legal and communications center in the downtown business district. This center has attracted new law firms, and brought back several that had abandoned the city (Dr. Clement Price, New Jersey historian and Newark resident; personal communication July 11, 1996).

The benefits of what economists call "agglomeration"—the geographic concentration of many and diverse types of workers, universities and technical institutes, and business firms, as well as high-tech cables and other in-place infrastructure—continue to enhance the value of doing business in cities (Persky, Sklar and Wiewel 1992, 4). In fact, metropolitan areas, surrounding and anchored by central cities, contain the majority of the American population; and metropolitan areas generate—although city residents do not receive—the overwhelming bulk of income in the United States. As of 1990, metropolitan areas accounted for 75% of the population, and 83% of income (U.S. Department of Commerce, in Persky, Sklar, and Wiewel, 9) Thus, cities remain a fundamental source of income for suburban residents (12). Moreover, most cities also provide cultural, medical, recreational, and higher-educational facilities heavily patronized by nonresidents (5).

Although in New Jersey the suburban economic-growth corridors along the orbits of interstate highways were the site of the overwhelming share of growth during the decade of the 1980s, in 1990, the top three employment municipalities in the state were still older cities: Newark, Atlantic City, and Jersey City (Hughes and Seneca 1992c, 20). Although Newark has lost 41.7% of its employment base since 1950, it still has a "significant, [although] vastly diminished," economic stature (24).

It is important to remember, however, that most of the jobs remaining in Newark are those requiring either college or more advanced degrees, which the majority of residents do not have. This is a significant reminder of the view that underlies the suggestions made in this chapter: Urban educational and social reform are symbiotic. Successful educational reform, leading to improved achievement by students, is not only dependent on a revitalizing city, but is itself a crucial component of more comprehensive change.

Such change will require concerted federal and state government action to jump-start economic growth in cities—and to spread the growth from downtown to the neighborhoods. Federal aid as a percentage of city budgets was reduced by nearly 64%, from an average of 17.7% in 1980 to 6.4% in 1990 (Simmens 1991, 8). This trend will need to be reversed. Investments in job creation, worker retraining, and infrastructure will be necessary. Quality education is required to assist underutilized inner city residents participation in an urban economic renaissance. As should be clear by now, however, at the same time that successful educational reform is an important ingredient of this renaissance for all urban residents, without a city's economic and political revitalization, educational revitalization in the ghetto is unlikely to occur. Both must be undertaken together.

Moreover, we must, for the first time, expect the large corporations to pay their share. Historically, society has cleaned up after the corporations: The costs of befouled water, air and soil, sustained unemployment and retraining costs as corporations close and relocate; as well as other problems created by industry and commerce, have been covered primarily by the American taxpayer. The large corporations have enjoyed almost unlimited freedom to escape from their responsibilities. One recent example is the following: The flight of corporations from Los Angeles has been a primary cause of the 40% unemployment rate among area blacks. After the 1992 riots in that city, a group of large corporations promised, at well-attended news conferences, to contribute $580 million in job creation investments. Four years later, in October of 1996, less than half the money had been raised, and the organization formed to coordinate the effort had closed. Only half of the 32 supermarkets that were supposed to bring lower prices and jobs to the area had been built (*New York Times* October 13, 1996).

One method of obtaining a corporate share of the cost to resuscitate the cities would be to enact a national urban tax on American-based corporations—payable no matter where in the global workshop they build their companies or make their money. Transnational corporations based in other countries that make profits from American sales or deals should pay this tax as well. I will propose further strategies for garnering corporate reparations later in the chapter.

The reinvigoration of city economies would enhance urban governments' access to political power at the state and federal levels. In addition, if minority voting districts were re-created, we could increase the number of black and Hispanic representatives, and thus augment the cities' political representation and power. The racism implicit in recent election redistricting, whereby some districts that were designed in the 1980s to allow voting blocks for racial groups have been dismantled, needs to be examined and rectified (*Star Ledger* June 30, 1995).

Resuscitation of central city neighborhoods would, of course, be expedited by renewed federal and state initiatives against poverty, housing and job discrimination, and against racial resegregation (Orfield and Easton, 1996; Kunen 1996). Admittedly, all this constitutes a "tall order." However, if we do not resuscitate our cities, we face an impossible situation regarding urban educational reform: Attempting to fix inner city schools without fixing the city in which they are embedded is like trying to clean the air on one side of a screen door.

Reforming the Schools as Part of a Broader Strategy for Social Change

Successful revitalization of the cities, and the spread of this new energy, enterprise, and profit to the neighborhoods, necessitates an education system that can prepare residents to participate. But, since educational upgrading of city schools is itself dependent on improvements in the lives and opportunities of inner city residents, educational reformers will need to link up with those who can create better social conditions.

We are beginning to see a resurgence of grassroots movements in this country (*New York Times* November 25, 1996; Walzak 1995). Rooted in labor unions, inner city neighborhoods, religious communities, and consumer activity, a burgeoning concern about safety, housing, jobs, the economy, and the environment is abroad in the land. Educational reformers need to work with people active in these movements, as well as with relevant established institutions, agencies, and nongovernmental organizations.

Educational reformers should join with the following:

- Community development organizations
- Groups that could create and fund WPA-type jobs
- Programs to train city residents for entry level as well as more sophisticated positions
- Legal services groups that offer counsel and guidance for negotiating the maze of social services, and that can initiate lawsuits to obtain full service if necessary

- Housing and tenants associations that work for better living conditions and sufficient low-income housing
- Health care providers who offer clinical services
- Coalitions for the homeless that offer temporary shelter when needed
- Voter registration organizations that not only assist in accessing the vote, but also in preparing lawsuits for redistricting efforts.

There are various sources of which I am aware that can provide information on the location and activities of people involved in social action groups. For example, the periodical *Poverty & Race*, published in Washington, DC by the Poverty and Race Research Action Council (a network of more than 8,300 activists, academics, and researchers) is an important source of information on activities relevant to progressive housing, legal services, the environment, education, immigration, employment, community development and organizing, and antipoverty and antidiscrimination work in cities nationwide. An additional source of information is Mickey Kaus of *The New Republic*, who has developed a proposal for public works programs, modeled on the WPA, that would create jobs for inner city residents (see also Wilson 1996a, 52–53).

Inner city community groups like the New Community Corporation in Newark, which has built homes, restaurants, day care centers, and supermarkets in the central city; or the Dudley St. Neighborhood Initiative in central city Boston, which successfully sought funding to renovate homes and organized the community against toxic waste dumping and the lack of social services there (Medoff and Sklar 1994); and similar groups in other cities are discussed in the monthly periodical, *The Neighborhood Works*, published in Chicago by a group of the same name. This periodical reports the activities of organizers across the nation who battle for jobs, build housing, and "make themselves heard."

Typically, however, groups like these do not interact with educators to renew neighborhood schools. Foundations and governmental granting agencies should link up school reform projects with grants to groups and agencies providing economic and social services to ghetto residents. Grant seekers will need to write proposals for projects that would increase and make meaningful the array of job, health care, housing and other services that are provided, and—importantly—write proposals for programs that would utilize ghetto schools as nuclei where referrals to these economic, political, and social services are made or where the services themselves are provided.

Coalitions of community activists, business, and local government groups in cities around the country are being funded by foundations such as the Local Initiatives Support Corporation, the nation's largest nonprofit community development support organization. St. Edmund's Redevelopment Corporation in inner city Chicago, Harlem Abyssinian Development Corporation in New York City, Tacolcy Economic Development Corporation in Miami, A Community of Friends in Los Angeles, as well as the New Community Corporation in Newark and the Boston Dudley St. Neighborhood Initiative mentioned above should all be involved in projects that connect with and reinforce school reform efforts (see Stodghill II 1996).

The goal of increased economic and political services in communities and at school sites is to ameliorate the worst effects of poverty, and to replace despair with hope and a sense of possibility. The aim is to create conditions for ghetto residents that will allow them to feel the sense of personal agency and self-determination that results from real economic and political possibilities—more common for middle-class and affluent families.

When inner city students and their families have access to the range of services that provide a realistic expectation that education will lead to better jobs, lives, and futures, as is expected in most middle-class and affluent homes, then the students will have a reason to make an educational effort. Realistic expectations that education will make a substantial, positive difference in the lives of their students may also motivate teachers and other school staff to a higher level of performance. At that point teachers, principals, and a quality curriculum can more easily make a difference in the lives of the inner city poor.

It is within this context of a broader strategy for social change that we should enact a number of educational reforms. Drawing on my experience in Newark, my reading of the school reform literature, and my interaction with colleagues involved in school reform in several cities, I will sketch what I perceive to be the most important practices of recent school reform efforts. It is important to remember, however, that to be successful in the long run, any educational initiatives that are chosen for inner city schools and districts will need to be combined with attempts to improve the economic and political milieus in which the schools are located.

State Control of Failing School Systems. A growing number of states (12 in December 1996) have passed laws allowing for state control of academically and/or financially bankrupt school systems. Laws in at least eight states—California, Connecticut, Illinois, Kentucky, New Jersey, New York, Ohio, and West Virginia—have resulted in the takeover of failing districts (Education Commission of the States 1996, 1997;

New York Times April 17, 1997). Although several problems, which I will discuss, typically accompany state takeovers of districts, these laws can be useful in that they can facilitate the removal of unqualified patronage appointments and nonperforming principals and teachers. Qualified individuals can be hired in their stead. The Illinois law allows teachers and principals in a long-term nonperforming school to be let go, and the school closed. In New York, community boards, and principals responsible for long-term underachieving schools can be removed (Hendrie, 1997; *New York Times* October 1, 1996). The New Jersey law allows a state superintendent 18 months in which to evaluate and remove unsatisfactory principals.

In Newark, the evaluation process determined in 1996 that 38 of 82 principals were unsatisfactory; 31 subsequently resigned, retired, or were fired (*Star Ledger* August 16, 1996, November 3, 1996). In the summer of 1996, the Newark state superintendent also laid off 634, or 7%, of the district's employees, almost all from groups whose numbers were excessive and who most probably had been patronage appointments: 124 from the central office, 124 bus attendants, 117, or 20% of, food service workers, and 40 custodians. The $26.3 million resulting from these layoffs was reallocated to services directly affecting the education of Newark students. Among these services are the following:

- Full-day kindergartens ($2.1 million)
- Guidance services for all primary and elementary students ($3.5 million)
- Addition of 81 security personnel to improve safety ($2.1 million)
- New alternative programs for students struggling in regular school ($1.1 million)
- Innovative instructional programs proposed by schools ($5 million)
- Support for special programs such as for substance abuse ($5 million)

In addition, the state superintendent in Newark created 28 new teaching positions and 80 new school-based staff development positions by reallocating $3.2 million of Title I funds (*Star Ledger* July 12, 1996).

There are problems that accompany state takeovers, however. One is that the years of state monitoring and of assigning penalties to districts that are perceived to be failing typically create a hostile relationship between state and district personnel. The punitive stance of state officials needs to be replaced by a supportive, collegial attitude. Indeed, in West Virginia, recent observers have attributed the success of a 1992 takeover of a district to the "goodwill" of state officials (Hoff 1996). However, more than goodwill is necessary. States that take control of local districts will need to ensure that increased funds are made available to provide sufficient technical assistance and other support necessary to improve educational quality. It is imperative to have money for pedagogical and technical training of teachers and principals, sources of computer expertise and of substantial curriculum improvement, as well as for equipment and capital needs. Moreover, funds must be backed up with accountability systems, needed to prevent their misuse.

A major problem can occur because state control is most often *not* accompanied by major infusions of funds for technical assistance or for upgrading curriculum and pedagogy; and safeguards against patronage and graft are not always established. In such cases, increases in student achievement have generally not occurred. For example, in Jersey City, in 1989 the first district overtaken by the state of New Jersey, money is still being lavished on the central administration, and very little has been spent on improving classroom instruction or curriculum. Student achievement has not risen (*Star Ledger* October 29, 1995, April 7, 1996).

In some cases, though, the mere presence of the state-assigned superintendent in a district can increase staff participation in reform. A university colleague of mine, active in educational reform in Newark schools both before and after the state came in, said that since the takeover, Newark teachers whom she has been attempting to engage in various projects for several years, now "return my phone calls and actually show up for meetings."

Thus, state authority that provides incentives and punishments can work against the inertia in big city systems. For example, reports from reform assessments in Chicago and Philadelphia find that much of the reform activity undertaken by teachers and administrators in restructured schools is "ceremonial" or amounts to going through the motions with little to show for a lot of activity (Consortium on Chicago School Research [Consortium] 1996, 72). Researchers argue that a "culture of resignation" among teachers and principals in many city schools prevents the psychological investment of staff in the hard work necessary to change an institution (New Jersey State Department of Education 1993, 4; Philadelphia Children Achieving Challenge, Executive Summary 1996, 9; Philadelphia Children Achieving Challenge 1996, 46). Moreover, the level of professional skill among urban teachers and principals is often undeveloped, and this can also affect the quality of reform that depends on their initiative and leadership (Christman and Macpherson 1996, 12, 34; Consortium 1995, 70; 1996, 72; New Jersey State Department of Education 1994b).

As a result of this culture of resignation and the undeveloped skills of many staff, top-down authoritative change backed by state sanctions can make an important contribution to reform in large urban districts. It is my belief that educational restructuring of city schools, in which power is often dispensed to teachers and principals, should be limited until the development of more constructive teacher and administrator skills and attitudes. However, in order to foster the development of these professional attitudes and behaviors, top-down control must be accompanied by effective nurturing of principals' and teachers' locally generated initiatives.

Renewal of School Leadership. Researchers studying school reform in Chicago argue that in order to lead a process that fosters the development of good schools, urban principals must develop strategies and skills that will enable them to "encourage" nonperforming teachers to quit; assess what good teaching is and recognize it in a job candidate; build teamwork and support teachers' individual initiative and faculty trust; find and strengthen ties to external networks and institutions; nurture a positive school vision and image; create an orderly, safe environment to promote instructional improvement and high academic expectations and demands; and apply sanctions (Consortium 1993, 26–29).

How this works in practice can be seen in the following example: During the planning of a Principals Leadership Institute in Newark in 1995, after the state came in, district principals were asked by facilitators to write anonymously what they considered to be the biggest problem they faced in making their school into a "good" school. The most common responses were statements like the following: "I have never seen a good school; I have no idea what it looks like." "I don't know how to run a good school; I've never been in one" (My notes from planning meeting July 24, 1996). The Newark Institute, begun in 1996 by the state superintendent in that city for all 82 principals and 161 assistant principals, introduces what I think are two very important components: visitation by principals and assistant principals to good urban schools in other cities, and significant amounts of expert assistance made available, on-site, to principals in their buildings. The institute makes available to school administrators direct access to experts in budgeting, interpretation of test scores, curriculum development, academic standard setting, and effective instructional leadership, among other areas. Funded by local foundations at a cost of over $500,000 in its first year, the institute also involves seminar sessions and retreats, and utilizes volunteers and paid consultants gathered by local colleges and universities as well as volunteers from several major nearby corporations.

Improvement of Teaching and Learning. In 1994-95, almost 8 years into the sweeping restructuring of Philadelphia's 22 comprehensive high schools into small charters (or learning communities, as they are now called), a team of 14 researchers assessed teaching and learning in five of the small schools. The researchers interviewed more than 300 students, shadowed 22 students over the course of a school day, and observed 122 classes. They concluded that the impact of reform was still "preliminary," in that

> the majority of students were disaffected by uninspired classes, inse-
> cure in buildings that were noisy and dilapidated, and offended by
> teachers who "don't teach" and school policies that punish or humili-
> ate them. . . . Only a small minority of students were in charters that
> offered real connection and caring along with rigorous course work.
> (Christman and Macpherson 1996, 12)

Students' complaints focused on their passive role in classroom work, teachers' lack of respect and concern for them, and the low academic standards that generally prevailed (Christman and Macpherson 1996, 11, 34; see also Philadelphia Children Achieving Challenge 1996, 31-32).

Other researchers have found poor teaching in restructured schools in Chicago (Hendrie 1996) and Newark (*New York Times* June 11, 1996; *Star Ledger* July 21, 1996). The improvement of teaching and learning is clearly of utmost importance for school reform, and does not occur because decision-making power has been restructured. Traditional staff development, often seen in terms of how many workshop days a state mandates, is typically "fragmented, ineffectual, and inefficient" (Corcoran 1995, 14-15). States and districts need to reorient staff development so that it is continuous and comprehensive, is directly connected to classroom practice and teachers' problems with curriculum development and implementation, involves visiting good schools and teachers, and provides extensive follow-up in teachers' own classrooms by those capable of providing technical assistance. Teachers need to join networks of professionals in other schools and cities struggling to improve classroom learning (Useem et al. 1995). My experience in Newark demonstrates that staff development ought not be confined to content knowledge and pedagogical skill, as vital as these are, but should also include the fostering in teachers of a proactive moral responsibility for respectful treatment of inner city youth.

However, the establishment of resources and structures for comprehensive and continuous efforts to improve teaching and learning is expensive, and involves considerably more than even a coherent and comprehensive array of staff development activities. In Philadelphia, for example, district reform plans in 1995 included the establishment of a "teaching and learning network," staffed by skilled personnel. Activities were created to provide support to teachers as they redesigned curricula and revised pedagogy and assessment procedures in accordance with emerging higher district standards. In the first 6 of 22 clusters of schools to participate in the reform, involving 67 of Philadelphia's schools, efforts to improve teaching and learning in one year (1995–96) cost $20 million.

The bulk of this sum was allocated as follows:

- $1.5 million for books and school libraries
- $1.7 million for "accommodation rooms" in elementary schools for children who are disruptive in class
- $3.7 million for teacher training and professional development
- $8.2 million for more computers, improved technology and access to computer networks, and the integration of the use of technology in classrooms
- $1 million for developing small learning communities (small schools or charters)
- $200,000 for leadership development in the small learning communities
- $2 million for the implementation of higher academic standards
- $2.1 million for salaries and benefits for personnel staffing the Teaching and Learning Network office (Philadelphia Children Achieving Challenge 1996, 61–62)

Quality curriculum, a necessary component of improved teaching and learning, is of course strengthened by infusions of books, libraries, computers, software, and other curriculum materials and equipment. But it is equally important that teachers be taught how to use the materials and equipment. A conversation with a colleague involved in reform assessment in Chicago on October 15, 1996 reminded me of my own experience in a New York City ghetto school in the late 1960s, and included her observation that "a lot of the extra money schools get here for materials is wasted. The [books and equipment] is stuffed in closets, and no one uses them. The teachers don't know how to use them." State and district plans must therefore include funds for training staff in the use of new materials.

Although in some localities teacher unions have been reluctant to support district reforms, improvement of teaching and learning has been fostered by peer assistance and review programs initiated by unions in several states. Such programs have been initiated by the American Federation of Teachers and National Education Association in Toledo, Cincinnati, and Columbus, Ohio; Rochester, New York; and Seattle, Washington. These have been successful in helping beginning teachers learn to teach, and for veterans who are having difficulty, to improve their teaching or to leave the classroom without evoking union grievances or delays. In each city, more teachers have been given help and have made major improvements in their teaching and more teachers have been dismissed than had ever occurred under the old systems of administrative review. In Toledo and Cincinnati, for example, roughly one third of the teachers who were referred to intervention each year of the program have left teaching by the end of the year through resignation, retirement, or dismissal (National Commission on Teaching and America's Future [National Commission] 1996, 99).

Preparation of New Teachers.   Educational reform needs to be bolstered by infusions of new teachers who are well prepared and motivated. I will describe goals and methods in the undergraduate urban teacher preparation program that I lead at Rutgers-Newark, as an example of a "best effort." My three colleagues in the education department and I have developed this program over the last decade from our understanding of urban systems, of learning and teaching, and in concert with our social values regarding the importance of educational equity.

Goals of the program include developing in new teachers respect for cultural and social diversity, and for the contributions of all groups to the development and functioning of our society. We attempt to imbue in our undergraduates a cultural sensitivity to urban poor children and their families, and to their moral, economic, and political right to an education equal to that offered students in affluent suburbs.

We also want to produce teachers who are highly educated in the arts and sciences, highly skilled pedagogically, and who are able to view teaching as a personally reflective yet collegial, collaborative enterprise. We want our graduates to be able to utilize student-centered teaching techniques where appropriate, and to value the varied abilities and kinds of intelligence of children from all backgrounds. We seek to demonstrate to our undergraduates, through numerous well-constructed fieldwork experiences in urban classrooms, that all students are capable of meeting the demands of cognitively complex activity.

We attempt to accomplish this with prospective teachers in the following ways. All of our students—whether in early childhood, elementary, or secondary education—major in one of the liberal arts, not in

education. Students must maintain a B overall grade point average, and must earn either an A or a B in all professional education courses and in their academic major. We require, in addition to a liberal arts background, participation in a professional program which includes an array of topics and activities that promotes a critical assessment of schools and city systems and a capacity to perform to a high standard in them. Students are taught the history of American cities, and of ways in which "ordinary" people have contributed to the U.S. past and have fought injustice (e.g., workers, African Americans, women). Students also study firsthand in local districts the political, bureaucratic nature of school systems. They read state and district reports that reveal the complex relationships between the two. In an extensive ethnographic assignment, students compare an urban and a suburban classroom and relate both to their own experiences as youngsters in school.

We introduce our undergraduates to teaching methods by assisting them in viewing urban public schools from the "bottom up": from the perspective of nondominant cultures and groups and of children living in poverty. For example, we assign a book on educating homeless children that presents viewpoints of the children themselves (Quint 1995); we discuss Lisa Delpit's critique of unmitigated use of process-centered approaches to teaching urban African American children writing and reading (Delpit 1996). Our students are also introduced to the idea that some children, feeling humiliated by teachers or the curriculum, act out the attitude "I will not learn from you" (Kohl 1994). In our classes we show and discuss videotapes of master teachers and administrators in urban settings, such as the documentaries "The Marva Collins Story" and "Good Morning, Miss Toliver." We then help our future teachers to construct lessons and unit plans that address the issues involved when one views schooling from the "bottom up." After this, they try out their activities with small groups of students in urban classrooms. At appropriate junctures, we provide undergraduates with information about and exposure to reforms currently being tried in various city schools, such as Accelerated Schools, the Comer approach, full-service schools, school-based management, and Success for All, and we offer them an opportunity to become involved in community work.

We instruct our undergraduates using a workshop approach, rather than through lectures, and model for them the strategies of interdisciplinary curriculum development and pedagogy, the techniques involved in using and adapting whole language, writing process, cooperative learning, and proactive classroom management strategies. Following Delpit (1996) and Natriello, McDill, and Pallas (1990), among others who have studied the learning behaviors of students who do not grow up hearing standard English at home or practicing the social behaviors that white middle-class advantage confers, we also stress the inadequacy of a rote basic skills approach to teaching these students, and show our future teachers how to combine cognitively demanding tasks within a structured, sequenced framework, when such a framework is necessary. All views regarding the teaching of reading are presented, and the challenging academic standards drafted by the National Council of Teachers of Mathematics (NCTM) and the National Academy of Sciences are used as resources for planning math and science lessons (NCTM 1989; National Research Council 1995).

Our program requires over 100 hours of field involvement prior to practice teaching. In addition to carrying out the ethnographic work mentioned above, students observe and assess curriculum and teaching in urban as well as suburban schools. Moreover, all methods courses involve trying out various pedagogical strategies in urban classrooms. During two and a half years of fieldwork experiences, a student in our program will probably meet some teachers who are not so good, and some who are excellent. With our undergraduates, we tease out the circumstances that lead to ineffective teaching and the attitudes and activities that foster success.

The practice teaching situation is the most difficult task not only for our undergraduates, but also for us. While the Rutgers-Newark Education Department is in the planning stages of creating a "professional development school," we do not yet have one. Thus, we are constantly seeking to develop cadres of highly skilled urban public school teachers with whom our student teachers could be placed. In most cases we are able to locate talented teachers.

One compensation for being without a Professional Development School is that through conscientious supervision and mentoring on our part, and by attempting to cluster student teachers in schools in which various reforms are being tried, we can help them to develop skills of collaborative planning and peer coaching that can overcome the negativity of other adults. This experience can produce beginning teachers who are able to perform well under the most adverse conditions. An additional advantage is that the public schools' cooperating teachers are often motivated to learn new techniques from our practice teachers, and we are thus helping to improve their skills as well.

Lastly, our program has not yet managed to devise a method of consistent mentoring of our graduates during their often difficult first year of teaching. Most locate teaching jobs in the northern New Jersey cities and towns not too far from the Rutgers-Newark campus, so we should be able to reach out to them; it is a task we are working toward accomplishing.

Programs to Address the Special Needs of Disadvantaged Students. The New Jersey Supreme Court ruled in 1990, 1994, and again in 1997, that disadvantaged students in poorer urban districts needed more than parity of expenditure and program quality of the regular education program with that of affluent suburban school districts (which would be reached through improvements in curriculum, teaching, and facilities, for example). They also need supplemental, compensatory initiatives to help them overcome their disadvantages, and to enable them to effectively utilize the regular educational program provided (*Abbott v. Burke* 1990, 287, 374; 1994, 444, 454; 1997, 58).

The Education Law Center in Newark has recently prepared a document that lists and describes programs with a solid research base showing improvement in the learning of urban poor students to whom the programs have been made available. These programs include

- Preschool and full-day kindergarten
- Reduced class size (in the context of improved pedagogy and teachers' skill in giving individualized attention)
- Bilingual, English as a second language instruction
- Programs for intensive curricular intervention—Success for All and the Comer Program (although lacking solid research showing success, anecdotal evidence supports the value of Reading Recovery and the Accelerated School methods as well).
- Programs to create safe schools
- School-to-work and school-to-college transition activities
- Full-service Schools (see below)
- Professional support for mainstreamed students and their teachers—a full 15% of New Jersey's 1.2 million students are classified and in special education. The percentages in cities are typically greater than the percentages in suburbs (*Star Ledger* October 8, 1996), and the percentage of children with profound disabilities is considerably greater in urban areas (Firestone, Goertz, and Natriello, 1997). Specialists in psychology, neurology, and other disciplines are needed to assist the development of students classified in one of the disability categories, as is professional support for teachers with mainstreamed "special ed" students in their

class but without the knowledge or skill to instruct them effectively.

Full-Service Schools.   In 1993, more than half of all states provided funds to stimulate the organization of school-based health programs, most often through competitive health department grants. However, the programs were few in number and widely scattered; only one tenth of the 7 million youth in the highest risk settings had access to health and social services in middle and high school sites (Dryfoos 1994, 15).

Until recently, New Jersey was a leader in full-service schools. In 1987, a $6 million foundation grant initiated the first substantial effort by a state to link schools and social service. Twenty-nine communities in the state won grants of $150,000 to $200,000 to set up centers at or near school sites (Dryfoos 1994, 241). As of 1994, the state had funded 42 schools in 30 districts with health, tutoring, and youth employment referral services. The Education Law Center reports that the initiative has stalled because state funding waned (1996, 19).

My own conception of full-service schools is more inclusive than found in these programs. I envision making the school a community center where the economic and political disenfranchisement of parents is addressed through a wide variety of services that include housing assistance, job training and career opportunities, preparation for General Educational Development (GED) certification, and college assistance. Parents may be considerably more likely to participate in school reform activities, and more involved in their children's education, if they see meaningful results for themselves from involvement at the school. Moreover, and of great importance to the overall goal of improving life in the city, by giving political and economic support services to parents at school sites, educators can make schools proactive change agents in the community at large.

FUNDING EDUCATIONAL REFORM

The above list of suggested educational reforms needs to be augmented by a discussion of funding. New Jersey, for example, has an aggregate current backlog of facility needs exceeding $10 billion, and these are greatest in the urban districts (Education Law Center, 1996, 6). Not only are buildings expensive to erect and maintain; most of the reforms I have recommended will also cost enormous sums, considerably more than districts currently have. In fact, reports from Chicago, Philadelphia, and Newark document the threat to educational reform from state and federal cuts to city budgets, state underfunding of formulas set by their own legislatures, and lack of other legal means whereby cities can raise money.

For example, in 1996, because of shortfalls of state and federal funding, the Philadelphia Board of Education was forced to cut $67 million from the reform agenda, $20 million from instructional expenditures, and $18 million from administrative and other nonteaching costs. The budget crisis has forced a scaling back of support for the reform agenda. In the Philadelphia teaching and learning network initiative discussed above, for example, the next 16 clusters of schools will be brought online with fewer resources than those of the first six. The first six clusters received $18 per student for improvement activities, but the next 16 will receive only half of that amount (Philadelphia Children Achieving Challenge 1996, 33–34).

Considerable amounts of money have already been spent on schools in America's inner cities, often with disappointing results. I do not believe that the reasons for the failure lie in the inability of urban children to learn or even in the inability of urban teachers to teach. I believe, rather, that both students and teachers are failing at least in part because they have lost hope. They have lost hope that hard work will produce results. In my months at Marcy School I heard 10-year-olds tell me that "there ain't no jobs out there, that's why kids drop out of school." As noted in chapter 2, a teacher wondered with me why her students, who could do the schoolwork in class, refused to even try to do well on the standardized tests. I believe that a reason for such "not trying" resides in anger and a sense of futility. And it is not just students who are angry and see a lack of possibility. The culture of resignation noted by Chicago and Philadelphia school researchers, and the degraded professional culture I spoke about in chapter 2, result to a degree from the loss of hope on the part of public school staff. If we can provide the conditions for a diminution of anger and a resurgence of hope in inner cities, by an aggressive assault on urban poverty and racial isolation, I believe that we will begin to see healthy returns on our investments in education there.

It is also important to make the point that it is less expensive to educate well than to pay later for the costs of an inadequate education. Low levels of literacy are highly correlated with welfare dependency and incarceration and their high costs (Educational Testing Service 1995; National Center for Education Statistics 1994). Nearly 40% of adjudicated juvenile offenders have learning disabilities that went untreated in school (Gemingnani 1994). Eighty-two percent of America's prisoners are high school dropouts (Hodgkinson 1992). The cost of incarcerating one young man is roughly $35,000 a year, more than tuition at Harvard University (Project South Washington 1996). Conservative estimates are that $1 invested in Head Start saves $3 in future costs to society (Stevens 1996). Natriello, McDill, and Pallas estimate that the loss to the nation because of the high school drop-out problem is approximately $50 billion every year in forgone lifetime earnings to those who did not complete high school, while, in addition, there are considerable losses in associated government tax revenues, greater welfare expenditures, greater costs of crime, and so on (1990, 42–43).

Despite these increased costs of failed inner city education, recent years have witnessed voter-approved tax and educational budget cuts in many states. Thus, the enormity of the task I have outlined here, and the chances for new policies and funding for programs that attack poverty and education in concert may appear bleak. It may seem as if the job of educational reform is impossible. Indeed, it *will* be impossible if we do not convince foundations, middle-class and affluent taxpayers, corporations, and politicians that such fundamental changes in the distribution of goods and services—and money—are not only necessary, but in their own interest. This task involves old-fashioned political struggle.

COMPLACENCY, RESIGNATION, AND FEAR

Chief Justice Weilentz of the New Jersey Supreme Court, in the potentially revolutionary *Abbott v. Burke* decision in 1990, wrote that

> there is solid agreement on the basic proposition that conventional education is totally inadequate to address the special problems of the urban poor. Something quite different is needed, something that deals not only with reading, writing, and arithmetic, but with the environment that shapes these students' lives and determines their educational needs. (372)

I am tempted to ask, How bad does it have to get in inner cities, and inner city schools, before we as a nation admit the truth of Justice Weilentz's statement? What will induce us to find the intolerable conditions there unacceptable? Perhaps self-interest is the prime mover. Therefore, it is important to note that it is increasingly difficult for suburban residents to escape the effects of inner city poverty and rage. Moreover, the problems of the cities are rapidly becoming the problems of the suburbs, where crowding and automobile congestion, poverty, and educational underfunding are all on the rise (Persky, Sklar, and Wiewel 1992, 5). Indeed, unemployment has become a problem in suburb as well as city. A 1996 *New York Times* report revealed sluggish growth in New Jersey's affluent suburbs, which had "long [been] the muscle in the region's economy." The report stated that the suburbs still lag behind the nation in job growth following the recession of 1992 (May 8, 1996).

Between 1993 and 1996, high schools in several of the most affluent New Jersey towns experienced serious drug and violence problems; the students in some middle-class New Jersey towns received instruction in broom closets and hallways, their sports programs eliminated, and their boards of education told by the governor to cut costs, despite increases in state taxes (*Star Ledger* January 31, 1996; *West Orange* [New Jersey] *Chronicle* February 15, 1996).

The fact that urban problems are increasingly the problems of the suburbs indicates that "we are all in this boat together," and—if we do not pull together—the boat may capsize and we will all sink. The lack of a Will to Cooperate (the lack of a social compact) is perhaps the biggest problem we face in revitalizing cities and city schools.

We lack a social will, but we do not lack social capacity. For there are, indeed, sufficient funds in this country to carry out all the initiatives listed here. The United States has one of the lowest tax rates of all advanced capitalist nations (only Turkey and Australia have lower tax burdens) (Mishel and Bernstein 1994, 86–87). In 1947 the effective tax rate on corporations was 50.9%; in 1993 it was 25.8% (102–103). In the 1950s, corporations paid 31% of the federal government's general revenues. In 1993, they paid just 15% (Bartlett and Steele 1994).

There are numerous tax inequities that, if eliminated, could provide considerable income for social investment. Social Security tax, for example, in 1996 applied only to the first $62,700 of earned income. If there were no ceiling on income that was taxed, and the wealthy were to pay Social Security tax on all their earned income, as do the majority of working Americans, the government would take in over $50 billion more every year (Zepezauer and Naiman 1996, 38, 167). Wise investment of these funds would yield enormous sums that could be used for social spending.

Moreover, even as a growing number of Americans with modest incomes are paying capital gains taxes on profits from the sale of stocks, land, or other assets, wealthy taxpayers can take advantage of a growing arsenal of exotic, but legal, Wall Street techniques to delay or entirely avoid taxes on their investment gains. According to David Bradford, an economist at Princeton University and a critic of the current income tax system, "The simple fact is that anyone sitting on a big pot of money today probably isn't paying capital gains taxes . . . the people who get stuck paying capital gains taxes [are] the ordinary investors . . . '' (*New York Times* December 1, 1996).

In addition to making taxes more equitable, there are other methods of garnering money for social spending. The government military budget, for example, still consumes huge portions of our resources. The Center for Defense Information, a Washington institute run by retired generals and admirals, estimates that we spend $327 billion a year on defense—if hidden costs like fuel for nuclear weapons are included (Zepezauer and Naiman 1996, 13–14). Subsidies of agribusiness are an estimated $18 billion a year; and 90% of these direct government subsidies go to the largest 18% of farms—the conglomerates—while 64% of all farmers receive nothing at all (Runge, Schnittker, and Penny 1995).

Over $12 billion a year in additional taxes could be collected from transnational companies without increasing current rates if present laws were enforced. Of the U.S.-based transnationals with assets over $100 million, 37% paid no federal taxes at all in 1991, and the average tax rate for those that did pay was just 1% of gross receipts. Of foreign-based transnationals, 71% paid no U.S. income tax on their operations in this country, that is, on the profits they earned in the United States, and the average rate for those that did pay was just 0.6% of gross receipts (Estes, 1993; Zepezauer and Naiman 1996, 70). As these examples suggest, there are huge sums of money that would be available to the federal government for social spending if the large corporations were to pay their share and if other tax inequities were remedied.

Materials published by a Boston group called United for a Fair Economy make available organizing resources to garner support for bills such as Congressional Bill H.R. 2534, the Corporate Responsibility Act, which would cut $800 billion in subsidies to corporate America, and H.R. 620, the Income Equity Act, which would boost the minimum wage and deny corporations the ability to deduct executives' excessive salaries from their taxes (United for a Fair Economy 1996; see also the periodical, *Too Much*, published by the Council on International and Public Affairs in New York City; and Derber 1996). Discussion of these bills and related issues with colleagues, students, and others is an example of the political work that needs to be undertaken if we are going to open up the coffers of corporate America to the benefit of the inner cities.

The coffers of the corporate sector are indeed full. Transnational corporations spend trillions of dollars on investment for future profits in the Third World and in former Communist countries of Eastern Europe, rather than in cities and neighborhoods at home. Articles in the business press describe the magnitude of these investments. The following, for example, appeared in *Business Week*: "'Borderless Finance: Fuel for Growth': As trillions of dollars and a barrage of financial instruments whirl around the globe, whole new industries will emerge—but not without a price" (Javetski 1994); or "Global Gamble: Morgan Stanley is Charging into the Third World. Will It Pay Off?" (Nathaus 1996). This article details Morgan Stanley's investments in Mexico, Brazil, China, Malaysia, India, and Indonesia (among 22 countries in which it is pursuing "many types of business"). The article states, "Morgan is not alone in betting on the Third World. It is waging a fierce battle with such U.S. arch rivals as Merrill Lynch, Goldman Sachs, J. P. Morgan, and too many foreign banks and brokers to mention" (64).

A 1993 article describes the foray of General Electric, America's third-most-profitable company, into the markets of China, India, and Mexico. The strategy is to penetrate fresh markets, rather than to hunt for cheap labor. "The day is not far off when [General Electric] will earn more money outside [U.S.] borders than inside. . . . Being national doesn't pay," stated the vice-chairman. One of General Electric's goals in China is to finance massive capital spending projects, such as a superhighway, and in Mexico, to build a $600 million natural-gas-burning power plant. "If [funding infrastructure development in the Third World] is wrong, it's a couple of billion dollars," stated the company chairman and chief executive officer. "If it's right, it's the future of the next century for this company" (Smart 1993).

The global power of corporate finance may have most of us convinced that the vast corporations, and the capitalist system that they represent, are all-powerful and that we are impotent. Or perhaps most of us are simply resigned to, for example, the poor being "always with us"; perhaps we are complacent in the face of drastic inequality because we ourselves are not yet suffering; and perhaps we are afraid for our slippery fortunes—often made in competition with and therefore always vulnerable to—the efforts of others.

But attitudes such as these are the bedrock of the status quo. Redlining of racially mixed neighborhoods does not occur without the support of the majority of the population—or without their silent assent. Corporate profits flow to other countries because such practices go unchallenged. We have been in a long period of social quiescence. There has not, in recent years, been sufficient will to challenge federal and state policies that maximize private wealth while minimizing the public good.

However, it may be that we are drawing near to a period of cultural and social ferment. The resurgence of a populist movement, noted above, may be a harbinger of change. My college students of the last several years are more concerned about poverty and racial discrimination than were students a decade ago. In fact, every 20 to 30 years during this century, Americans have responded to social distress and unrestrained corporate expansion and profiteering with a flowering of egalitarian ideals. After the massive, unregulated global flow of capital and industrial exploitation at home in the late nineteenth century, came the Progressive Era and the popular expansion of the American Socialist Party. After the untrammeled corporate spending and expansion of the 1920s came the New Deal and the growth of the labor movement and of the U.S. Communist Party. After the quiescent 1950s and the alleged entrenchment of a "corporate mentality" in all our psyches came the turbulent and egalitarian 1960s. We need to entertain the possibility—and work for the eventuality—that another new day will dawn.

Those of us who are not resigned, complacent, or afraid must band together to engage in struggles to change others' attitudes and to alter existing political and economic priorities and laws. Educational reformers, housing activists, Legal Aid attorneys, health care progressives, community organizers, and those who are in a position to create jobs and fund social change need to work together. Together we can summon from ourselves and others the outrage, the combativeness, and the courage that will transform our inner cities, and our inner city schools.

References

Abbott v. Burke 100 N.J. 269 (1985).

Abbott v. Burke 119 N.J. 287 (1990).

Abbott v. Burke 135 N.J. 444 (1994).

Abbott v. Burke M622, Slip Op., May 14, 1997.

Anyon, Jean. 1994a. The Retreat of Marxism and Socialist Feminism: Postmodern and Poststructural Theories in Education. *Curriculum Inquiry* 24 (2): 115–134.

Anyon, Jean. 1994b. Teacher Development and Reform in an Inner City School. *Teachers College Record* 96 (1): 14–31.

Anyon, Jean. 1995a. Educational Reform, Theoretical Categories, and the Urban Context. *Access: Critical Perspectives on Culture and Policy Studies in Education (New Zealand)* 14 (1): 1–11.

Anyon, Jean. 1995b. Inner City School Reform: Toward Useful Theory. *Urban Education* 30 (1): 56–70.

Association for Children of New Jersey. 1992. *Keeping the Focus on Children: Accountability for Educational Improvement in the Special Needs Districts.* Newark: Author.

Ayres, Leonard P. 1909. *Laggards in Our Schools: A Study of Retardation and Elimination in City School Systems.* New York: Russell Sage Foundation.

Baker v. Carr 369 U.S. 189 (1962).

Baltzell, E. Digby. 1958. *Philadelphia Gentlemen: The Making of a National Upper Class.* Glencoe, Ill: Free Press.

Banfield, Edward C. and James Q. Wilson. 1963. *City Politics.* New York: Vintage Books.

Baratz, Joan. 1969. Teaching reading in an Urban Negro School System. Pp. 92–116 in *Teaching Black Children to Read*, ed. Joan Baratz and Roger Shuy. Washington, DC: Center for Applied Linguistics.

Baratz, Joan. 1970. Beginning Readers for Speakers of Divergent Dialects. Pp. 77–83 in *Reading Goals for the Disadvantaged*, ed. J. Allen Figurel. Newark, Del: International Reading Association.

Barbaro, Fred. 1972. Political Brokers. *Society* 9 (September/October): 42–54.

Bartholomew, Harland and Associates. 1944. A Preliminary Report on the Background and Character of the City of Newark, New Jersey. St. Louis, Mo: Author. Typescript.

Bartholomew, Harland and Associates. 1945. A Preliminary Report on Housing Conditions and Policy for Newark, New Jersey. St. Louis, Mo: Author. Typescript.

Bartlett, Donald L. and James B. Steele. 1994. *America: Who Really Pays the Taxes?* Portland, Ore: Touchstone Press.

Berkeley, Ellen Perry. 1971. Newark: Bellweather City. *Architectural Forum* (September): 40–45.

Bernard, Richard M. and Bradley R. Rice, eds. 1985. *Sunbelt Cities: Politics and Growth Since World War II.* Austin: University of Texas Press.

Berry, Brian. 1979. *The Open Housing Question: Race and Housing in Chicago, 1966–1976.* Cambridge, Mass: Ballinger.

Braun, Robert. 1979. Thorny Issues of School Financing—an Analysis. (Newark) *Star Ledger*, November 18, 1979.

Brophy, Paul C. 1993. Emerging Approaches to Community Development. Pp. 213–230 in *Interwoven Destinies: Cities and the Nation*, ed. Henry G. Cisneros. New York: W. W. Norton.

Brown, John Seely. 1991. Research That Reinvents the Corporation. *Harvard Business Review* (January/February): 101–117.

Bruce, William George. 1904a. Questions Regarding Teachers. *American School Board Journal* (January): 6.

Bruce, William George. 1904b. School Administrators. *American School Board Journal* (March): 13.

Burr, Nelson R. 1942. *Education in New Jersey: 1630–1871.* Princeton, NJ: Princeton University Press.

Butts, R. Freeman. 1978. *Public Education in the United States: From Revolution to Reform.* New York: Holt, Rinehart and Winston.

Butts, R. Freeman and Lawrence A. Cremin. 1953. *A History of Education in American Culture.* New York: Holt, Rinehart and Winston.

Callahan, Raymond C. 1962. *Education and the Cult of Efficiency: A Study of the Social Forces That Have Shaped the Administration of the Public Schools.* Chicago: University of Chicago Press.

Carnegie Forum on Education and the Economy. 1986. *A Nation Prepared: Teachers for the 21st Century.* New York: Carnegie Corporation.

Carnoy, Martin. 1982. Economics and Education. Pp. 519–529 in *The Encyclopedia of Educational Research*, 5th ed., Vol. 2, ed. Harold E. Mitzel. New York: Macmillan.

Carnoy, Martin and Henry Levin. 1985. *Schooling and Work in the Democratic State.* Stanford, Ca: Stanford University Press.

Cazden, Courtney. 1970. The Neglected Situation in Child Language Research and Education. Pp. 81–101 in *Language and Poverty: Perspectives on a Theme*, ed. Frederick Williams. Chicago: Markham.

Centolanza, Louis R. 1986. The State and the Schools: Consequences of Curricular Intervention, 1972–1980. Ed.D. diss., Rutgers University.

Chamber of Commerce of Greater Newark. 1989. *Greater Newark: A Microcosm of America.* Chatsworth, Ca: Windsor.

Christman, Jolley Bruce, and Pat Macpherson. 1996. *The Five School Study: Restructuring Philadelphia's Comprehensive High Schools.* Philadelphia: Research for Action.

Cisneros, Henry G., ed. 1993. *Interwoven Destinies: Cities and the Nation.* New York: W. W. Norton.

Clark, Kenneth. 1965. *Dark Ghetto: Dilemmas of Social Power.* New York: Harper and Row.

Cohen, David. 1982. Policy and Organization: The Impact of State and Federal Educational Policy on School Governance. *Harvard Educational Review* 52 (4): 474–499.

Cohen, Michael. 1990. Key Issues Confronting State Policymakers. Pp. 251–288 in *Restructuring Schools: The Next Generation of Educational Reform,* ed. Richard F. Elmore and Associates. San Francisco: Jossey-Bass.

Cohen, Ronald D. 1990. *Children of the Mill: Schooling and Society in Gary, Indiana, 1906–1960.* Bloomington and Indianapolis: Indiana University Press.

Comer, James P. 1980. *School Power: Implications of an Intervention Project.* New York: Macmillan, Free Press.

Conforti, Joseph M. 1972. Newark: Ghetto or City? *Society* 4 (October): 20–32.

Conforti, Joseph M. 1974. The Equity Package: Cities, Families and Schools. *Society* 11 (November/December): 22–33.

Consortium on Chicago School Research. 1993. *A View from the Elementary Schools: The State of Reform in Chicago.* Chicago: Author.

Consortium on Chicago School Research. 1995. *Charting Reform: Chicago Teachers Take Stock.* Chicago: Author.

Consortium on Chicago School Research. 1996. *Charting Reform in Chicago: The Students Speak.* Chicago: Author.

Cook, Fred J. 1974. Who Rules New Jersey? Pp. 73–96 in *Theft of the City: Readings on Corruption in Urban America,* ed. John A. Gardiner and David Olson. Bloomington and London: Indiana University Press.

Corcoran, Thomas C. 1995. *Transforming Professional Development for Teachers: A Guide for State Policymakers.* Washington, DC: National Governors' Association.

Corson, David B. 1921. Some Ideals and Accomplishments of the Newark School System. National Education Association Proceedings and Addresses: 707–713. Newark, NJ.

Corson, David B. 1924. Leading School Systems in New Jersey: The Newark System. *New Jersey Journal of Education* 13 (March): 1–26.

Council of the Great City Schools. 1987. *Challenges to Urban Education: Results in the Making.* Washington, DC: Author.

Council of the Great City Schools. 1994a. *Critical Educational Trends: A Poll of America's Urban Schools.* Washington, DC: Author.

Council of the Great City Schools. 1994b. *National Urban Education Goals: 1992–1993 Indicators Report.* Washington, DC: Author.

Council on International and Public Affairs. 1996. *Too Much.* New York: Author.

Cuban, Larry. 1990. Reforming Again, and Again, and Again. *Educational Researcher* 19 (January–February): 3–13.

Cubberly, Ellwood P. 1905. *School Funds and Their Apportionment.* New York: Teachers College Press.

Cubberly, Ellwood P. 1919. *Public Education in the United States*. Boston: Houghton Mifflin.

Cullinan, Bernice E. 1974. *Black Dialects and Reading*. Urbana, Ill: National Council for Teachers of English.

Cunningham, John T. 1988. *Newark*. rev. ed. Newark: New Jersey Historical Society.

Curvin, Robert. 1975. The Persistent Minority: The Black Political Experience in Newark. Ph. D. diss., Princeton University.

Curvin, Robert. 1977. Black Ghetto Politics in Newark After World War II. Pp. 145–160, in *Cities of the Garden State: Essays in the Urban and Suburban History of New Jersey*, ed. Joel Schwartz and Dan Prosser. Dubuque, Iowa: Kendall-Hunt.

Darling-Hammond, Linda. 1992. Teaching and Knowledge: Policy Issues Posed by Alternate Certification for Teachers. *Peabody Journal of Education* 67 (3): 123–154.

Darling-Hammond, Linda. 1996a. The Right to Learn and the Advancement of Teaching: Research, Policy, and Practice for Democratic Education. *Educational Researcher* 25 (6): 5–17.

Darling-Hammond, Linda. 1996b. Restructuring Schools for High Performance. Pp. 144–194 in *Rewards and Reform: Creating Educational Incentives That Work*, ed. Susan Fuhrman and Jennifer O'Day. San Francisco, Ca: Jossey-Bass.

Darling-Hammond, Linda, Jacqueline Ancess, and Beverly Falk. 1995. *Authentic Assessment in Action: Studies of Schools and Students at Work*. New York: Teachers College Press.

Darling-Hammond, Linda, and E. Sclan. 1996. Who Teaches and Why: Dilemmas of Building a Profession for Twenty-First Century Schools. Pp. 67–101 in *Handbook of Research on Teacher Education*, ed. J. Sikula, T. Butter, and E. Guyton. New York: Macmillan.

David, Jane L. 1990. Restructuring in Progress: Lessons from Pioneering Districts. Pp. 209–250 in *Restructuring Schools: The Next Generation of Educational Reform*, ed. Richard F. Elmore and Associates. San Francisco: Jossey-Bass.

Decter, Stephen A. 1959. The Politics of Municipal Charter Revision: Newark, NJ, 1947–1953. Senior thesis, Princeton University.

Delpit, Lisa. 1996. *Other People's Children*. New York: New Press.

Deming, W. Edwards. 1982. *Quality, Productivity, and Competitive Position*. Cambridge, Mass: MIT Press.

Derber, Charles. 1996. *The Wilding of America: How Greed and Violence are Eroding Our National Character*. New York: St. Martin's Press.

Dolce, Philip C. 1976. *Suburbia: The American Dream and Dilemma*. New York: Anchor Books.

Douglas, Philip Le B. 1972. Reform in Newark: The Response to Crisis, 1953–1972. Senior thesis, Princeton University.

Drake, St. Clair and Horace R. Cayton. 1945. *Black Metropolis: A Study of Negro Life in a Northern City*. New York: Harcourt Brace.

Dryfoos, Joy. 1994. *Full-Service Schools: A Revolution in Health and Social Services for Children, Youth, and Families*. San Francisco: Jossey-Bass.

Edmonds, Ron. 1979. Effective schools for the Urban Poor. *Educational Leadership* 37 (October): 15–18.

Edsall, Thomas Byrne and Mary D. Edsall. 1991. *Chain Reaction: The Impact of Race, Rights, and Taxes on American Politics.* New York: W. W. Norton.

Education Commission of the States. 1995a. *School Finance Litigation Activities.* Denver: Author.

Education Commission of the States. 1995b. School Finance Litigation List (Active Lawsuits and Year Filed). Denver: Author.

Education Commission of the States. 1996. Files on Academic and Financial Bankruptcy of School Districts. Denver: Author.

Education Commission of the States. 1997. Academic Bankruptcy Policy Brief. Denver: Author.

Education Law Center. 1996. Plaintiffs' Brief in Support of Motion in Aid to Litigants' Rights. (April 18). Newark, NJ: Author. Typescript.

Education Trust. 1996. *Education Watch: The 1996 Education Trust State and National Data Book.* Washington, DC: Author.

Educational Testing Service. 1991. *The State of Inequality.* Princeton, NJ: Author.

Educational Testing Service. 1995. *Literacy and Dependency: The Literacy Skills of Welfare Recipients in the United States.* Princeton, NJ: ETS Policy Information Center.

Eiger, Norman. 1976. The Newark School Wars: A Sociohistorical Study of the 1970 and 1971 Newark School System Strikes. Ed.D. diss., Rutgers University.

Elmore, Richard F. and Associates. 1990. *Restructuring Schools: The Next Generation of Educational Reform.* San Francisco: Jossey-Bass.

Elmore, Richard F., Penelope Peterson, and Sarah McCarthey. 1996. *Restructuring in the Classroom: Teaching, Learning, and School Organization.* San Francisco: Jossey-Bass.

Estes, Paul. 1993. *Who Pays? Who Profits? The Truth About the American Tax System.* Vancouver, Wash: IPS.

Fannon, Frantz. 1967. *Black Skin, White Masks.* New York: Grove Press.

Faust, Dean. 1994. Financing World Growth. *Business Week* (October 3): 100–104.

Field, Alexander James. 1976. Educational Expansion in Mid-Nineteenth Century Massachusettes: Human-Capital Formation or Structural Reinforcement? *Harvard Educational Review* 46 (4): 521–552.

Fine, Michelle, ed. 1994. *Chartering Urban School Reform: Reflections on Public High Schools in the Midst of Change.* New York: Teachers College Press.

Firestone, William, Margaret Goertz, and Gary Natriello. 1994. *The Myth of Bottomless Pits and Crumbling Lighthouses: Two Years of New Jersey's Quality Education Act.* New Brunswick, NJ: Center for Educational Policy Analysis at Rutgers University.

Firestone, William, Margaret Goertz, and Gary Natriello. 1997. *From Cashbox to Classroom: The struggle for fiscal reform and educational change in New Jersey.* New York: Teachers College Press.

Firestone, William A., Gary Natriello, and Margaret Goertz. 1994. The QEA: Myth and Reality. *New Jersey Reporter* (September/October): 17–25.

Fossey, Richard. 1996. Kidding Ourselves about School Dropout Rates. *The Harvard Education Letter* (May/June): 5–7.

Freire, Paulo. 1970. *Pedagogy of the Oppressed*. New York: Herder and Herder.

Fullan, Michael (with Suzanne Steigelbauer). 1991. *The New Meaning of Educational Change*. New York: Teachers College Press.

Galishoff, Stuart. 1988. *Newark, The Nation's Unhealthiest City: 1832–1895*. New Brunswick, NJ: Rutgers University Press.

Garreau, Joel. 1991. *Edge City: Life on the New Frontier*. New York: Doubleday.

Gemingnani, Robert. 1994. Juvenile Correctional Education: A Time for Change. Office of Juvenile Justice and Delinquency Prevention Update on Research. *Juvenile Justice Bulletin* (October).

Gersman, Elinor Mondale. 1969. Education in St. Louis, 1880–1900: A Case Study of Schools in Society. Ph.D. diss., Washington University.

Ginzberg, Eli. 1993. The Changing Urban Scene: 1900–1960 and Beyond. Pp. 33–47 in *Interwoven Destinies: Cities and the Nation*, ed. Henry G. Cisneros. New York: W. W. Norton.

Glazer, Nathan. 1993. City Leadership in Human Capital Investment. Pp. 250–272 in *Interwoven Destinies: Cities and the Nation*, ed. Henry G. Cisneros. New York: W. W. Norton.

Goertz, Margaret E. 1991. *A Quest for Equal Educational Opportunity in NJ: Abbott v. Burke and the Quality Education Act of 1990*. Working paper no. 19, Woodrow Wilson School of Public and International Affairs, Princeton University.

Goertz, Margaret E. 1992. The Development and Implementation of the Quality Education Act of 1990. Consortium for Policy Research in Education, Eagleton Institute of Politics, Rutgers University. Unpublished paper.

Goodlad, John I. 1994. *Educational Renewal: Better Teachers, Better Schools*. San Francisco: Jossey-Bass.

Goodlad, John I. 1990. *Teachers for Our Nation's Schools*. San Francisco: Jossey-Bass.

Gordon, David M. 1978. Capitalist Development and the History of American Cities. Pp. 25–63 in *Marxism and the Metropolis: New Perspectives in Urban Political Economy*, ed. William K. Tabb and Larry Sawers. New York: Oxford University Press.

Governor's Select Commission on Civil Disorder, State of New Jersey. 1968. *Report for Action*. Trenton, NJ: Author.

Graff, Harvey J. 1979. *The Literacy Myth: Literacy and Social Structure in the Nineteenth-Century City*. New York: Academic Press.

Graham, Hugh Davis. 1984. *The Uncertain Triumph: Federal Education Policy in the Kennedy and Johnson Years*. Chapel Hill: University of North Carolina Press.

Grant, Gerald. 1988. *The World We Created at Hamilton High School*. Cambridge, Mass: Harvard University Press.

Greater Newark Chamber of Commerce. 1971. *The Report of the Survey of the Public Schools of Newark, New Jersey*. 7 Vols. Newark, NJ: Author.

Groh, George W. 1972. *The Black Migration: The Journey to Urban America*. New York: Weybright and Talley.

Grubb, Norton, and Marvin Lazerson. 1974. *Education and Industrialism: Documents in Vocational Education, 1870–1970*. P. 328 in *The One Best System: A History of American Urban Education*. Cambridge, Mass: Harvard University Press.

Hacker, Andrew. 1992. *Two Nations: Black and White, Separate, Hostile, Unequal*. New York: Ballantine Books.

Haggard, Ernest A. 1954. Social Status and Intelligence: An Experimental Study of Certain Cultural Determinants of Measured Intelligence. *Genetic Psychology Monographs* 49: 141–186.

Hale-Benson, Janice E. 1986. *Black Children: Their Roots, Culture, and Learning Styles*. rev. ed. Baltimore, Md: Johns Hopkins University Press.

Hampel, Robert. 1986. *The Last Little Citadel: American High Schools Since 1940*. Boston: Houghton Mifflin.

Hardin, Russell. 1982. *Collective Action*. Baltimore: Johns Hopkins University Press.

Hendrie, Caroline. 1996. 109 Chicago Schools Put on Academic Probation. *Education Week*, October 9, 1996, 3.

Hendrie, Caroline. 1997. Crew Packs Arsenal of New Powers in N.Y.C. *Education Week*, January 15, 1997, 1.

Herrick, Mary J. 1984. *The Chicago Schools: A Social and Political History*. Beverly Hills, Ca: Sage.

Hess, G. Alfred. 1991. *School Restructuring, Chicago Style*. Newbury Park, Ca: Corwin Press.

Hess, G. Alfred. 1995. *Restructuring Urban Schools: A Chicago Perspective*. New York: Teachers College Press.

Hirsch, Susan E. 1978. *Roots of the American Working Class: The Industrialization of Crafts in Newark, 1800–1860*. Philadelphia: University of Pennsylvania Press.

Hodgkinson, Harold L. 1992. *A Demographic Look at Tomorrow*. Washington, DC: Institute for Educational Leadership/Center for Demographic Policy.

Hoff, David. 1996. West Virginia Leaves District Better Than It Found It. *Education Week*, September 18, 1996.

Hofstadter, Richard. 1955. *The Age of Reform*. New York: Alfred A. Knopf.

Hogan, David J. 1985. *Class and Reform: School and Society in Chicago, 1880–1930*. Philadelphia: University of Pennsylvania Press.

Holmes Group. 1986. *Tomorrow's Teachers: A Report of the Holmes Group*. East Lansing, Mich: Author.

Homel, Michael. 1985. *Down From Equality: Black Chicagoans and the Public Schools, 1920–1941*. Chicago: University of Chicago Press.

Hopfenberg, Wendy, Henry M. Levin, and Associates. 1993. *The Accelerated Schools: Resource Guide*. San Francisco: Jossey-Bass.

Hughes, James W. and Joseph J. Seneca. 1992a. *New Jersey Cities in the 1980s: An Employment Report Card*. Rutgers Regional Report, Issue paper no. 3, Faculty of Planning. New Brunswick, NJ: Rutgers University.

Hughes, James W. and Joseph J. Seneca. 1992b. *The New Jersey Manufacturing Employment Hemorrhage*. Rugters Regional Report, Issue paper no. 4. Faculty of Planning. New Brunswick, NJ: Rutgers University.

Hughes, James W. and Joseph J. Seneca. 1992c. *The Suburban Employment Perimeter: New Jersey Municipal Job Growth in the 1980s.* Rutgers Regional Report, Issue paper no. 5. Edward J. Bloustein School of Planning and Public Policy. New Brunswick, NJ: Rutgers University.

Hughes, James W. and Joseph J. Seneca. 1995. *New Dimensions of National and Regional Output and Productivity: New Jersey's Economic History Revisited.* Rutgers Regional Report, Issue paper no. 12. Edward J. Bloustein School of Planning and Public Policy. New Brunswick, NJ: Rutgers University.

Jackson, Kenneth T. 1976. The Effect of Suburbanization on the Cities. Pp. 89–110 in *Suburbia: The American Dream and Dilemma.* ed. Philip C. Dolce. Garden City, New York: Anchor Books.

Jackson, Kenneth T. 1985. *Crabgrass Frontier: The Suburbanization of the United States.* New York and Oxford: Oxford University Press.

Jackson, Kenneth T. and Barbara Jackson. 1971. The Black Experience in Newark: The Growth of the Ghetto, 1870–1970. Pp. 36–60, in *New Jersey Since 1860: New Findings and Interpretations,* ed. William C. Wright. Trenton: New Jersey Historical Commission.

Javetski, Bill. 1994. Borderless Finance: Fuel for Growth. *Business Week,* Special 1994 bonus issue, Pp. 40–50.

Jehl, Jeanne and Michael W. Kirst. 1993. Getting Ready to Provide School-Linked Services: What Schools Must Do. *Education and Urban Society* 25 (2): 153–165.

Jencks, Christopher, and Paul E. Peterson, eds. 1991. *The Urban Underclass.* Washington, DC: Brookings Institute.

Judd, Dennis R. and Todd Swanstrom. 1994. *City Politics: Private Power and Public Policy.* New York: HarperCollins.

Kain, John. 1968. Housing Segregation, Negro Employment and Metropolitan Decentralization. *Quarterly Journal of Economics* 26: 110–130.

Kaplan, Harold. 1963. *Urban Renewal Politics: Slum Clearance in Newark.* New York: Columbia University Press.

Kasarda, John D. 1989. Urban Industrial Transformation and the Underclass. *Annals of the American Academy of Political Science* 501 (January): 20–31.

Kasarda, John D. 1993. Cities as Places Where People Live and Work: Urban Change and Neighborhood Distress. Pp. 81–124 in *Interwoven Destinies: Cities and the Nation,* ed. Henry G. Cisneros. New York: W. W. Norton.

Kasinitz, Philip and Jan Rosenberg. 1994. *Missing the Connection: Social Isolation and Employment on the Brooklyn Waterfront.* Working papers, Michael Harrington Center for Democratic Values and Social Change, Queens College/City University of New York.

Katznelson, Ira and Margaret Weir. 1985. *Schooling for All: Class, Race and the Decline of the Democratic Ideal.* New York: Basic Books.

Kelly, Don Quinn. 1972. Black Political Activity and the Formation of Public Policy on Education of Blacks in the United States—Two Eras: The State of Alabama from 1884 to 1910 and the City of Newark, New Jersey, from 1964 to June, 1972. Ph.D. diss., Columbia University.

Kiefer, Barbara Z. and Johanna S. DeStefano. 1985. Cultures Together in the Classroom: "What You Sayin?" Pp. 159–172 in *Observing the Language Learner*, ed. Angela Jaggar and M. Trika Smith-Burke. Urbana, Ill: National Council of Teachers of English.

King, Sabrina Hope. 1993. The Limited Presence of African American Teachers. *Review of Educational Research* 63: 115–150.

Kohl, Herbert. 1967. *36 Children*. New York: New American Library.

Kohl, Herbert. 1994. *"I Won't Learn from You" and Other Thoughts on Creative Maladjustment*. New York: New Press.

Kotlowitz, Alex. 1991. *There Are No Children Here: The Story of Two Boys Growing Up in the Other America*. New York: Doubleday, Anchor Books.

Kozol, Jonathan. 1967. *Death at an Early Age: The Destruction of the Hearts and Minds of Negro Children in the Boston Public Schools*. Boston: Houghton Mifflin.

Kozol, Jonathan. 1991. *Savage Inequalities: Children in America's Schools*. New York: Crown Publishers.

Kunen, James S. 1996. Back to Segregation. *Time Magazine* 147 (18): 39–45.

Kurp, Ralph K. 1967. Public Schools in the City of Newark, New Jersey: 1850–1965. Ph.D. diss., Rutgers University.

Kusick, Marilyn R. 1974. Social Reform as a Tool of Urban Reform: The Emergence of the Twentieth-Century Public School in Newark, New Jersey, 1890–1920. Ph.D. diss., Rutgers University.

Labov, William. 1969. Some Sources of Reading Problems for Negro Speakers of Non-Standard English. Pp. 29–67 in Joan Baratz and Roger Shuy, eds., *Teaching Black Children to Read*. Washington, DC: Center for Applied Linguistics.

Laccetti, Silvio R., ed. 1990. *New Jersey Profiles in Public Policy*. Palisades Park, NJ: Commonwealth Books.

Ladd, Helen F. and John Yinger. 1989. *America's Ailing Cities: Fiscal Health and the Design of Urban Policy*. Baltimore: Johns Hopkins University Press.

Laitin, David D. 1986. *Hegemony and Culture*. Chicago: University of Chicago Press.

Lake, Robert W. 1981. *The New Suburbanites: Race and Housing in the Suburbs*. New Brunswick, NJ: Center for Urban Policy Research, Rutgers University.

Lazerson, Marvin. 1971. *Origins of the Urban School: Public Education in Massachusetts, 1870–1915*. Cambridge, Mass: Harvard University Press.

Learning Communities Network, Inc. 1996. Just the Facts? *Uncommon Sense* 1 (2): 1, 4–6.

Lewis, Anne C. 1996. Urban Middle-Grades Reform: Foundations Keep Trying. *Harvard Education Letter* 11 (4): 5–6.

Lieberman, Ann, ed. 1995. *The Work of Restructuring Schools: Building from the Ground Up*. New York: Teachers College Press.

Louis, Arthur M. 1975. The Worst American City, *Harpers Magazine* (January): 67–71.

Madaus, G. 1988. The Influence of Testing on the Curriculum. Pp. 83–121 in

Critical Issues in Curriculum, ed. Lauren Tanner. Chicago, Ill: Universtiy of Chicago Press.

Mahan, David James. 1968. The Influence of the Efficiency Movement on a Large School System: A Case Study of the St. Louis Public Schools. Ed.D. diss., Washington University.

Massell, Diane and Susan Fuhrman. 1994. *Ten Years of State Education Reform, 1983-1993.* New Brunswick, NJ: Eagleton Institute of Politics, Rutgers University.

Massey, Douglas S. and Nancy Denton. 1989. Hypersegregation in U.S. Metropolitan Areas: Black-Hispanic Segregation along Five Dimensions. *Demography* 26 (3): 373–391.

Massey, Douglas S. and Nancy A. Denton. 1993. *American Apartheid: Segregation and the Making of the Underclass.* Cambridge, Mass: Harvard University Press.

Mayor's Commission on Group Relations. 1959. *Newark: A City in Transition.* Vol. 1, *The Characteristics of the Population.* Newark, NJ: Author. Mimeographed.

McDermott, Ray. 1987. Achieving School Failure: An Anthropological Approach to Literacy and Social Stratification. Pp. 82–118 in *Education and Cultural Process: Anthropological Approaches,* 2nd ed., ed. George Spindler. Prospect Heights, Ill: Waveland.

McLaughlin, John. 1996. The Learning Curveball. Special section of *Star Ledger.* (July).

McLaughlin, John. 1997. The Judging Will Put an End to the Fudging. *Star Ledger,* May 15, 1997, 34.

Medoff, Peter and Holly Sklar. 1994. *Streets of Hope: The Fall and Rise of an Urban Neighborhood.* Boston: South End Press.

Meier, August and Elliott Rudwick. 1966. *From Plantation to Ghetto.* New York: Hill and Wang.

Meier, Deborah. 1995. *The Power of Their Ideas: Lessons for America from a Small School in Harlem.* Boston: Beacon Press.

Memmi, Albert. 1965. *The Colonizer and the Colonized.* Boston: Beacon Press.

Memmi, Albert. 1968. *Dominated Man.* Boston: Beacon Press.

Middle States Association of Colleges and Schools. 1973. The Written Report of the Visiting Committee for the Middle States Association Evaluation of the Central High School (Newark, NJ), March 13, 14, 15, 1973. Typescript. Available at the Newark Library.

Mirel, Jeffrey. 1993. *The Rise and Fall of an Urban School System: Detroit, 1907–1981.* Ann Arbor: University of Michigan.

Mishel, Lawrence and Jared Bernstein. 1994. *The State of Working America, 1994–1995.* Armonk, New York: Economic Policy Institute and M. E. Sharpe.

Model Cities Application. 1967. Application to the Department of Housing and Urban Development for a Grant to Plan a Comprehensive City Demonstration Program. Newark, NJ: Office of the Mayor.

Model Cities Program. 1969. Newark, NJ: Office of the Mayor.

Mortimore, Peter and Pam Sammons. 1987. New Evidence on Effective Elementary Schools. *Educational Leadership* 45 (September): 4–8.

Muncey, Donna E. and Patrick J. McQuillan. 1993. Preliminary Findings from a Five-Year Study of the Coalition of Essential Schools. *Phi Delta Kappan* 74 (6): 486–489.

Muncey, Donna E. and Patrick J. McQuillan. 1996. *Reform and Resistance in Schools and Classrooms: An Ethnographic View of the Coalition of Essential Schools.* New Haven: Yale University Press.

Murphy, Joseph. 1990. The Educational Reform Movement of the 1980s: A Comprehensive Analysis. Pp. 3–56 in *The Educational Reform Movement of the 1980s: Perspectives and Cases*, ed. Joseph Murphy. Berkeley, Ca: McCutchan.

Nathaus, Leah. 1996. Global Gamble: Morgan Stanley is Charging into the Third World. Will it Get Burned? *Business Week* February 12, 1996, 63–72.

National Advisory Commission on Civil Disorders. 1968. *Report of the National Advisory Commission on Civil Disorders.* New York: E. P. Dutton and Co.

National Association for the Advancement of Colored People. 1961. Study of the Newark School System. In *Hearings Before the U.S. Commission on Civil Rights, Newark, New Jersey*, 1962. Washington, DC.

National Center for Education Statistics: U.S. Commission on Civil Rights. 1994. *Literacy Behind Prison Walls: Profiles of the Prison Population from the Adult Literacy Survey.* Washington, DC: U. S. Department of Education.

National Commission on Excellence in Education. 1983. *A Nation at Risk.* Washington, DC: Department of Education.

National Commission on Teaching and America's Future. 1996. *What Matters Most: Teaching for America's Future. Report of the National Commission on Teaching and America's Future.* New York: Teachers College, Columbia University.

National Council of Teachers of Mathematics. 1989. *Curriculum and Evaluation Standards for School Mathematics.* Reston, Va: Author.

National Education Association. 1940. City Teachers: Their Preparation, Salaries, and Experience. *Research Bulletin* 18 (1).

National Research Council. 1995. *National Science Education Standards.* Washington, DC: National Academy Press.

Natriello, Gary, and Morgan Collins. 1993. *Necessary but Not Sufficient: The Quality Education Act and At-Risk Students.* New Brunswick, NJ: Center for Educational Policy Analysis, Rutgers University.

Natriello, Gary, and Morgan Collins. 1994. *Necessary but Not Sufficient: The Impact of the Quality Education Act on At-Risk Students.* New Brunswick, NJ: Center for Educational Policy Analysis, Rutgers University.

Natriello, Gary, Edward L. McDill, and Aaron M. Pallas. 1990. *Schooling Disadvantaged Children: Racing Against Catastrophe.* New York: Teachers College Press.

New Jersey Advisory Committee to the U.S. Commission on Civil Rights. 1968. *Public Housing in Newark's Central Ward.* Trenton: Author.

New Jersey Department of Labor and Industry, Division of Employment Security. 1960 and 1961. *New Jersey Covered Employment Trends by Geographical Areas of the State.* Trenton: Author.

New Jersey State Department of Education. 1984. *Report to the Acting Executive Superintendent, Newark School District.* Trenton: Author.

New Jersey State Department of Education. 1993. *Newark Public Schools, Level III External Review.* Trenton: Author.

New Jersey State Department of Education. 1994a. *1992–1993 Certificated Full-time Staff Report by District Position and Race.* Trenton: Author.

New Jersey State Department of Education. 1994b. *Comprehensive Compliance Investigation of the Newark Public Schools.* Trenton: Author.

New Jersey State Department of Education. 1995. *Comprehensive Plan.* Trenton: Author.

Newark Board of Education. 1933. *Newark Schools in the Depression.* Newark, NJ: Author.

Newark Board of Education. 1960–1969. *Minutes.* Newark, NJ: Author.

Newark Board of Education. 1961. *Newark Board of Education Data Sheet.* Newark, NJ: Author. Typescript.

Newark Board of Education. 1968. *Data Sheet for Newark Schools.* Newark, NJ: Author. Typescript.

Newark Board of Education, Bureau of Municipal Research. 1965. *List of Anti-Poverty Programs of the Newark Board of Education.* Trenton, NJ: Author. Typescript.

Newark Board of Education. Department of Reference and Research, 1923. *School Survey.* Newark, NJ: Author. Mimeographed.

Newark Board of Education, Department of Reference and Research. 1936. *Nationality Survey of the Elementary Schools.* Newark, NJ: Author. Mimeographed.

Newark Board of Education, Department of Reference and Research. 1969. *Report of City-Wide Testing Program.* Newark, NJ: Author. Mimeographed.

Newark Board of Education, Office of Planning, Evaluation and Testing. 1992. *Restructuring Urban Schools in Newark, NJ: An Evaluation of the Cluster Schools Program.* Newark, NJ: Author.

Newark Central Planning Board. 1944. *Preliminary Report on the Scope of the City Plan.* Newark, NJ: Author. Typescript.

Newark Central Planning Board. 1947. *The Master Plan for the Physical Development of the City of Newark, N.J.* Newark: Author. Typescript.

Newark Central Planning Board. 1949. *Newark Municipal Yearbook, 1948–49.* Newark, NJ: Author.

Newark Central Planning Board. 1951. *Newark Municipal Yearbook, 1950–51.* Newark, NJ: Author.

Newark Central Planning Board. 1961. *Re: New Newark.* Newark, NJ: Author.

Newark Public Library. 1995. *Lasting Impressions: Greater Newark's Jewish Legacy. An Exhibition.* Newark, NJ: Author.

Newark Teachers Union. 1953. *A Vanishing Profession.* Newark, NJ: Author.

O'Leary, Wesley. 1923. The Development of Vocational Schools, Continuation Schools and Manual Training. Pp. 14–16 in *Proceedings of the Public Confer-*

ence on the School Curriculum of New Jersey. Trenton: Department of Public Instruction.

Oakes, Jeannie. 1990. *Multiplying Inequalities: The Effects of Race, Social Class, and Tracking on Opportunities to Learn Mathematics and Science.* Santa Monica, Ca: Rand Corporation.

Odden, Allen and Lawrence Picus. 1992. *School Finance: A Policy Perspective.* New York: McGraw-Hill.

Office of the Mayor. Commission on Group Relations. 1959. *Report of the Commission on Group Relations,* Vol. 1. Newark, NJ: Author. Typescript.

Orfield, Gary. 1993. *The Growth of Segregation in American Schools: Changing Patterns of Separation and Poverty since 1968.* A Report of the Harvard Project on School Desegregation to the National School Boards Association. Washington, DC: Author.

Orfield, Gary, and Carole Ashkinaze. 1991. *The Closing Door: Conservative Policy and Black Opportunity.* Chicago: University of Chicago Press.

Orfield, Gary and Susan Easton. 1996. *Dismantling Desegregation: The Quiet Reversal of Brown v. Board of Education.* New York: The New Press, distributed by W. W. Norton.

Orr, Eleanor Wilson. 1987. *Twice as Less: Black English and the Performance of Black Students in Mathematics and Science.* New York: W. W. Norton.

Perlmann, Joel. 1988. *Ethnic Differences: Schooling and Social Structure among the Irish, Italians, Jews, and Blacks in an American City, 1880–1935.* New York: Cambridge University Press.

Persky, Joseph, Elliott Sklar, and Wim Wiewel. 1992. *Does America Need Cities?: An Urban Investment Strategy for National Prosperity.* Washington, DC: Economic Policy Institute and the U.S. Conference of Mayors.

Peterson, Paul E. 1976. *School Politics: Chicago Style.* Chicago: University of Chicago Press.

Peterson, Paul. 1985. *Politics of School Reform, 1870–1940.* Chicago: University of Chicago Press.

Philadelphia Children Achieving Challenge. 1996. *A First-Year Evaluation Report.* Philadelphia: Author.

Philadelphia Children Achieving Challenge. 1996. *A First-Year Evaluation Report, Executive Summary.* Philadelphia: Author.

Philadephia Education Fund. 1996. *Research and Policy Perspectives.* Philadelphia: Author.

Piccigallo, Philip. 1989. Renovating Urban Schools is Fundamental to Improving Them. *Phi Delta Kappan* 70 (January): 402–406.

Piven, Frances Fox, and Richard Cloward. 1970. *Regulating the Poor: The Functions of Public Welfare.* New York: Pantheon.

Planners Associates, Inc. 1970. *Summary Report, Newark Board of Education Title I E.S.E.A. Evaluation, 1969–1970.* Newark, NJ: Author.

Pomper, Gerald. 1966. Ethnic and Group Voting in Nonpartisan Municipal Elections. *Public Administration Quarterly* 30 (Spring): 79–97.

Pomper, Gerald, ed. 1986. *The Political State of New Jersey.* New Brunswick: Rutgers University Press.

Popper, Samuel. 1952. Newark, NJ, 1870–1910: Chapters in the Evolution of an American Metropolis. Ph.D. diss., New York University.

Price, Clement Alexander. 1975. The Afro-American Community of Newark, 1917–1947: A Social History. Ph.D. diss., Rutgers University.

Price, Clement Alexander. 1980. *Freedom Not Far Distant: A Documentary History of Afro-Americans in New Jersey*. Newark: New Jersey Historical Society.

Project South Washington. 1996. Crime and Incarceration Quiz. *Poverty & Race* 5 (6): 11–12.

Purkey, Stewart and Martha Smith. 1983. Effective Schools: A Review. *Elementary School Journal* 83 (4): 427–452.

Quint, Sharon. 1995. *Schooling Homeless Children*. New York: Teachers College Press.

Randall, Prudence B. 1971. The Meanings of Progressivism in Urban School Reform: Cleveland, 1901–1909. Ph.D. diss., Case Western Reserve University.

Ravitch, Diane. 1983. *The Troubled Crusade: American Education, 1945–1980*. New York: Basic Books.

Reock, Ernest C. Jr. 1993. *State Aid for Schools in New Jersey: 1976–1993. Part I: Report*. New Brunswick: Center for Government Services, Rutgers University.

Reock, Ernest C. Jr. 1996. *State Aid for Schools in New Jersey: 1976–1996*. New Brunswick: Center for Government Services, Rutgers University.

Reynolds v. Sims 377 U.S. 533 (1964).

Rich, Wilbur C. 1996. *Black Mayors and School Politics: The Failure of Reform in Detroit, Gary, and Newark*. London and New York: Garland.

Robinson v. Cahill 118 N.J. Super (1972).

Robinson v. Cahill 62 N.J. 473 (1973).

Robinson v. Cahill 69 N.J. 449 (1976).

Robinson v. Cahill 70 N.J. 155 (1976).

Rogers, David. 1968. *110 Livingston St.: Politics and Bureaucracy in the New York City Schools*. New York: Random House.

Rosenfeld, Gerry. 1971. *"Shut Those Thick Lips!" A Study of Slum School Failure*. New York: Holt, Rinehart and Winston.

Rothman, Robert. 1993. Obstacle Course: Barriers to Change Thwart Reformers at Every Twist and Turn. *Education Week* (February 10): 9–12.

Runge, Ford, John Schnittker, and Timothy Penny. 1995. *Ending Agricultural Entitlements: How to Fix Farm Policy*. Madison, Wis: Progressive Foundation.

Said, Edward. 1978. *Orientalism*. New York: Pantheon.

Salmore, Barbara G., and Stephen A. Salmore. 1993. *New Jersey Politics and Government: Suburban Politics Comes of Age*. Lincoln: University of Nebraska.

San Antonio Independent School District v. Rodriguez 411 U.S. 1 (1973).

Sarason, Seymour. 1971. *The Culture of the School and the Problem of Change*. Boston, Mass: Allyn and Bacon.

Sarasan, Seymour. 1996. *Revisiting "The Culture of School and the Problem of Change."* New York: Teachers College Press.

Sassen, Saskia. 1991. *The Global City: New York, London, Tokyo*. Princeton, NJ: Princeton University Press.

Schotland, Joseph H. 1956. Statement on Report of Survey Institute, Inc. on the Administrative Management of the Business Operations of the Newark School System. Newark, NJ: Author. Typescript.

Schrag, Peter. 1967. *Village School Downtown: Politics and Education—A Boston Report*. Boston: Beacon Press.

Schwartz, Joel and Daniel Prosser. 1977. *Cities of the Garden State: Essays in the Urban and Suburban History of New Jersey*. Dubuque, Iowa: Kendall/Hunt.

Sciarra, David. 1997. *Plaintiffs' brief in support of motion in aid to litigants' rights*. Newark, NJ: Education Law Center.

Seneca, Joseph J. 1990. The Structure and Performance of the New Jersey Economy. Pp. 58–85 in *New Jersey: Profiles in Public Policy*, ed. Silvio R. Laccetti. Palisades Park, NJ: Commonwealth Books.

Sepinwall, Harriet Lipman. 1986. The History of the 1875 "Thorough and Efficient" Amendment to the New Jersey Constitution in the Context of Nineteenth Century Social Thought on Education. Ed.D. diss., Rutgers University.

Serrano v. Priest (5 Cal. 3d 584, 487) P. 2nd 1241, 96 Cal. Rptr 601 (1971).

Simmens, Lance. 1991. *City Fiscal Conditions, 1980–90*. Washington, DC: U.S. Conference of Mayors.

Sizer, Theodore. 1992. *Horace's School: Redesigning the American High School*. Boston: Houghton Mifflin.

Slavin, Robert E. et al. 1992. *Success for All: A Relentless Approach to Prevention and Early Intervention in Elementary Schools*. Arlington, VA: Educational Research Service.

Smart, Tim. 1993. GE's Brave New World: Welch Sees the Future. It's China, India, Mexico. *Business Week* November 8, 1993, 64–70.

Smith, Marshall S. and Jennifer O'Day. 1991. Systemic School Reform. Pp. 233–267 in *The Politics of Curriculum and Testing: The 1990 Yearbook of the Politics of Education Association*, ed. Susan H. Fuhrman and Betty Malen. New York: Falmer Press.

Smitherman, Geneva. 1975. *Black Language and Culture: Sounds of Soul*. New York: Harper and Row.

Smitherman, Geneva. 1977. *Talking and Testifying: The Language of Black America*. Boston: Houghton Mifflin.

Stellhorn, Paul Anthony. 1982. Depression and Decline, Newark, New Jersey: 1929–1941. Ph.D. diss., Rutgers University.

Sternlieb, George. 1966. *The Tenement Landlord*. New Brunswick, NJ: Urban Studies Center, Rutgers University.

Sternlieb, George, and Mildred Barry. 1967. *Social Needs and Social Resources: Newark*. New Brunswick, NJ: Graduate School of Business Adminstration, Rutgers University.

Stevens, Lois. 1996. Speaking Out for Head Start. *Entry Point: The Quarterly Newsletter of RESULTS* (Summer).

Stodghill II, Ron. 1996. Bringing Hope Back to the 'Hood. *Business Week* (August 19): 70–73.

Strayer, George D. 1942. *The Report of a Survey of the Public Schools of Newark, New Jersey.* New York: Teachers College Bureau of Publications.

Strayer, George D. 1944. *The Report of a Survey of the Public Schools of Boston, Massachussettes.* Boston: City of Boston Printing Department.

Strayer, George D. 1951. *Administrative Management of the School System of New York City; Report of a Survey of the Board of Education and the Board of Higher Education.* New York. Available from Teachers College Library Special Collections.

Tabb, William K. 1970. *The Political Economy of the Black Ghetto.* New York: W. W. Norton.

Taggart, Robert J. 1970. Programs of City Superintendents for Schools in Michigan, 1870–1915. Ph.D. diss., University of Michigan.

Tilly, Chris. 1990. *Short Hours, Short Shrift: Causes and Consequences of Part-time Work.* Washington, DC: Economic Policy Institute.

Tractenberg, Paul. 1974. Robinson v. Cahill: The "Thorough and Efficient" Clause. *Law and Contemporary Problems* 38, (Winter–Spring): 311–332.

Tractenberg, Paul. 1977. Pupil Performance in Basic Skills in the Newark School System Since 1967. Pp. 235–243 in *Newark 1967–1977: An Assessment,* ed. Stanley Winters. Newark: New Jersey Institute of Technology.

Tractenberg, Paul. 1995. Statement of Professor Paul L. Tractenberg on Behalf of the Education Law Center about the State Education Department's Comprehensive Plan for Educational Improvement and Financing. Newark, NJ: Rutgers University Law School. Typescript.

Turp, Ralph K. 1967. Public Schools in the City of Newark, New Jersey: 1850–1965. Ed.D. diss., Rutgers University.

Tyack, David B. 1967. *Turning Points in American Educational History.* Waltham, Mass: Blaisdell.

Tyack, David. 1974. *The One Best System: A History of American Urban Education.* Cambridge, Mass: Harvard University Press.

Tyack, David and Larry Cuban. 1995. *Tinkering toward Utopia: A Century of Public School Reform.* Cambridge, Mass: Harvard University Press.

Tyack, David and Elisabeth Hansot. 1982. *Managers of Virtue: Public School Leadership in America, 1820–1980.* New York: Basic Books.

Tyack, David, Robert Lowe, and Elisabeth Hansot. 1984. *Public Schools in Hard Times: The Great Depression and Recent Years.* Cambridge, Mass: Harvard University Press.

United for a Fair Economy. 1996. *Share the Wealth.* Boston: Author.

U.S. Bureau of the Census. *Census of the Population 1960, 1970, 1980, 1990, 1994, 1995.* Washington, DC: Author.

U.S. Bureau of the Census. 1970. *General Social and Economic Characteristics, Poverty Status in 1969 of Families and Persons.* Washington, DC: Author.

U.S. Bureau of the Census. 1990. *Social Characteristics of Persons, School Enrollment, and Educational Attainment.* Washington, DC: Author.

U.S. Bureau of the Census. 1994. *Statistical Abstract of the United States* (114th ed.). Washington, DC: Author.

U.S. Commission on Civil Rights. 1967. *Racial Isolation in the Public Schools*, Vol. 1. Washington, DC: Author.

U.S. Commission on Civil Rights in Newark. 1962. *Hearings*. Washington, DC: Author.

U.S. Department of Education, National Center for Educational Statistics. 1994. *Common Core of Data Survey, December, 1994*. Washington, DC: Author.

U.S. Department of Education, National Center for Educational Statistics. 1995. *Statistics of State School Systems. Revenues and Expenditures for Public Elementary and Secondary Education. Common Core of Data Surveys 1995*. Washington, DC: Author.

U.S. Department of Education. National Center for Educational Statistics. 1996. *Urban Schools: The Challenge of Location and Poverty*. Washington, DC: Author.

U.S. General Accounting Office. 1997. *School Finance: State Efforts to Reduce Funding Gaps Between Poor and Wealthy Districts*. Washington, DC: Author.

U.S. Immigration Commission. 1911. *The Children of Immigrants in Schools*, Vol. IV. Reprint Francesco Cordasco and Scarecrow Reprint Corporation, 1970. Washington, DC: Government Printing Office.

Useem, Elizabeth et al. 1995. Urban Teacher Curriculum Networks and Systemic Change. Paper presented at the annual meeting of the American Educational Research Association, San Francisco, April.

Vinovskis, Maris, A. 1985. *The Origins of Public High Schools: A Reexamination of the Beverly High School Controversy*. Madison: University of Wisconsin Press.

Walzak, Lee. 1995. America's New Populism. *Business Week* (March 13): 75–78.

Warren, Donald, ed. 1989. *American Teachers: Histories of a Profession at Work*. New York: Macmillan.

Washnis, George. 1974. *Community Development Strategies: Case Studies of Major Model Cities*. New York: Praeger.

Wasley, Patricia. 1994. *Stirring the Chalkdust: Tales of Teachers Changing Classroom Practice*. New York: Teachers College Press.

Webster Junior High School. 1968. Self-Study Report. Newark, NJ: Author. Mimeographed.

Wehlage, Gary, Gregory Smith, and Pauline Lipman. 1992. Restructuring Urban Schools: The New Futures Experience. *American Educational Research Journal* 29 (1): 51–93.

Weick, Karl. 1976. Educational Organizations as Loosely Coupled Systems. *Administrative Science Quarterly* 24 (1): 1–19.

Whyte, William H. Jr. 1956. *Organization Man*. New York: Simon and Schuster.

Wiener, Morton, and Ward Cromer. 1967. Reading and Reading Difficulty: A Conceptual Analysis. *Harvard Educational Review* 37: 620–643.

Wilkerson, Doxey A. 1939. *Special Problems of Negro Education: Staff Study Number 12*. Prepared for the Advisory Committee on Education. Washington, DC: U.S. Government Printing Office.

Wilkinson, Pierce. 1976. The Impact of Suburbanization on Government and Politics in Contemporary America. Pp. 59–88 in *Suburbia: The American Dream and Dilemma*, ed. Philip C. Dolce. Garden City, New York: Anchor Books.

Wilson, William Julius. 1987. *The Truly Disadvantaged: The Inner City, the Underclass, and Public Policy*. Chicago: University of Chicago Press.

Wilson, William Julius. 1991. Public Policy Research and the Truly Disadvantaged. Pp. 460–482 in *The Urban Underclass*, eds., Christopher Jencks, and Paul E. Peterson. Washington, DC: Brookings Institute.

Wilson, William Julius. 1996a. Work. *The New York Times Magazine*, August 18, 1996: 26.

Wilson, William Julius. 1996b. *When Work Disappears: The World of the New Urban Poor*. New York: Knopf.

Winters, Stanley B., ed., 1977. *Newark, 1967–1970: An Assessment*. Newark: New Jersey Institute of Technology.

Winters, Stanley B., ed., 1990. *Newark: The Durable City*. Newark: New Jersey Institute of Technology.

Wong, Mun et al. 1992. Under Siege: Children's Perception of Stress. Paper presented at the annual meeting of the American Psychological Association, April.

Wright, Marion M. Thompson. 1941. *The Education of Negroes in New Jersey*. New York: Teachers College Press.

Wrigley, Julia. 1982. *Class Politics and Public Schools: Chicago, 1900–1950*. New Brunswick, NJ: Rutgers University Press.

Zepezauer, Mark and Arthur Naiman. 1996. *Take the Rich Off Welfare*. Tucson: Odonian Press.

Zook, Jim. 1993. 10 Years later, Many Eductors See Little Progress for the "Nation at Risk". *Chronicle of Higher Education*, April 21, A19, A24–25.

Index

About the Author

Jean Anyon, Ph.D., Associate Professor at Rutgers University, taught elementary grades in inner city schools in Bedford-Stuyvesant, NY; Washington, DC; and Philadelphia. She received her academic degrees from the University of Pennsylvania and New York University. Since 1982 she has been Chairperson of the Education Department at Rutgers University in Newark, New Jersey. She is also Director of the Institute for Research in Urban Education on the Rutgers–Newark Campus. She has published widely on the relation of social class and race to issues of curriculum, equity, classroom practice, and school reform. Several articles of hers have become classics and are widely reprinted in volumes edited by others. This is her first book. Her second, a collection of essays currently being edited with Roslyn Mickelson, is entitled, *By Design and Neglect: Homelessness and Education in the United States and Brazil.*